Critical Theory and Disability

Critical Theory and Disability explores social and ontological issues encountered by present-day disabled people, applying ideas from disability studies and phenomenology. It focuses on disabling contexts in order to highlight and criticize the ontological assumptions of contemporary society, particularly those related to the meaning of human being. In empirical terms, the book explores critically social practices that undermine disabled people's well-being, drawing on cases from contemporary Bulgaria. It includes in-depth examination of key mechanisms such as disability assessment, personal assistance (direct payments), and disability-based discrimination. On this basis, wider sociological and ontological claims are made concerning the body, identity, otherness, and exclusion.

ABOUT THE SERIES

Critical Theory and Contemporary Society explores the relationship between contemporary society as a complex and highly differentiated phenomenon, on the one hand, and Critical Theory as a correspondingly sophisticated methodology for studying and understanding social and political relations today, on the other.

Each volume highlights in distinctive ways why (1) Critical Theory offers the most appropriate concepts for understanding political movements, socioeconomic conflicts and state institutions in an increasingly global world and (2) why Critical Theory nonetheless needs updating in order to keep pace with the realities of the twenty-first century.

The books in the series look at global warming, financial crisis, post–nation state legitimacy, international relations, cinema, terrorism, and other issues, applying an interdisciplinary approach, in order to help students and citizens understand the specificity and uniqueness of the current situation.

Series Editor
Darrow Schecter, Reader in the School of History,
Art History and Humanities, University of Sussex, UK

BOOKS IN THE SERIES

Critical Theory and Film, Fabio Vighi

Critical Theory and the Critique of Political Economy, Werner Bonefeld

Critical Theory and Contemporary Europe, William Outhwaite

Critical Theory of Legal Revolutions, Hauke Brunkhorst

Critical Theory in the Twenty-First Century, Darrow Schecter

Critical Theory and the Digital, David Berry

Critical Theory and Libertarian Socialism, Charles Masquelier

Critical Theory and Disability

A phenomenological approach

TEODOR MLADENOV

Bloomsbury Academic
An imprint of Bloomsbury Publishing Inc

B L O O M S B U R Y
NEW YORK · LONDON · OXFORD · NEW DELHI · SYDNEY

Bloomsbury Academic

An imprint of Bloomsbury Publishing Inc

1385 Broadway	50 Bedford Square
New York	London
NY 10018	WC1B 3DP
USA	UK

www.bloomsbury.com

BLOOMSBURY and the Diana logo are trademarks of Bloomsbury Publishing Plc

First published 2015

Paperback edition first published 2016

Library of Congress Cataloging-in-Publication Data

A catalog record for this book is available from the Library of Congress.

ISBN: HB: 978-1-6289-2199-1
PB: 978-1-5013-2216-7
ePDF: 978-1-6289-2201-1
ePub: 978-1-6289-2200-4

Series: Critical Theory and Contemporary Society

Typeset by Deanta Global Publishing Services, Chennai, India

Contents

Acknowledgments

The present work stems from my professional experience at the Center for Independent Living—Sofia and is greatly indebted for its understanding of disability and social policy to the Center's founder and leader Kapka Panayotova.

The work is based on a doctoral research project, the idea for which emerged in the summer of 2008. A generous studentship from the Graduate School at King's College London enabled me to commence the project's implementation in October 2009. The work started under the supervision of Steven Wainwright and Clare Williams from the Centre for Biomedicine and Society (CBAS), hosted at that time by King's. Steve and Clare supported my research during its initial stage, allowed me considerable freedom to explore my ideas, and provided me with valuable feedback on the early versions of the first several case studies. During this introductory phase, I also received useful comments on my work from Alison Harvey and Barbara Prainsack. In addition, I benefited from discussions with Edison Bicudo, a friend and fellow doctoral traveler, as well as with Christian Haddad from the University of Vienna and Thomas Tierney from the College of Wooster, both of whom were visiting CBAS at that time.

When CBAS moved to Brunel University at the beginning of 2011, the supervision of my doctoral research was transferred to Alan Cribb and Gerard Lum from the Department of Education and Professional Studies at King's. Alan and Gerard made the second phase of my work on the project an intellectually rewarding experience. I am greatly indebted for their conceptual input, as well as for their feedback that significantly improved the readability and internal consistency of the text. My research experience at King's was also enriched by the Journal Club convened by Kathryn Ehrich, the Disability Studies Reading Group convened by Deborah Chinn, and the Theory and Methods Reading Group convened by Sharon Gewirtz.

Six of the chapters in the book are revised versions of articles already published elsewhere. The part of Chapter 1 on the Bulgarian context and the whole of Chapter 7 are based on "Breaking the silence: disability and sexuality in contemporary Bulgaria," in *Disability in Eastern Europe and the*

ACKNOWLEDGMENTS

Former Soviet Union, ed. Michael Rasell and Elena Iarskaia-Smirnova (London: Routledge, 2014). Chapter 3 is a revised version of "Deficient bodies and inefficient resources: the case of disability assessment in Bulgaria," *Disability & Society* 26, no. 4 (2011); Chapter 4—of "Personal assistance for disabled people and the understanding of human being," *Critical Social Policy* 32, no. 2 (2012); Chapter 5—of "'There is no place for you here': a phenomenological study of exclusion," *Critical Disability Discourse* 4 (2013); Chapter 6—of "Like Everest: defamiliarization and uncanniness in media representations of inaccessibility," *Disability & Society* 28, no. 4 (2013); and Chapter 8—of "The UN Convention on the rights of persons with disabilities and its interpretation," *ALTER—European Journal of Disability Research* 7, no. 1 (2013). I would like to acknowledge the publishing companies for granting permissions to reproduce the articles in this book.

Early versions of the chapters benefited from feedback provided by the anonymous reviewers and editors of the aforementioned journals and the Routledge volume, as well as the two anonymous reviewers of Bloomsbury Academic. In particular, I would like to emphasize the contributions of Michael Rasell from the University of Lincoln, Elena Iarskaia-Smirnova from Saratov State Technical University, Catherine Duchastel from York University (Canada), Len Barton from the Institute of Education (London), and Darrow Schecter from the University of Sussex (Darrow's comments influenced the final arrangement of the chapters). I am also grateful for the assistance of Matthew Kopel and Kaitlin Fontana from Bloomsbury Academic.

The support of friends and family was invaluable. Rayna and Geoff von Gerard helped selflessly with settling down in London. Milena Stateva and Yvo Pokern were impeccable as hosts and interlocutors. Besides reading my texts and commenting insightfully on my analyses, Lili Angelova kept things meaningful in times when meaning was falling apart. She also made the work possible in emotional terms. Rosi Mihaylova's unconditional belief in what I was doing was yet another condition for its possibility. Misho and Tsetska Angelovi were consistently caring and cheerful, never missing an opportunity to crack a joke. I am profoundly grateful for all the *sirene* and *rakiya* brought from Bulgaria by Rosi, Misho, and Tsetska or shared by our friends in London.

1

Introduction

Disability studies is an interdisciplinary domain of sociopolitical inquiry located at the intersection of various disciplines such as sociology, social policy, political science, literary theory, history, and philosophy. As a distinct field of academic activity, disability studies emerged in the 1980s, mainly in Britain and North America. It has its roots in the disabled people's movements of 1960s and 1970s that empowered groups and individuals to seek deinstitutionalization and independent living, as well as de-medicalization of disability.[1] Disability activism has embraced the *social model of disability* as its "big idea."[2] Stemming from principles originally formulated by the members of the British disabled people's organization, Union of the Physically Impaired Against Segregation, the social model defines "disability" as the restrictions of activity faced by people with specific bodily differences or "impairments" when they encounter disabling social and material contexts.[3] This has been a crucial insight with major theoretical and practical implications. Similarly to the feminists' distinction between (biological) sex and (social) gender, the distinction between (biological) impairment and (social) disability, as expounded by the social model, has shifted the focus in thinking about disabled people's problems from the individual and his/her body toward society and its organization. This has inspired several generations of disability scholars and activists to highlight and criticize the social and political conditions of disabled people's structurally engendered problems, referring to them in terms of oppression, exclusion, marginalization, stigmatization, inequality, and discrimination.[4] Nevertheless, over the 30 years or so of its development, disability studies has refrained from exploring the ontological dimension of disabled people's situation. Apart from several notable recent exceptions,[5] scholars within the discipline have been reluctant to explicitly engage in thinking about the meaning of being—and of human being in particular—in its relation to disability. In other words, they have been reluctant to engage with existential-ontological questions.

This reluctance has its sociopolitical reasons. Leading disability studies scholars have warned that excessive theorizing alienates the discipline from its social base.[6] The attempts at analytical sophistication have been regarded as furthering the distance between theory and practice, thus widening the gap between academic inquiry and activists' struggles for social change. While the social model still keeps this vital link alive, its elaboration along philosophical lines would arguably break it down. Is such a breakdown inevitable? One response is that a more nuanced understanding would benefit academics and activists alike. Thus Darrow Schecter notes in his discussion of Georg Simmel's philosophical sociology that "for the sociologist no less than for the activist, it is important to be able to understand and interpret social action instead of just classifying it in terms of hermetic categories and rigidly schematic notions of interest."[7] The benefit of reflexivity that philosophy brings to social sciences has been repeatedly emphasized by critical theorists:

> Philosophy . . . enables social scientists to identify and explore questions that might not otherwise be raised. Without philosophically informed social theory of the right sort whole ranges of phenomena might be sealed off from investigation and the potential political impact of the research diminished to that extent.[8]

Another response is that in modernity the struggle for disability emancipation is increasingly waged on the terrain of ontology.[9] For example, the clash between Deaf people (the capital "D" indicates that the word is used as a cultural category) and the promoters of cochlear implants has been described as "a clash in *ways of being*."[10] In a similar vein, Rod Michalko points out that "disability finds its sensibility within the ways in which a collective conceives of *what it means to be human* and how it makes a place for the individual in what it socially organizes as a human community."[11] Critical philosophical analysis ensures that the ontological assumptions of the modern society—and particularly those related to the meaning of human being—are not taken for granted. Existential-ontological suspicion, then, is a major prerequisite for challenging the *status quo*, including the one of disabling social and material contexts.

Key ideas

Proceeding from these presumptions, the present work sets out to explore the existential-ontological aspects of disability—"ontological," because they are related to the question of being and its meaning, and "existential," because they encompass these modes of being that directly concern human existence. The work takes as its conceptual point of departure the British social model's definition of disability, its distinction between "impairment" and "disability," and its attendant critique of the "individual model" and medicalization.[12] At the same time, the inquiry deliberately seeks to go beyond the social model's classical formulations and to clarify and reformulate its ontological presuppositions—a task that will be approached head-on in Chapter 2. The subsequent chapters will focus on the ways in which the meaning of one's being is associated with practices such as disability assessment, personal assistance, disability activism, disability-based discrimination, media representations of disability, discourses on sexuality and disability and disability rights legislation, henceforth referred to as "disability-related practices."

Following the approach of "practice theory," I consider "practices" to be patterned networks of interrelated activities mediated by humans and nonhuman entities.[13] This inquiry will draw on cases from Bulgaria, my home country, and will be particularly interested in the investigation of those practices that constitute or challenge *dis/ablism*. The term combines the notion of "disablism," that is, rendering people inferior on the basis of their impairments,[14] with the notion of "ableism," that is, promoting certain psychophysical features as superior or "fully human."[15] Both "disablism" and "ableism" are terms coined by analogy to critical concepts with similar meaning and function such as sexism, racism, and agism. Since I take disablism to be the negative complement of ableism—unlike Campbell, who insists that the two words "render quite radically different understandings of the status of disability to the norm"[16]—I combine the two terms by writing "dis/ablism."

In order to explore disability-related practices, this investigation will resort to the methodological and conceptual tools of phenomenology—an approach that looks at the concrete (everyday, familiar, immanent) in order to uncover the general (transcendent). Drawing on ideas developed by Martin Heidegger and Maurice Merleau-Ponty that will be presented below, I consider phenomenology to be an approach that focuses on the details of everyday involved and engaged human living and finds there answers (or new questions) concerning being and meaning.[17] The significance of studying phenomenologically the existential-ontological aspects of disability by looking at disability-related practices is twofold. First, any attempt to understand disability will be incomplete without analyzing the way in which the meaning of disability is related to the meaning of human being in general. Second, any attempt to challenge dis/ablism—for instance, in the area of social policy or human rights legislation—will remain questionable if it does not pay heed to the existential-ontological implications of the practical measures proposed.

The relationship between the general and the concrete—sociologically, the "macro-level" and the "micro-level," philosophically, the "transcendent" and the "immanent"—generates a major methodological tension that will be repeatedly thematized throughout the book. My initial idea was to highlight the relationship between disability and the meaning of human being by conceptualizing certain existential-ontological tendencies of modernity concerning disabled and nondisabled people alike. Critical theorists—including those within disability studies—have analyzed such tendencies under broad headings such as medicalization, methodological and political individualism (and neoliberal individualism in particular), productivism, consumerism, instrumental rationality, and technological "enframing." In developing the project for my research, I summarized these notions into three modes of *reduction of the human*—objective, subjective, and instrumental. This critical framework was strongly influenced by Heidegger's version of phenomenology, and—more specifically—by his critique of the metaphysics of presence and modernity.[18]

My main argument contains three elements that I consider to be fundamental for the understanding of "disability" within disability studies: (a) bodily differences, (b) mediation, and (c) restrictions of activity. My contribution to the discipline consists in exploring these elements and their interrelations in the light of the existential-ontological considerations suggested by the aforementioned critical phenomenological framework. Thus I argue that mediation (element b) incorporates existential-ontological reductions, and that restrictions of activity (element c) amount to undermining of disabled people's being. Consequently, my main argument can be formulated thus: bodily differences usually identified as "impairments" (element a) are translated into restrictions of activity (element c) and, on a deeper level, into undermining of disabled people's very existence through the mediation (element b) of inhabiting a world constituted by disability-related practices that incorporate general patterns of existential-ontological reduction.[19] The question concerning the ontological status of bodily differences (element a) will be addressed in the discussion of bodily realism in Chapter 2, and subsequent chapters will explore dis/ablist mediation (element b) and its effects in terms of restrictions of activity and undermining of disabled people's being (element c).

Undermining of being

Element (c) of my main argument incorporates the idea that the restrictions of activity faced by people with impairments in their everyday encounters with dis/ablism have an ontological dimension that amounts to undermining of disabled people's very existence. This negative existential-ontological aspect has been highlighted by disability scholars in various ways, although its genesis and structure have remained obscure. For example, as early as in 1966, Hunt expresses anger over the fact that disabled people are frequently treated as "less than people."[20] More recently, Hughes states that "[f]or most people 'it goes without saying' that they are human beings. For disabled people in many historical contexts 'it has to be said'."[21] Similarly, Campbell underlines throughout her recent book that, in modernity, disability is systematically regarded as "inherently negative" and "ontologically intolerable."[22] The existential-ontological negation of disabled people is also implicated in the already obsolete but persevering term "invalid" that connotes lack of worth ("valid" comes from the Latin *valere*, which means "to be worth"). The word is still used to refer to disabled individuals in many countries, particularly in Eastern Europe.[23] In Bulgaria the term, albeit formally abandoned in 2005 with the introduction of the new Law for the Integration of People with Disabilities, nevertheless persists—not only in media reports and popular parlance, but also in institutional discourse.[24] Such persistence reflects something deeper than a mere habit of speech—it reflects the work of *privation*.

On the level of ontology, "privation" could be regarded as the operation of defining an entity as a lacking version of another entity. The first entity does not have an independent ontological status, relying for its being and meaning on the second entity that is regarded as ontologically complete. Privation is a paradigmatic operation of modernity. It is at work every time a binary opposition is set up, which is why all binary oppositions tend to be hierarchically structured. Thus women are consistently rendered as privative versions of men, premodern people—as privative versions of moderns, the Orient—as a privative version of the Occident and so forth.[25] Through privation, the other is framed as a lacking variation of the same and this essential sameness is regarded as the basis for inclusion. Yet such an inclusion is actually *inclusive exclusion* (I borrow the term from Agamben)[26] through which real difference—that is, difference able to "make a difference"[27]—is effaced.

Phenomenologists have been vocal critics of ontological privation. Exemplary in this respect is the work of Emmanuel Levinas, whose entire oeuvre could be regarded as a systematic effort to overcome the logic of privation and to restore to the subordinate term (the "other") its independence, dignity, and ability to bring about "real difference."[28] Within disability studies, it has repeatedly been suggested that in modernity disabled people are systematically framed as privative versions of able-bodied people.[29] For example, in the binary opposition of sightedness versus blindness, blindness is overwhelmingly reduced to a privation of sight:

the conventional version of the binary opposition of sightedness/blindness privileges the former. This opposition imagines blindness not merely as opposite to sight but as the negation of it, generating a conception of blindness as lack—lack of knowledge, lack of normalcy, lack of ability.[30]

But:

> The deviation from one modality of existence (e.g. seeing) to another (e.g. blindness) can only be called a loss, and therefore the person has problems, if the first modality is used as the standard for judgements about the second. Purely in terms of physical existence, which can be of infinite variation, any modality may be used as the standard.[31]

Thus in modern society the "otherness" of living with a specific bodily difference identified as impairment is consistently being translated into the privative "sameness" of deficient normality or ab-normality. This situation has its conceptual antecedents. The modern mind-body distinction received its original formulation in the first half of the seventeenth century in the works of René Descartes, who thus articulated philosophically a way of relating to phenomena that had already started to dominate his times.[32] The mind-body distinction is inherently hierarchically structured, which entails relations of power—by prioritizing the mind over the body, it subjugates the latter, incorporating at that a host of other hierarchical binaries such as culture versus nature, internal versus external, reason versus passion, active versus passive etc. Drew Leder points out that to posit a strict boundary of separation between the mind and the body leads to nature being deprived of its "soul" and becoming dead, passive matter, amenable to limitless interventions on behalf of the active subject.[33] Consequently,

> Descartes's ontology is thus intertwined with a project of mastery. . . . Prior to the advent of mechanism, certain prohibitions remained against human tampering with nature. Insofar as natural bodies were seen by pre-modern thinkers as alive and exhibiting intrinsic ends, there were limits placed upon their use. . . . However, when nature was reconceived as lifeless mechanism, such constraints were lifted. *Res extensa*, devoid of intrinsic subjectivity, could be reshaped in a limitless fashion.[34]

Feminist scholars have been particularly articulate in exposing this political aspect of the Cartesian mind-body dualism, linking it in a genealogical fashion to the alleged ontological dependence of the feminine on the masculine.[35] If the body is ontologically inferior to the mind, and the feminine is conceived as inherently "corporeal," while the masculine is considered as inherently "rational," then the feminine tends to be regarded as a privative version of the masculine. Similar analyses have been applied to disability. Thus Abberley points out that "the mode of being of disabled people can be seen as constituting a paradigmatic negation of masculinity," conceived as "mastery over nature"[36];

Hughes states that "[t]he strong, well-formed, non-disabled, masculine body is the benchmark and against this benchmark a woman is found wanting and a disabled person—man or woman—is weak and vulnerable"[37]; and Shakespeare notes that, similarly to women, "disabled people could also be regarded as Other, by virtue of their connection to nature; their visibility as evidence of the constraining body; and their status as constant reminders of mortality."[38] Importantly, with disability the aforementioned privation works through a kind of a double other-ing—in modernity disabled people are systematically framed as the other of the other. They are not only associated with the corporeal, but their corporeality is conceived as *intrinsically deficient* as well. Obviously, this mechanism affects disabled women in the first place,[39] but given that disabled men are subjected to feminization on the basis of their impairments,[40] they are not exempt from double other-ing either.

By exposing the existential-ontological dimension of the restrictions faced by disabled people, my ethico-political hope is to open up a space for re-imagining and positively re-valuing different ways of being human. To be able to do this, though, it is not enough to imagine *different individuals*—what is needed is to imagine *different worlds* that incorporate different existential-ontological presuppositions. By inspiring and leading such a foundational change, disabled people become "entitled bearers of a fresh view of reality," "introducing issues and perspectives with the potential to refigure the social order."[41] Similarly, Fisher argues that through encounters with disability a new ethics can develop—one of interdependence rather than independence, autonomy, calculation, and entrepreneurship: "Through their personal experiences of parenting and caring for their children many parents develop insights into the values of mutuality and interdependence that transcend dominant notions of 'normality' and autonomy that are based on ontological separateness."[42] Hughes sees the task of disability studies in the twenty-first century as developing a critical social ontology that is capable of granting ontological recognition to disabled people.[43] The present inquiry incorporates these ethical commitments.

Modernity and its ontological reductions

In the preceding section, I explained how restrictions of activity (element c. of my main argument) can be regarded as undermining disabled people's very being. Now, I turn toward the idea that mediation (element b. of the main argument) incorporates ontological reductions. The basic premise is that, on the most general level, modernity encompasses a family of interrelated existential-ontological patterns or tendencies that can be mapped on the social, political, economic, technological, and cultural history of the Western world. These tendencies have their own prominent philosophical articulators, although their genesis and persistence is by no means confined to philosophy.[44] Phenomenologists such as Martin Heidegger and Maurice Merleau-Ponty have singled out the fathers of philosophical modernity René Descartes and Immanuel Kant[45] as the articulators of the fundamental presuppositions of modernity, yet it is not unusual to trace the genealogy of the modern ontological presuppositions back to Plato.[46] A defining feature of these presuppositions is ontological reductionism, which is just another name for traditional ontology. As Hubert Dreyfus puts it:

> Traditional ontology has always sought to understand the everyday world by finding something on the level of the occurrent, such as substance, sense data, or representations in transcendental consciousness, that is supposed to be intelligible without reference to anything else, and then sought to show how everything else can be seen to be intelligible because it is built up out of these self-sufficient elements.[47]

Let us consider Descartes's famous statement "*I think, therefore I am*" that grounds being in thinking.[48] First, Descartes sharply differentiates the mind from the body as two radically different substances—the mind is essentially a "thinking thing" (*res cogitans*), whereas the body—an "extended thing" (*res extensa*). As Merleau-Ponty points out, within this Cartesian framework there are "two senses, and two only, of the word 'exist': one exists as [an extended] thing or else one exists as a consciousness."[49] Second, building on his radical distinction, in his *Meditations*, Descartes endeavors to identify himself exclusively with his mind, subjecting his embodiment to radical doubt.[50] Thus the mind gets ontological priority over the body, which consequently becomes "a secondary and non-essential aspect of [one's] true nature."[51] The sociopolitical consequences of this reasoning were already highlighted in the preceding section. Here, it is important to emphasize that both the "thinking things" and the "extended things" posited by Descartes are based on the notion of *substantiality* that is characterized by self-sufficient presence in space and endurance through time. This means that Descartes equates being with something occurrent—he substituted the ontology of the world with "that of certain entities within-the-world."[52]

When Heidegger begins his major work *Being and Time*, originally published in 1927, with the stipulation that the question of being (*Sein*) has been forgotten, he has this traditional ontological stance in mind.[53] On this reading, to challenge the "forgetfulness of being" is just another way to critically approach ontological reductionism—that is, the tendency to reduce being to entities, to understand being exclusively in terms of beings. This leads to "de-worlding"[54]—entities are extracted from their constitutive contexts and are regarded as self-sufficient or self-explanatory. As far as the human way of being is concerned, modern de-worlding amounts to reducing humans to objects, subjects, or resources. To be an object means to be a passive entity, a (docile) body liable to scientific and especially biomedical scrutiny, normalization, and corrective interventions. To be a subject means to be a self-conscious, self-driven, self-reliant, isolated "I," able to make autonomous decisions and to intentionally control and manipulate objects—an understanding of human being epitomized by the radical individualism of neoliberalism. Finally, to be a resource means to be a useful entity, available for instrumental purposes in the framework of productivist and/or consumerist social orders.

Phenomenologists have time and again highlighted and criticized reductive understandings of being, and of human being in particular. Heidegger begins his *Zollikon Seminars*—a series of workshops and lectures addressed to medical practitioners in the period 1959–69—stating clearly that "human existing in its essential ground is never just an object which is present-at-hand; it is certainly not a self-contained object," and that "all conventional, objectifying representations of a capsule-like psyche, subject, person, ego, or consciousness in psychology and psychopathology must be abandoned in favour of an entirely different understanding."[55] Unlike "present-at-hand" (*vorhanden*) entities whose way of being is self-enclosed, humans are essentially decentered, ecstatic, always already beyond themselves, as will be explained below. Merleau-Ponty's *Phenomenology of Perception* can also be read as a sustained critique of the reduction of human beings to self-contained subjects or objects, especially when it comes to issues of embodiment. As far as the reduction of humans to resources is concerned, in his analysis of modernity Heidegger criticizes the technological way of being that tends toward imposing a total domination over late modernity by transforming each and every entity into a "standing-reserve" [*Bestand*]—a resource constantly available for instrumental utilization:

> As soon as what is unconcealed no longer concerns man even as object, but does so, rather, exclusively as standing-reserve, and man in the midst of objectlessness is nothing but the orderer of the standing-reserve, then he comes to the very brink of a precipitous fall; that is, he comes to the point where he himself will have to be taken as standing-reserve.[56]

It is important to underline that the reductive existential-ontological patterns or tendencies of modernity outlined above are not to be found in "transcendental consciousness," nor in some "empirical reality" that is independent of human existence. Ontological reductions are constantly being (re)constituted and (re) articulated through one's everyday involvement with entities and others within the meaningful context of a world. For Heidegger, being "is" not—rather, it *obtains*.[57] That is why Heidegger prefers to write "it gives/there is being" (*es gibt Sein*) instead of "being is" (*Sein ist*).[58] Being—or, more precisely, the meaning of being, the understanding of what it means *to be*, for "[b]eing is given in the understanding of being"[59]—obtains in meaning-engendering contexts or worlds constituted by social practices. This means that ontological reductions "are" not either—they *obtain* in specific social and historical situations. In order to grasp them as socially and historically contingent, though, one needs to substitute the traditional atomistic "substance ontology" with a radically contextualized and holistic "event ontology."[60] The phenomenological notion of "world" and the understanding of human being (Dasein) as "being-in-the-world" and of human body as "lived body" provide for such a substitution.

World, being-in-the-world, Dasein

In *Being and Time* Heidegger introduced the notion of "being-in-the-world" (*In-der-Welt-sein*) in order to designate the most basic state of human being or, in Heidegger's terms, "Dasein."[61] The notion was part of his attempt to overcome not only Cartesian mind-body dualism, but also his teacher Husserl's prioritizing of subjectivity.[62] Consequently, being-in-the-world is said to be *ontologically primordial* in the sense that it makes intelligible both the subjective and the objective modes of being, as well as the being of instruments: "*all* the modes of Being of entities within-the-world are founded ontologically upon the worldhood of the world, and accordingly upon the phenomenon of Being-in-the-world."[63] As "a structure which is primordially and constantly *whole*,"[64] being-in-the-world suggests a holistic understanding of human being that does not abstract "an individual" from the context s/he inhabits. Accordingly, the preposition "in" that mediates between "being" and "world" does not designate a location in space but it denotes *involvement*— that is, habitation, dwelling, familiarity.[65] In other words, the human being is able to be "in space" only on the basis of being-in-the-world.[66] The same reasoning applies to time. Hubert Dreyfus illustrates this foundational state of human being with expressions such as "He is *in* love" or "He is *in* the working class."[67] Heidegger insists that such an involved or engaged way of being has ontological priority over the detached, objectifying, and objectified residing in tridimensional space and linear time (i.e., the time of the clock and the calendar). This means that one is able to relate to entities *as such*—that is, as entities—only on the basis of one's ability to inhabit, dwell, or be familiar with a meaning-engendering context. This meaning-engendering context is "the world." The term, then, designates all the relations obtaining among humans and nonhuman entities that constitute the background of meaningfulness. From a phenomenological perspective, "the world" is the context on the basis of which it is possible to relate to entities as meaningful and as such the world is the "there" that gets inhabited by humans and where meaning obtains. Accordingly, the human way of being is designated as "Da-sein" that literally translates from German as "there-being."

Dasein is neither a subject nor an object. Rather, Dasein is the condition one enters when one begins to make sense of entities, others and oneself: "We can think of Dasein as a condition into which human beings enter, either individually or collectively, at a historical juncture when Being becomes an issue for them."[68] William Blattner points out that Dasein should be approached in terms of "ability-characteristics," not "state-characteristics."[69] The abilities that are proper to Dasein are abilities at understanding, at giving and receiving meaning: "to exist as Da-sein means to hold open a domain through its capacity to receive-perceive the significance of the things that are given to it [Da-sein] and that address it [Da-sein] by virtue of its own 'clearing' [*Gelichtetheit*]."[70] In other words, to be Dasein means to be able to relate to entities *as* entities of a particular kind, for example, as instruments—available, "ready-to-hand" (*zuhanden*) things,[71] or else as objects—self-contained, occurrent, "present-at-hand" (*vorhanden*) things.[72] Dasein understands being. That is why the definitive feature of Dasein on the ontic level—that is, the feature that distinguishes Dasein from other entities—is that it is ontological: "Dasein is ontically distinctive in that it *is* ontological."[73] On the one hand, Dasein's abilities at understanding being are realized by *engaging* with entities and others within the world—that is, by *inhabiting* a world. That is why the most basic state of Dasein is being-in-the-world.[74] On the other hand, in its being-in-the-world Dasein gets involved with entities and others in such a way as to let them be *as* entities and others.

Every activity of Dasein implies understanding of being and every understanding of being implies understanding of one's own being, that is, self-understanding. Heidegger captures this essential self-referentiality of Dasein with the term "mineness" (*Jemeinigkeit*).[75] Dasein cannot not relate; Dasein cannot not understand; and Dasein cannot not self-understand. Dasein relates by doing and by not doing; by speaking and by keeping silent; and also by being in a mood. To be Dasein is to be "thrown" into relating, understanding, and self-understanding. Dasein's characteristics are essentially ability-characteristics and these ability-characteristics are essentially self-interpretive ability-characteristics[76]—not in cognitive terms though, for the (self)understanding that is in question actually *grounds* cognition.

What would it mean for Dasein to be "disabled" then? On the existential-ontological level of analysis, to be disabled would mean to be restricted in one's possibilities for self-understanding in such a way, so that one's very existence is undermined. In order for a human being to understand herself or himself as *X* (worker, mother, student), s/he must be able to *inhabit a world as X*. This means that, in the first place, there should be a world that would let one be as *X*. The world that disabled people find themselves thrown into disciplines them into assuming a self-understanding of deficiency, inferiority, in-validity. The fight of disabled people for emancipation is therefore essentially an existential-ontological fight—a fight for a new world where different self-understandings would be possible. These issues will be looked at in more detail in the chapters on discrimination (Chapter 5) and media representations of inaccessibility (Chapter 6).

Lived body

The analysis of Dasein's being-in-the-world developed in *Being and Time* is exclusively focused on *practical* engagement. That is why Heidegger's phenomenological descriptions of this mode of being emphasize the role of the "hand," as for example in the activity of hammering.[77] Importantly, "hand" here should not be taken to mean an anatomical organ but the bodily aspect of the ability to inhabit a world. In an essay on Heidegger entitled "Heidegger's ear" Derrida points out that, for Heidegger, the ear is similar to the hand in that it is not "an organ with which graspable or perceptible things are received or perceived."[78] The reason is that the hand is "always engaged in speaking and *logos*"[79]—that is, the hand is always engaged in the disclosure of meaning, including its own meaning. Within the framework of the existential-ontological analysis presented in *Being and Time*, the "hand" is the bodily aspect of the ability to inhabit a world where it is possible to relate to entities either as "ready-to-*hand*" (*zuhanden*)—that is, as available instruments, or as "present-at-*hand*" (*vorhanden*)—that is, as occurrent objects.[80]

This leads to the more general question concerning the relationship between the human *body* and being-in-the-world. In *Being and Time* Heidegger avoids such a discussion with the stipulation that Dasein's "'bodily nature' hides a whole problematic of its own."[81] Heidegger was most probably concerned that if the human way of being gets related to *a* body *before* the analysis of being-in-the-world is fully developed, this would distort the analysis by reducing Dasein to an occurrent, present-at-hand entity.[82] From the perspective of existential phenomenology, the body can be properly *human* only within the broader structure of a world.[83] Nevertheless, Heidegger's analysis of being-in-the-world remains incomplete without an account of the body. Hubert Dreyfus, among others, regards this omission with unease:

> without the body there could be no account of why there are just these regions [of existential spatiality]. We would not be able to understand, for example, why the accessibility of right and left is not symmetrical, or why we must always "face" things in order to cope with them. On Heidegger's account these would just remain unexplained asymmetries in the practical field. This is not inconsistent, but it is unsatisfying.[84]

"Not inconsistent, but unsatisfying" is a good way to denote Heidegger's disregard of the body. "Not inconsistent," because it does not prevent Heidegger from laying the ground for a holistic and practice-oriented understanding of human being as being-in-the-world; "unsatisfying," because this understanding is incomplete without a phenomenological account of the body. Such an account was later provided by Maurice Merleau-Ponty in his *Phenomenology of Perception*, who "pursued the general project of division I of *Being and Time* in an essential direction neglected by Heidegger, but without which Heidegger's phenomenology is seriously compromised."[85] Merleau-Ponty built on Heidegger's analysis of being-in-the-world in order to conceptualize the body in a nonreductive way. He designated the body that is an integral part of being-in-the-world as "lived body"—referring to the German word *Leib*—and distinguished it from the traditional Cartesian understanding of the body as an inanimate, machine-like "organism"—in German, *Körper*.[86] The same distinction was also rendered by Merleau-Ponty in terms of "phenomenal body" versus "objective body," where:

> the objective body is not the true version of the phenomenal body, that is, the true version of the body that we live by: it is indeed no more than the latter's impoverished image, so that the problem of the relation of soul to body has nothing to do with the objective body, which exists only conceptually, but with the phenomenal body.[87]

So, the objective body is an "impoverished image" of the lived or phenomenal body, where "impoverished" should be taken to mean "de-worlded." The "lived body" (*Leib*), however, is always already meaningful because it is bound in a *co-constitutive relationship* with the world: "I am conscious of my body *via* the world," but also "I am conscious of the world through the medium of my body."[88] Consequently, the notion of "lived body" provides the opportunity to think about the body without losing sight of the world. For example, when Merleau-Ponty states that "[w]e must . . . avoid saying that our body is *in* space, or *in* time. It *inhabits* space and time,"[89] he is not referring to the objective, but to the lived (phenomenal) body. It is the former which is abstracted from the world, not the latter. Accordingly, "[w]e remain physically upright not through the mechanism of the skeleton or even through the nervous regulation of muscular tone, but because we are caught up in a world."[90] To "remain physically upright" then is to engage with a whole array of interrelated practices and meanings and should not be reduced to objective structures and processes.

The implications of this way of conceptualizing the body for analyses of disability are far-reaching, as will be demonstrated in the case studies of media representations in Chapter 6 and sexuality in Chapter 7. Chapter 2 develops the argument by emphasizing that the *strongly realist* view of the body espoused by some disability scholars may render the body as "overendowed with nature and over-determined by its natural limitations,"[91] which invites "biological reductionism."[92] In contrast, to regard the body as "lived" is to re-inscribe its materiality into the meaningful context of the worlds inhabited by humans. Such a *weakly realist* re-inscription helps in uncovering the mechanisms that translate the bodily differences identified as impairments into undermining of disabled people's existence. Proceeding from these presumptions, I consider the phenomenological notion of "world" and the attendant understanding of human being (Dasein) as "being-in-the-world" and of human body as "lived body" as constituting the conceptual bedrock of the present investigation. These ideas will be further elaborated in Chapter 2 and will then be used in the case studies in Chapters 3–8 as guidelines for the critical phenomenological analysis of disability.

Methodological considerations

The present work is an interdisciplinary inquiry into disability. The two main disciplines that it draws on are sociology and philosophy. In this section, I will first highlight some general methodological—or "metatheoretical"[93]—issues that stem from my engagement with particular ideas and schools of thought within and across these two disciplines. After that, I will proceed with more specific methodological considerations about the techniques of inquiry utilized in the chapters to follow.

Sociology

The investigation draws first and foremost on the critical sociological approach to disability developed within disability studies. More specifically, it takes as its point of departure the British social model of disability[94] while also considering its recent developments, revisions, and critiques along poststructuralist, feminist, phenomenological, and critical realist lines.[95] I consider the most salient feature of disability studies to be its methodological holism, as opposed to methodological individualism.[96] This is certainly a defining characteristic of the social model. The latter has been regarded as "an *holistic* approach that explains specific problems experienced by disabled people in terms of the *totality of disabling environments and cultures*."[97] My contention is that methodological holism and its attendant antireductionist attitude to the questions concerning disability are also pivotal for disability studies in general. As Schillmeier puts it, "[t]he very strength of disability studies has been, precisely, to propose alternatives to challenge the reductionist perspective(s) of modern epistemological politics."[98] Within the discipline, this anti-reductionist research ethos translates into focusing on the environing world and emphasizing interrelatedness and interdependence.[99]

The present investigation is also influenced by ideas developed in the domain of sociology of the body.[100] The analyses of embodiment elaborated by sociologists of the body have a direct bearing on issues related to disability.[101] Most importantly for my purposes, the sociology of the body is inherently concerned with overcoming binary oppositions—the central one of course being the opposition between body and society. Crossley even argues that, besides being "a major issue for the sociologists of the body," the resolution of the problem of dualism "sometimes appears to be the very *raison d'etre* of sociological interest in the body."[102] In brief, the sociology of the body's antireductionist stance and its philosophically dense critiques of Cartesianism informed by phenomenology[103] provide good reference points for understanding modern ontological reductions.

In my sociological approach to disability I also draw on ideas from the domain of science and technology studies (STS),[104] and particularly from actor-network theory (ANT).[105] From STS/ANT, I borrow concepts such as boundary-work, boundary object, translation, mediation, black-boxing, distribution, assemblages, and networks—these concepts are particularly prominent in the case studies presented in the chapters on disability assessment (Chapter 3), discrimination (Chapter 5), and the UN Convention on the Rights of Persons with Disabilities (Chapter 8). Over the past decade the STS/ANT approach has already been applied to disability with promising results.[106] In metatheoretical terms, I find STS concepts to be useful for bridging the gap between the micro- and macro-levels of sociological analysis. Accordingly, I do not subscribe to ANT's rejection of critical theory. For example, Bruno Latour dismisses critiques of modernity, particularly the critique of modern reductionism[107]—yet if we have deluded ourselves into believing in subjects and objects throughout the modern period, as Latour argues, then the exposure of this delusion is bound to constitute a radical critique of modernity and of its reductive ontological presuppositions.

Philosophy

As far as philosophy is concerned, the present work can be located within the tradition of critical philosophy as initiated by Kant in his epochal attempt to overcome both rationalism and empiricism.[108] Roughly speaking, this tradition insists on exploring the conditions for the possibility of relating meaningfully to entities before exploring the entities themselves.[109] Yet Kant's philosophy tends to depict these conditions as subjective, disembodied, and ahistorical:

> in focusing the search for the conditions of ontological determinability on the transcendental subject as a detached, disembodied ego, Kant chose the wrong starting point. He remained trapped within the Cartesian understanding of the subject as a thinking substance, which led him to think of Dasein as a worldless entity, an occurrent compound of body and soul.[110]

In order to overcome this residual Cartesianism while remaining faithful to Kant's critical project, critical philosophers needed to challenge, first, the priority of the subject, second, the priority of the present, and third, the priority of the rational form. As Pippin puts it, "[t]heoretically, the question was: how has it come to be that we require experience to be categorized in various, ineliminable ways, in just *these* ways? No one in [the critical] tradition was content with Kant's reliance on some innate 'logical form' in human judgment as an answer."[111] Historically, this discontent with the Kantian solution stimulated a series of consecutive philosophical attempts at re-conceptualizing mediation. To put things briefly and schematically: Kant saw the possibility for a dialectical reconciliation between the subjective and the objective poles in the mediation of the transcendental subjectivity; later, Hegel historicized Kant's transcendental subjectivity, emphasizing its intrinsic relation with social and historical objectivity; on his behalf, Marx rendered Hegel's historicized yet still all too idealist mediation in exclusively materialist terms (i.e., in terms of relations of production) while nevertheless retaining its rational teleology.[112] From the perspective of this critical tradition, Heidegger's philosophy can be regarded as an attempt to *radicalize the understanding of mediation* beyond any subjective, objective, and/or instrumental reference points. Heidegger endeavored to do this by emphasizing the ontological significance of being-in-the-world.

Thus Heidegger's focus on the ontological determination—that is, the being (*Sein*)—of beings (*Seiendes*) can be genealogically related to Kant's work on the conditions for the possibility of knowledge. But whereas Kant located these conditions in the mediation of the transcendental subject, Heidegger regarded the ontological determination of entities as mediated by the social practices of inhabiting a world. The methodological corollary is that one should attend to the everyday, involved, and embedded reality of the human being-in-the-world in order to tackle the question of being. Such an analysis focuses first of all on "those entities within-the-*environment* which we encounter as closest to us."[113] The interrogation of the finite Dasein in the context of its everyday living takes precedence over metaphysical speculation:

> The theme of our analytic is to be Being-in-the-world, and accordingly the very world itself; and these are to be considered within the horizon of average everydayness—the kind of Being which is *closest* to Dasein. We must make a study of the everyday Being-in-the-world; with the phenomenal support which this gives us, something like the world must come into view.[114]

This methodological injunction delineates an important point of contact between the phenomenological approach informed by Heidegger's critical philosophy and the critical sociological approach outlined above. The point of contact is the focus on the everyday, involved social practices in view of their significance for human existence in general. So far, disability studies scholars have engaged with Merleau-Ponty's version of phenomenology,[115] but Heidegger's thought has remained largely disregarded. Indeed, two relatively recent books—Campbell's *Contours of Ableism* (2009) and Schillmeier's *Rethinking Disability* (2010)—make extensive use of Heidegger's concepts, yet without taking phenomenology as their methodological point of departure. Unlike them, the present work explicitly endeavors to approach disability from a phenomenological perspective. This perspective is informed by Heidegger's critical philosophy, in conjunction with Merleau-Ponty's work on the body.[116]

Case study method

The present investigation proposes a phenomenologically informed conceptual framework for critical analysis of disability-related practices. Such an endeavor is, first, itself grounded in social practices (as the section entitled "Personal reflections" below makes clear), and second, in need of an appropriate research method for providing analytically rich accounts of practices. The latter consideration underpins the choice of the case study method. In procedural terms, case studies allow for considerable flexibility in defining the topic, the scope of the description, and the sources of information. Consequently, this research method facilitates conceptual innovation[117]—a major aspiration of the present work. In addition, case studies are regarded as more appropriate for exploring generative mechanisms, whereas cross-case study approaches might be more useful for studying effects.[118] This makes the case study method particularly suitable for my purposes, considering my focus on the mechanisms that translate bodily differences into undermining of disabled people's existence. Last but not least, by focusing on a single issue, entity, or event, case studies allow for a significant depth of analysis, thus facilitating analytically thorough and holistic accounts. Indeed, this very feature is often adduced as an argument against the "generalizability" of case studies, but a less formal view of generalization and a less detached understanding of the researcher's role grant more credibility to case studies' inferences.[119]

The last point suggests that the choice of the case study method has also been prompted by my metatheoretical affiliations discussed above. Case studies allow the inquirer to attend to the everyday practices that constitute human being-in-the-world while paying heed to the inquirer's own context-dependent, first-person perspective—a major methodological concern of phenomenology.[120] In other words, the method that looks at the minute details of a single case allows for a more engaged analysis than the cross-case study approach seeking conclusions on the basis of a large sample of cases:

> Great distance to the object of study and lack of feedback easily lead to a stultified learning process, which in research can lead to ritual academic blind alleys, where the effect and usefulness of research becomes unclear and untested. As a research method, the case study can be an effective remedy against this tendency.[121]

Unsurprisingly, phenomenologists have been particularly keen on the case study method. Outstanding examples can be found in the analytically and empirically rich descriptions of different cases of perception developed by Merleau-Ponty in his *Phenomenology of Perception*. Similarly, Heidegger often grounds his philosophical reflections on detailed descriptions of concrete, familiar, everyday activities, entities, or moods. Examples include the activity of hammering in *Being and Time*, the peasant shoes in "The origin of the work of art,"[122] the jug in "The thing"[123] and boredom in *The Fundamental Concepts of Metaphysics*.[124] Phenomenologically influenced social scientists have also developed seminal studies of cases. For example, through a detailed investigation of the activity of "throwing like a girl," Young famously discloses the ways in which patriarchal norms get incorporated in bodily habits, resorting to Merleau-Ponty's work on the body.[125] Garfinkel's ethnomethodology, which draws on the phenomenology of Husserl, Schütz, and Heidegger,[126] is primarily concerned with meticulously describing individual cases of everyday social practices. Actor-network theorists, whose links with phenomenology are mediated by poststructuralism but are nevertheless discernible, deploy their analyses on the level of the "local" by "following the actors" through the "heterogeneous networks" they inhabit—Law and Callon's unpacking of a case of military aircraft project provides a good illustration of this approach.[127] All these examples suggest that the case study method is a preferred tool for inquiries drawing on or influenced by phenomenology.

Overview of the cases

In Chapters 3–8 I develop case studies of different disability-related practices. Chapter 3 is concerned with the objective and instrumental modes of reduction of the human and their translation into restrictions of activity through the mediation of the medicalized and productivist disability assessment as is legally codified and practiced in contemporary Bulgaria. The next case, presented in Chapter 4, focuses on the subjective mode of reduction by exploring the tension between individualist and collectivist understandings of human being implied in a specific mechanism for the provision of personal assistance for disabled people. Chapter 5 revisits the issue of objective reduction—it explores the spatio-temporal patterns that underlie the reduction of human beings to passive, object-like entities. Such patterns, it is argued, underpinned the exclusion, from the domain of the human, of a group of disabled people in a case of disability-based discrimination that gained considerable publicity in Bulgaria some years ago. In the process of developing the case studies on personal assistance and discrimination (Chapters 4 and 5) I became increasingly preoccupied with the mundane, familiar details of everyday interactions. Thus in the case studies following Chapter 5, I shifted emphasis from the macro- to the micro-level of analysis and incorporated several new conceptual tools in my investigation of disability. Chapter 6 explores the mechanism of "defamiliarization" and the attendant experience of "uncanniness" associated with disability in recent media representations of the inaccessible architectural environment in Sofia. Chapter 7 looks at everyday understandings of the body and their role in sustaining dis/ablism by analyzing popular discourses on sexuality in its relation to disability. Finally, Chapter 8 highlights the ubiquity of interpretation and the importance of its extra-juridical dimension for the constitution of juridical solutions to disability-related problems, particularly of those solutions outlined in the UN Convention on the Rights of Persons with Disabilities.

The six case studies presented in the six consecutive chapters following Chapters 1 and 2 were developed in the same chronological order. What unifies them is the focus on the existential-ontological aspects of disability. The shift of emphasis from the macro- toward the micro-level of investigation reflects both the weakening or "decentering" (as the theorists of deconstruction might put it) of my initial quasi-structuralist position and the explicit recognition of the pivotal role of bodily difference in the constitution of the phenomenon of disability. Yet it does not represent a turn toward methodological individualism or to naïve realism. From its very beginning until its end, my research has been grounded in methodological holism. The shift of its emphasis helped to extend this holism toward the body—or, rather, to reinsert the question about the ontology of the body into the holistic understanding of disability developed so far.

The cases are taken from present-day Bulgaria. The choice of the topics has been suggested by: (1) the significance of the issues for disabled people's wellbeing, and accordingly—for disability studies and politics; (2) my own previous observations and thoughts on these issues, stemming from my decade-long professional engagement with disabled people's organizations—on this ground, I chose topics with which I already had some familiarity, such as disability assessment (Chapter 3), personal assistance (Chapter 4), and media representations of inaccessibility (Chapter 6); (3) the availability of information—this consideration prompted, for example, the inclusion of the cases on discrimination (Chapter 5), sexuality (Chapter 7), and the UN Convention (Chapter 8). It should be noted here that the discipline of disability studies is still virtually nonexistent in the Bulgarian context, which means that available and readily utilizable information is scarce. My sources were national and international legislation, policy documents, juridical decisions, electronic and print media reports, online discussion forums, internet sites as well as my personal and professional experience in the Bulgarian disability rights movement.

The Bulgarian context

Since the fall of the state socialist regime in 1989, Bulgaria has experienced a turbulent "transition" from a centrally planned economy toward a free market economy and from one-party rule toward parliamentary democracy. This transformation has been accompanied not only by a number of significant social and cultural changes, but also by a number of continuities. The new order ostensibly undermined all kinds of boundaries—national, ideological, cultural. Traveling abroad became easier and people gained unprecedented access to previously scarce or explicitly forbidden cultural resources, a process that has been greatly enhanced by the internet since the mid-1990s. Nevertheless—or probably precisely as a reaction to such disorienting openness—negative attitudes toward *difference* along major sociocultural axes like ethnicity, gender, sexual orientation, and disability have remained relatively stable. Public discussion on such issues was largely silenced during the state socialist period, when the problems of difference were expected to automatically wither away with the abolition of class exploitation. They did not disappear,[128] but neither did they dissolve with the development of the free market and parliamentary democracy after 1989. The results of recent sociological studies strongly suggest that "at the moment in Bulgaria (and to a different but approximating degree in all postsocialist countries) many real problems exist in relation to the perception and approach towards difference."[129]

The interplay between change and continuity over the past two decades of transition is especially pronounced with regard to issues of disability, although Bulgarian sociologists rarely consider this form of difference in their analyses. Two examples will clarify the point. As might be expected, individualism has quickly become the dominant way of structuring relationships with others and with the self in the new, aspiringly neoliberal order.[130] Nevertheless, disabled people continue to be denied individual agency. This is particularly evident when one considers the ongoing hegemony of paternalistic personal assistance schemes first introduced by the government in 2002.[131] As will be argued in Chapter 4, these schemes have proved time and again incredibly resistant to reforms along the lines of the independent living philosophy and practice. The other example is related to the already mentioned term "invalid." In 2005, a major legislative change finally substituted this problematic label with the more appealing "person with disability" (in Bulgarian: *chovek s uvrezhdane*). The substitution was promoted by progressive disabled people's organizations, reflecting the self-perception of the majority of disabled people in Bulgaria, particularly those of working age, as suggested by a nationally representative survey conducted in 2001.[132] Yet everyday use, supported by the media, continues to resist this linguistic transformation—for a great number of Bulgarians, as for most of Bulgarian journalists, disabled people are still "invalids."

Illuminating such historical tendencies makes it easier to uncover the dynamics of dis/ablism in Bulgaria. Reports highlighting exclusion, discrimination, oppression, and even physical violence experienced by disabled Bulgarians have been mounting over the first decade of the new millennium, mainly due to the efforts of grassroots organizations of disabled people.

These have included: nationwide studies criticizing Bulgarian disability policy as a whole[133]; critical analyses of disability legislation[134]; accounts of inaccessible built environment, of which many recent examples can be found in the media, as Chapter 6 testifies; cases of discrimination adjudicated by the Bulgarian Commission for Protection against Discrimination (www.kzd-nondiscrimination.com), one of which is extensively studied in Chapter 5; and reports on the degrading and inhuman conditions within residential institutions.[135] In sum, the restrictions of disabled people's activity and the attendant undermining of their very existence have been well documented by Bulgarian human rights advocates, occasionally supported by the media. The history of this pervasive dis/ablism refers back to the state socialist responses to disability but, more importantly, dis/ablism has survived the demise of the old regime. In 2007, an international comparative study covering 14 European countries put Bulgaria in one of the last places (twelfth) in terms of the overall inclusion of disabled people in the country.[136] All these observations raise questions about those features of the present Bulgarian context that are associated with dis/ablism. Several such features can be outlined that might not be specifically Bulgarian when considered individually, but constitute a more or less distinctive physiognomy when taken together.

First, disability-related regulations, concepts, and practices in Bulgaria have been heavily medicalized. Historically speaking, such medicalization can be traced back to the influence of the Soviet approach of *defectology* during state socialist times.[137] At present, it is most conspicuous in the standard method for certifying disability status for welfare purposes—the "Medical expert assessment of the ability to work" that will be explored in detail in Chapter 3. The medicalization of disability permeates everyday discourse too, as argued in Chapter 7. Second, Bulgarian disability policy-making is dominated by the so-called "nationally representative organizations of and for disabled people" as defined in the Bulgarian Law for the Integration of People with Disabilities of 2005. These large membership-based umbrella structures have been criticized for reproducing and sustaining paternalistic and charity-focused approaches to disability.[138] Yet they have retained their exclusive position as the government's "legitimate partner" where disability policy is concerned, enjoying annual government subsidies.[139] Third, disability-related thought and action in accord with the social model of disability and the independent living philosophy (Chapter 4) is confined to a few grassroots civil society entities. At present, these groups are small in size, financially fragile, and often excluded from local and/or national policy-making.[140] So far, disability has not been pursued as a legitimate and valuable field of study by Bulgarian social and political scientists or by those working in the field of humanities. This list of features is far from exhaustive but it nevertheless provides some clues for imagining the present physiognomy of dis/ablism in Bulgaria and the factors that are associated with it.

The physiognomy of dis/ablism in Bulgaria is also marked by intersectionality. The present investigation pays heed to the intersection of disability and gender in the chapter on sexuality (Chapter 7), where it is argued that the gendered expectations of the male-centered worldview rooted in the metaphysics of presence contribute significantly to the existential-ontological invalidation of disabled people. Unlike gender, class and its intersection with disability remain outside of the scope of the work, chiefly because of Bulgaria's specific socio-historic situation. State socialism greatly undermined the significance of this axis of difference. Indeed, since the fall of the regime in 1989, market-oriented transformations of the Bulgarian society along the lines of deregulation and privatization have resulted in the emergence and gradual increase of class divisions. But their impact on disabled people's lives is still incommensurable with the one characteristic of "advanced" capitalist countries with firmly established and easily recognizable class systems such as Britain or the United States.

As far as ethnicity is concerned, it is important to note that Roma people constitute a large (about 5 percent according to official data) and heavily segregated group of the Bulgarian population. Bulgarian Turks are another large ethnic group, but they are much better included socially and politically and, in general, are not subjected to discrimination in the way and to the degree that Roma people are. Disabled Roma people therefore experience multiple forms of oppression in the Bulgarian society. The studies presented in the book do not tackle this issue because ethnicity did not figure as an axis of difference in the particular cases that were analyzed. Thus the description and critical analysis of ethnic difference in its relation to dis/ablism in Bulgaria remains a sociopolitically and analytically important task for future phenomenological investigations of the lives of disabled people in Bulgaria.

Personal reflections

Disability studies scholars have insisted that those who engage with disability research should be reflexively aware of their "own values, priorities and processes of interpretation,"[141] including their biographies. On their behalf, phenomenologists have repeatedly emphasized the inextricable historicity of human existence that "always carries forward its past, whether it be by accepting or disclaiming it. We are, as Proust declared, perched on a pyramid of past life, and if we do not see this, it is because we are obsessed by objective thought."[142] What past do I carry forward and how has it influenced my present investigation? Born in Bulgaria in 1976, I spent the first 13 years of my life in a state socialist country, while after 1989 I experienced the rise and consolidation of neoliberal capitalism. I grew up in Bulgaria, yet since 2005 I have spent extensive periods in England. Accordingly, although my first language is Bulgarian, for a number of years now I have been reading, writing, and even thinking in English. I was originally trained as a psychologist, but eventually turned toward sociology and philosophy. Being "able-bodied," I have often felt as a stranger in the disabled people's community, but recognizing dis/ablism has alienated me much more from the community of the "able-bodied" experts and professionals. My research occupies a "no man's land" between sociology and philosophy. In sum, my past has been one of crossing boundaries between regimes, cultures, languages, communities, and domains of knowledge. These boundary-experiences bring about anxiety but can also be illuminating. For a social scientist, to be a stranger can be advantageous.[143] Reflecting on his own personal and intellectual biography, Lennard Davis notes: "Perhaps it is true that the outsider is fully the only one who can write. And perhaps writers are never fully part of that which they write about."[144] Not having a "proper" place, experiencing oneself as an outsider both "at home" and "abroad" makes one able to see the same as other, thus enhancing one's perception of what usually remains imperceptible because of its familiarity—a theme developed in the chapters on discrimination (Chapter 5) and media representations of inaccessibility (Chapter 6). Without constituting a privileged vantage point, my personal experiences of the "in-between" nevertheless inform my analyses of disability.

Professional background

Before commencing the present work, I was involved for almost a decade in the Bulgarian disability rights movement by organizing advocacy events, supervising community development workers, conducting disability equality trainings, translating awareness-raising materials, doing emancipatory research, and writing social policy analyses. An image would best convey the spirit of the times. It is a photograph taken during a public action on December 3, 2003, which depicts a row of people in wheelchairs against a row of police officers in front of the Council of Ministers in Sofia.[145] Wheelchair users are demanding government funding for personal assistance, while the police officers are protecting the institution. Ironically, the entrance to the building is architecturally inaccessible, thus making the presence of the police somehow redundant. The public action was one of the many organized by the Center for Independent Living (CIL)—Sofia (www.cil.bg), a Bulgarian nongovernmental, nonprofit organization of disabled people. Since 1996, the organization has advocated for equal opportunities for disabled people by promoting the independent living philosophy and the social model of disability.

I have taken part in numerous projects implemented by CIL—Sofia, including nationwide disability awareness campaigns and campaigns for changing disability legislation in the direction of social inclusion, deinstitutionalization, and antidiscrimination. In addition, CIL—Sofia has promoted critical thought and reflection by producing a host of print and electronic materials—newsletters, journals, pamphlets, manuals, analyses, and reports, covering issues such as accessibility, personal assistance, inclusive education, participation in the labor market, and participation in the policy-making. Most of the case studies presented in this book draw on my experiences, observations, and reflections accumulated over the years of my professional engagement with CIL—Sofia and refer to materials publicized by the organization. This engagement has shaped my thinking about disability, although I have gradually developed a critical attitude toward some of the ideas underlying disability activism. Still, I find myself committed to its ethos.

So far, I have not been physically or behaviorally different in ways which would invite my framing as "disabled." I recognize that people whose lives are entangled in disability-related practices have access to insights that are hardly accessible to me due to my different positionality. I therefore sympathize with the slogan "Nothing about us without us!," which privileges disabled people's experience in thought and action. Yet both the meanings of "us" and of "experience" should not be taken for granted. The positing of a collective subject·is a politically strong and often necessary gesture but it tends to be exclusive and to reproduce the oppressions it is meant to overthrow in the first place.[146] A broader understanding of "us" and of "experience" would grant some experiential legitimacy to my own investigations. Notwithstanding my able-bodied-ness, over the years of my involvement in the disability movement in Bulgaria, I have time and again witnessed dis/ablism in areas such as built environment, interpersonal communication, personal assistance, disability assessment, welfare provision, legal regulation, medical treatment, media representations, schooling, political representation, and research. These encounters with dis/ablism are a major motivation behind my present investigation and shape its presuppositions and conclusions.

Conceptual background

If one accepts that "philosophy begins . . . as an inheritance"[147] and not in a vacuum, then it is crucial to turn to one's conceptual history in order to understand one's conceptual present. A good deal of my formal training in psychology at the Sofia University (1995–2000) was informed by classical psychoanalysis and some of its psychodynamic embranchments, which at that time were gaining prominence in academic circles. During the same period, though, I got involved in an extra-curricular group for studying and practicing the postmodern psychotherapeutic approach of Solution Focused Brief Therapy (SFBT).[148] Steve de Shazer, one of the founders of the approach, uses Wittgenstein's language philosophy and the poststructuralism of Derrida and Lacan in order to conceptualize SFBT practice.[149] I was heavily influenced by de Shazer's way of looking at the therapeutic situation, and, by extension, at the human world.

In 2005–06 I spent one year at the University of Sussex, UK, to study Social and Political Thought. There, the sociopolitical aspects of the philosophy of Kant, Hegel, Marx, Nietzsche, Benjamin, Gramsci, Heidegger, Foucault, Derrida, and other critical thinkers were discussed extensively and in considerable depth under telling course headings such as "Text and critique in social and political thought" and "Methodological approaches to the history of ideas." My master's dissertation at Sussex was devoted to exploring the relevance of certain ideas in Nietzsche, Heidegger, Foucault, and Derrida for disability studies. Although since then I have revised some of my understandings, I consider many of the insights gained at Sussex as pivotal for my subsequent thinking.

As far as the confrontation between "continental" and "analytic" philosophical traditions is concerned, I prefer to regard it as artificial and ideological,[150] or even as a *rationalization*—"[i]t rationalises a willingness not to read, at least a willingness not to render oneself capable of reading well."[151] My own intellectual history, although primarily informed by "continental" authors, nevertheless crosses the boundary between the two camps (which adds yet another case to the list of my "in-between" experiences referred to above). My reading of Heidegger has been strongly influenced by Hubert Dreyfus, who explains Heidegger's ideas by taking on board notions from Dewey and Wittgenstein, Bourdieu and Kuhn, Searle and Foucault—thus creatively combining pragmatism and analytic philosophy of language, critical sociology and philosophy of science, analytic philosophy of mind and poststructuralism.[152] I find many of the concepts that are influential within the "analytic" domain particularly engaging and useful— such as Wittgenstein's "language games" and "forms of life," as well as his critique of "private language"[153]; Austin's distinction between "constative" and "performative" utterances[154]; and Ryle's critique of Descartes's mind-body dualism and his distinction between "knowing how" and "knowing that."[155] These ideas have been helpful in building my understanding of the phenomenological concept of "world," which constitutes the conceptual core of the present thesis.

Relational background

The present investigation is also shaped by its relational background. Obviously, there are many people who have influenced it—I have recognized them in my acknowledgments. Yet what I want to highlight here are not personal relations, but relations of research production. These relations have diverse manifestations in contemporary academia. For one thing, researchers are submitted to a ubiquitous pressure to "get published" that more or less imperceptibly influences the articulation of their ideas. The point is that:

> Knowledge within the Academy serves a variety of purposes. It is a commodity by which academics do far more than exchange ideas; it is the very means of exchange for the academic political economy. Tenure, promotion, peer recognition, research grants, and countless smaller codes of privilege are accorded through the adding up of articles, books, papers in "refereed" journals and conferences.[156]

These "economic, job survival or advancement pressures to produce in appropriate ways"[157] constitute an increasingly instrumentalized research ethos that in Britain is promoted through the system of the periodic research assessments (currently termed "Research Excellence Framework") that serves to determine the allocation of public funding for academic research. The prospects for continuing one's work in academia often hang on the number and "quality" of one's publications in highly ranked peer-reviewed journals that would provide for a good research assessment submission of the host institution. Whatever I have written here has been affected by this institutionally embedded instrumental rationality that regards one's conceptual work as a means for advancing one's employment chances. For example, most of the chapters were originally written in view of their submission as self-standing articles for peer-reviewed publication. This had some impact on the content, mostly due to the methodological requirements of the targeted outlets. Sometimes, more empirical evidence was expected, at other times the practical relevance of the research was to be emphasized, yet at other times the theoretical underpinnings had to be strengthened. At one point, this tension between theory and practice manifested itself explicitly within a single feedback—the paper I had submitted to a peer-reviewed journal was returned for revision with one referee suggesting "to enhance the theoretical and conceptual basis of the work" and the other recommending "the theory [to be] boiled down to its essentials." On the one hand, the field of social policy—and probably of contemporary Anglo-Saxon sociology as well—is reluctant to engage in philosophical debates. On the other hand, the field of philosophy tends to regard "empirical" studies as insufficiently rigorous in conceptual terms or as uncritical with regard to their own presuppositions. This presents immense challenges for interdisciplinary endeavors, such as the present one, that happen to occupy the aforementioned "no man's land" between sociology and philosophy. No matter how successfully these challenges were addressed here, it seems futile to disentangle the final result from the disciplining (in both the negative and the positive, Foucaultian sense of the word) influences of the context of knowledge production that it inhabited.

Activists in the disability movement have been highly suspicious of academics—especially of "able-bodied" ones—for "hijacking" the movement's ideas for personal career gains. The aforementioned conditions of research production in contemporary academia that reduce intellectual activity to an instrument for securing one's job in a precarious employment situation add a structural dimension to this risk of misappropriation. Since on the one hand my background is rooted in disability activism, yet on the other hand I am an "able-bodied" researcher who has for the past several years been positioned within an academic field, I have experienced the full force of this contradiction. But whereas there is an undeniable instrumental, self-interested aspect to what I have done here, which has influenced its form and content, there are also many instances of struggle with such one-dimensional instrumentality. Without disavowing the former, as an author I identify most fully with those moments of the text that manage to articulate resistances to the ubiquitous logic of instrumental rationality.

Notes

1 Rannveig Traustadóttir, "Disability studies, the social model and legal developments," in *The UN Convention on the Rights of Persons with Disabilities: European and Scandinavian Perspectives*, eds. Oddný Mjöll Arnardóttir and Gerard Quinn (Leiden and Boston: Martinus Nijhoff Publishers, 2009), 4–7.

2 Frances Hasler, "Developments in the disabled people's movement," in *Disabling Barriers—Enabling Environments*, ed. John Swain, Vic Finkelstein, Sally French, and Mike Oliver (London: SAGE, 1993), 280.

3 Union of the Physically Impaired Against Segregation, *Fundamental Principles of Disability* (London: Union of the Physically Impaired Against Segregation,

1976); Michael Oliver, *Understanding Disability: From Theory to Practice* (London: Macmillan, 1996).

4 Len Barton, "Struggle, support and the politics of possibility." *Scandinavian Journal of Disability Research* 1, 1 (1999): 13–22.

5 For example, Fiona Kumari Campbell, *Contours of Ableism: The Production of Disability and Abledness* (Basingstoke: Palgrave Macmillan, 2009); Bill Hughes, "Being disabled: towards a critical social ontology for disability studies." *Disability & Society* 22, 7 (2007): 673–84; Michael Schillmeier, *Rethinking Disability: Bodies, Senses, and Things* (New York: Routledge, 2010).

6 Colin Barnes, Mike Oliver and Len Barton, "Disability, the academy and the inclusive society," in *Disability Studies Today*, eds. Colin Barnes, Mike Oliver, and Len Barton (Cambridge: Polity Press, 2002), 257–8.

7 Darrow Schecter, *The Critique of Instrumental Reason from Weber to Habermas* (London: Continuum, 2010), 29–30.

8 Fred Rush, "Introduction," in *The Cambridge Companion to Critical Theory*, ed. Fred Rush (Cambridge: Cambridge University Press, 2004), 9.

9 Hughes, "Being disabled."

10 Campbell, *Contours of Ableism*, 94.

11 Rod Michalko, *The Difference that Disability Makes* (Philadelphia: Temple University Press, 2002), 14, emphasis added.

12 Victor Finkelstein, *Attitudes and Disabled People: Issues for Discussion* (New York: World Rehabilitation Fund, 1980); Michael Oliver, *The Politics of Disablement* (London: Macmillan, 1990); Oliver, *Understanding Disability*; Union of the Physically Impaired Against Segregation, *Fundamental Principles*.

13 Theodore Schatzki, "Introduction: Practice theory," in *The Practice Turn in Contemporary Theory*, eds. Theodore Schatzki, Karin Knorr Cetina, and Eike von Savigny (New York: Routledge, 2001).

14 Carol Thomas, *Sociologies of Disability and Illness: Contested Ideas in Disability Studies and Medical Sociology* (Basingstoke: Palgrave Macmillan, 2007), 13.

15 Campbell, *Contours of Ableism*, 5.

16 Ibid.

17 Martin Heidegger, *Being and Time*, trans. John Macquarrie and Edward Robinson (Oxford: Blackwell, 1962 [1927]); Maurice Merleau-Ponty, *Phenomenology of Perception*, trans. Colin Smith (New York: Routledge, 2002 [1945]).

18 Heidegger, *Being and Time*.

19 It might immediately be objected that at least some impairments are *intrinsically* restrictive—that is, restrict human activity and/or undermine human existence *independently of* mediation. I will discuss this issue in Chapter 2.

20 Paul Hunt, "A Critical Condition," in *The Disability Reader: Social Science Perspectives*, ed. Tom Shakespeare (London: Cassell, 1998 [1966]), 14.

21 Hughes, "Being disabled," 677.

22 Campbell, *Contours of Ableism*.

23 See International Disability Network, *International Disability Rights Monitor (IDRM): Regional Report of Europe, 2007* (Chicago: International Disability Network, 2007).

24 Applied to a person, the word "invalid" (in Bulgarian: *invalid*) has the same negative connotations in Bulgarian as in English.

25 Luce Irigaray, *This Sex Which is Not One*, trans. Catherine Porter with Carolyn Burke (Ithaca, NY: Cornell University Press, 1985 [1977]); Bruno Latour, *We Have Never Been Modern*, trans. Catherine Porter (Cambridge, MA: Harvard University Press, 1993 [1991]); Edward W. Said, *Orientalism* (New York: Vintage Books, 1978). In the case of "the feminine," for example, "[h]istorically, the reduction of sexual difference has been the reduction of the *feminine* other to what Irigaray calls the 'masculine' economy of the same. . . . Within this economy the feminine other is not thought in her alterity or specificity *qua* feminine but only as the dependent opposite of the masculine, the not-masculine. In effect, 'the feminine' translates as the inferior of the masculine, the copy of the original masculine, the pathologized masculine, the castrated masculine and so on." Stella Sandford, "Levinas, feminism and the feminine," in *The Cambridge Companion to Levinas*, eds. Simon Critchley and Robert Bernasconi (Cambridge: Cambridge University Press, 2002), 143–4.

26 Giorgio Agamben, *Homo Sacer: Sovereign Power and Bare Life*, trans. Daniel Heller-Roazen (Stanford, CA: Stanford University Press, 1998 [1995]).

27 Michalko, *Difference*.

28 For Levinas, overcoming the logic of privation is very much related to overcoming Hegelian dialectics that seeks unity in difference. Both these points—the overcoming of privation and the overcoming of dialectics—are at the heart of Levinas's project: "The whole of this work [*Totality and Infinity*] aims to show a relation with the other not only cutting across the logic of contradiction, where the other of A is the non-A, the negation of A, but also across dialectical logic, where the same dialectically participates in and is reconciled with the other in the Unity of the system." Emmanuel Levinas, *Totality and Infinity: An Essay on Exteriority*, trans. Alphonso Lingis (The Hague: Martinus Nijhoff Publishers, 1979 [1961]), 150.

29 Campbell, *Contours of Ableism*; Schillmeier, *Rethinking Disability*; Minae Inahara, "This body which is not one: the body, femininity and disability." *Body & Society* 15, 1 (2009): 47–62.

30 Michalko, *Difference*, 27.

31 Finkelstein, *Attitudes*, 11.

32 René Descartes, *Key Philosophical Writings*, ed. Enrique Chávez-Arvizo, trans. Elizabeth S. Haldane and G. R. T. Ross (Hertfordshire: Wordsworth Editions, 1997). See also Nick Crossley, *The Social Body: Habit, Identity and Desire* (London: SAGE, 2001).

33 Drew Leder, "A tale of two bodies: the Cartesian corpse and the lived body," in *Body and Flesh: A Philosophical Reader*, ed. Donn Welton (Oxford: Blackwell, 1998).

34 Ibid., 119–20.

35 Elizabeth Gross, "What is feminist theory?" in *Feminist Challenges: Social and Political Theory*, eds. Carole Pateman and Elizabeth Gross (Sydney: Allen & Unwin, 1986); Sandra Harding, *The Science Question in Feminism* (Ithaca, NY: Cornell University Press, 1986); Irigaray, *This Sex*.

36 Paul Abberley, "The concept of oppression and the development of a social theory of disability." *Disability, Handicap & Society* 2, 1 (1987): 16.

37 Bill Hughes, "Wounded/monstrous/abject: a critique of the disabled body in the sociological imaginary." *Disability & Society* 24, 4 (2009): 400.

38 Tom Shakespeare, "Cultural representation of disabled people: dustbins for disavowal?" *Disability & Society* 9, 3 (1994): 292.

39 Rosemarie Garland Thomson, *Extraordinary Bodies: Figuring Physical Disability in American Culture and Literature* (New York: Columbia University Press, 1997), 29.

40 Michalko, *Difference*, 20–1; see also Chapter 7.

41 Thomson, *Extraordinary Bodies*, 38.

42 Pamela Fisher, "Experiential knowledge challenges 'normality' and individualized citizenship: towards 'another way of being'." *Disability & Society* 22, 3 (2007): 291.

43 Hughes, "Being disabled."

44 Nevertheless, it is justifiable to engage with philosophy in order to understand the existential-ontological tendencies of modernity because "issues in philosophy often simply express most economically and dramatically a variety of issues that pervade the social and cultural fabric, and philosophical language, if nothing else, can be an economical way of discussing a number of these issues." Robert B. Pippin, *Modernism as a Philosophical Problem*, 2nd edn (Oxford: Blackwell, 1999), 8.

45 Heidegger, *Being and Time*; Merleau-Ponty, *Phenomenology of Perception*.

46 Martin Heidegger, *Plato's Sophist*, trans. Richard Rojcewicz and André Schuwer (Bloomington and Indianapolis: Indiana University Press, 1997 [1924–25]).

47 Hubert L. Dreyfus, *Being-in-the-World. A Commentary on Heidegger's Being and Time, Division I* (Cambridge, MA: MIT Press, 1991), 122.

48 Descartes, *Key Philosophical Writings*, 92.

49 Merleau-Ponty, *Phenomenology of Perception*, 230.

50 Descartes, *Key Philosophical Writings*, 92; see also David R. Cerbone, "Heidegger and Dasein's 'bodily nature': what is the hidden problematic?" *International Journal of Philosophical Studies* 8, 2 (2000): 210.

51 Crossley, *Social Body*, 10.

52 Heidegger, *Being and Time*, 131.

53 Ibid., 21. In Macquarrie and Robinson's translation of *Being and Time* used here, the German term *Sein* is translated in English as "Being," with a capital "B." Following Dreyfus (*Being-in-the-World*, xi) and Blattner (*Heidegger's Being and Time: A Reader's Guide*, London: Continuum, 2006, 14), I prefer to avoid capitalization because it might suggest that "being" is some kind of super-entity. Heidegger's point is precisely that "being" is not an entity but the foundation of any entity's most basic intelligibility—"being" is that on the basis of which entities are encountered *as entities*. As Blattner ("Heidegger's Kantian idealism revisited." *Inquiry* 47, 4 (2004): 330) puts it, Heidegger's "being" denotes "a framework of constraints that determines *whether* something is."

54 Dreyfus, *Being-in-the-World*, 139.

55 Martin Heidegger, *Zollikon Seminars: Protocols, Conversations, Letters*, ed. Medard Boss, trans. Franz Mayr and Richard Askay (Evanston, IL: Northwestern University Press, 2001 [1959–69]), 3–4.

56 Martin Heidegger, *The Question Concerning Technology, and Other Essays*, trans. William Lovitt (New York: Harper & Row, 1977), 26–7.

57   William Blattner, "Temporality," in *A Companion to Heidegger*, eds. Hubert L. Dreyfus and Mark A. Wrathall (Oxford: Blackwell, 2005), 318.

58   Heidegger, *Being and Time*, 255, see n. 1.

59   Alexandar Kanev, *Heidegger and the Philosophical Tradition* (Sofia: East-West, 2011), 28.

60   Charles Guignon, "Being as appearing: retrieving the Greek experience of Phusis," in *Companion to Heidegger's* Introduction to Metaphysics, eds. Richard Polt and Gregory Fried (New Haven and London: Yale University Press, 2001). Richard Rorty renders the difference between atomism and holism as the difference "between the assumption that there can be entities which are what they are totally independent of all relations between them, and the assumption that all entities are merely nodes in a net of relations." Richard Rorty, "Wittgenstein, Heidegger, and the reification of language," in *The Cambridge Companion to Heidegger*, ed. Charles Guignon (Cambridge: Cambridge University Press, 1993), 345. Rorty compares Heidegger's holism in *Being and Time* with that of Wittgenstein in *Philosophical Investigations*: "From the point of view of both *Philosophical Investigations* and *Being and Time*, the typical error of traditional philosophy is to imagine that there could be, indeed that there somehow *must* be, entities which are atomic in the sense of being what they are independent of their relation to any other entities (e.g., God, the transcendental subject, sense-data, simple names)." Ibid., 347.

61   Heidegger, *Being and Time*, 78.

62   Dreyfus, *Being-in-the-World*, 301.

63   Heidegger, *Being and Time*, 254.

64   Ibid., 225.

65   Ibid., 79–80; see also Martin Heidegger, *Poetry, Language, Thought*, trans. Albert Hofstadter (New York: Harper & Row, 1971), and Cerbone, "Heidegger," 214.

66   Heidegger, *Being and Time*, 82; see also John Pickles, *Phenomenology, Science and Geography: Spatiality and the Human Sciences* (Cambridge: Cambridge University Press, 1985), 154–70.

67   Dreyfus, *Being-in-the-World*, 43.

68   Gregory Fried and Richard Polt, "Translators' introduction," in *Introduction to Metaphysics*, ed. Martin Heidegger, trans. Gregory Fried and Richard Polt (New Haven and London: Yale University Press, 2000), xii.

69   Blattner, *Heidegger's* Being and Time.

70   Heidegger, *Zollikon Seminars*, 4.

71   Heidegger, *Being and Time*, 98.

72   Ibid., 67–8.

73   Ibid., 32.

74   Ibid., 78.

75   Ibid., 68.

76   Blattner, *Heidegger's* Being and Time.

77   Heidegger, *Being and Time*, 98.

78   Jacques Derrida, "Heidegger's ear: Philopolemology (*Geschlecht* IV)," in *Reading Heidegger: Commemorations*, ed. John Sallis, trans. John P. Leavey, Jr. (Bloomington and Indianapolis: Indiana University Press, 1993), 187.

79 Ibid., 187.
80 Heidegger, *Being and Time*, 67–8 and 98.
81 Ibid., 143.
82 Richard R. Askay, "Heidegger, the body, and the French philosophers." *Continental Philosophy Review* 32, 1 (1999): 29–35; see also Cerbone, "Heidegger."
83 Cerbone, "Heidegger," 225.
84 Dreyfus, *Being-in-the-World*, 137.
85 Blattner, *Heidegger's* Being and Time, 171.
86 Merleau-Ponty, *Phenomenology of Perception*, 329–30. In his English translation of Merleau-Ponty's *Phenomenology of Perception*, Colin Smith renders the French expression *corps vivant* as "living body"; the link between the latter and the German word *Leib* is explicitly made on p. 329. In the English translation of Heidegger's *Zollikon Seminars* by Franz Mayr and Richard Askay, *Leib* is given simply as "body" and is counterposed to *Körper* or "corporeal thing." In the English translation of Medard Boss's *Existential Foundations of Medicine and Psychology* by Stephen Conway and Anne Cleaves (New York and London: Jason Aronson, 1979 [1971]), *Leib* is rendered as "bodyhood," and a footnote is given explaining that "[t]his word is congruent with the German *Leib*, which has the connotation of body as lived bodylines" (p. 126, n. 2). The English term "lived body," preferred, for example, by phenomenologists such as Drew Leder (*The Absent Body*, Chicago: The University of Chicago Press, 1990), suits best my purposes here. Leder states: "To be a lived body is always also to be a physical body with bones and tendons, nerves and sinews, all of which can be scientifically characterized. These are not two different bodies. *Korper* is itself an aspect of *Leib*, one manner in which the lived body shows itself." Ibid., 6.
87 Merleau-Ponty, *Phenomenology of Perception*, 501–2.
88 Ibid., 94–5.
89 Ibid., 161.
90 Ibid., 296, n. 18.
91 Hughes, "Being disabled," 677.
92 Ibid., 679.
93 George Ritzer, *Modern Sociological Theory*, 5th edn (Boston: McGraw-Hill, 2000), 489–92.
94 Finkelstein, *Attitudes*; Oliver, *Politics of Disablement*; Oliver, *Understanding Disability*; Union of the Physically Impaired Against Segregation, *Fundamental Principles*.
95 For example, Campbell, *Contours of Ableism*; Mairian Corker and Tom Shakespeare (eds), *Disability/Postmodernity: Embodying Disability Theory* (London: Continuum, 2002); Hughes, "Being disables"; Hughes, "Wounded/monstrous/abject"; Bill Hughes and Kevin Paterson, "The social model of disability and the disappearing body: towards a sociology of impairment." *Disability & Society* 12, 3 (1997): 325–40; Kevin Paterson and Bill Hughes, "Disability studies and phenomenology: the carnal politics of everyday life." *Disability & Society* 14, 5 (1999): 597–610; Michalko, *Difference*; Schillmeier, *Rethinking Disability*; Tom Shakespeare, *Disability Rights and Wrongs* (New York: Routledge, 2006); Tom Shakespeare and Nicholas

Watson, "The social model of disability: an outdated ideology," in *Research in Social Science and Disability, Vol. 2: Exploring Theories and Expanding Methodologies*, eds. Sharon N. Barnartt and Barbara M. Altman (Stamford, CT: JAI Press, 2001); Thomas, *Sociologies*; Shelley Tremain (ed.), *Foucault and the Government of Disability* (Ann Arbor: The University of Michigan Press, 2005).

96   See Barry Barnes, *The Elements of Social Theory* (London: UCL Press, 1995), 10–36.

97   Colin Barnes, "Direct payments and their future: an ethical concern?" *Ethics & Social Welfare* 1, 3 (2007): 350, emphasis added.

98   Schillmeier, *Rethinking Disability*, 96.

99   See, for example, Fisher, "Experiential knowledge"; Dan Goodley, "Becoming rhizomatic parents: Deleuze, Guattari and disabled babies." *Disability & Society* 22, 2 (2007): 145–60; Solveig M. Reindal, "Independence, dependence, interdependence: some reflections on the subject and personal autonomy." *Disability & Society* 14, 3 (1999): 353–67.

100   Crossley, *Social Body*; Hancock Philip, Bill Hughes, Elizabeth Jagger, Kevin Paterson, Rachel Russel, Emmanuelle Tulle-Winton, and Melissa Tyler, *The Body, Culture and Society* (Buckingham: Open University Press, 2000).

101   Thomas, *Sociologies*, 138–41.

102   Crossley, *Social Body*, 1–2.

103   Ibid.; Leder, *Absent Body*.

104   Thomas F. Gieryn, "Boundary-work and the demarcation of science from non-science: strains and interests in professional ideologies of scientists." *American Sociological Review* 48, 6 (1983): 781–95; Susan Leigh Star and James R. Griesemer, "Institutional ecology, 'translations' and boundary objects: amateurs and professionals in Berkeley's Museum of Vertebrate Zoology, 1907–39." *Social Studies of Science* 19, 3 (1989): 387–420. For an excellent overview of the field see Sergio Sismondo, *An Introduction to Science and Technology Studies* (Oxford: Blackwell, 2004).

105   Bruno Latour, *Reassembling the Social: An Introduction to Actor-Network-Theory* (Oxford: Oxford University Press, 2005) and *We Have Never Been Modern*, trans. Catherine Porter (Cambridge, MA: Harvard University Press, 1993 [1991]).

106   Campbell, *Contours of Ableism*; Ingunn Moser, "Disability and the promises of technology: technology, subjectivity and embodiment within an order of the normal." *Information, Communication & Society* 9, 3 (2006): 373–95; Schillmeier, *Rethinking Disability*; Myriam Winance, "Trying out the wheelchair: the mutual shaping of people and devices through adjustment." *Science, Technology & Human Values* 31, 1 (2006): 52–72.

107   Latour, *Modern*, 115–16. Latour's relationship with critical theorizing is far from straightforward, notwithstanding that sometimes he presents it as such. For discussions of the similarities between Latour's and Heidegger's views on technology see Lynnette Khong, "Actants and enframing: Heidegger and Latour on technology." *Studies in History and Philosophy of Science* 34, 4 (2003): 693–704, and Soren Riis, "The symmetry between Bruno Latour and Martin Heidegger: the technique of turning a police officer into a speed bump." *Social Studies of Science* 38, 2 (2008): 285–301.

108   Immanuel Kant, *The Critique of Pure Reason*. 2nd edn, trans. Norman Kemp Smith (London: Palgrave Macmillan, 2003 [1787]).

109 On the relationship between Kantian critical philosophy and early Critical Theory see Fred Rush, "Conceptual foundations of early Critical Theory," in *The Cambridge Companion to Critical Theory*, ed. Fred Rush (Cambridge: Cambridge University Press, 2004), 10.

110 Béatrice Han-Pile, "Early Heidegger's appropriation of Kant," in *A Companion to Heidegger*, eds. Hubert L. Dreyfus and Mark A. Wrathall (Oxford: Blackwell, 2005): 89. The connection between Descartes and Kant is explicitly highlighted by both Heidegger (*Being and Time*, 248) and Merleau-Ponty (*Phenomenology of Perception*, x).

111 Pippin, *Modernism*, 63.

112 Schecter, *Critique*, 9–17.

113 Heidegger, *Being and Time*, 94.

114 Ibid.

115 See, for example, Hughes and Paterson, "The social model"; Paterson and Hughes, "Disability studies and phenomenology"; Jackie Leach Scully, "Disability and the thinking body," in *Arguing About Disability: Philosophical Perspectives*, eds. Kristjana Kristiansen, Simo Vehmas, and Tom Shakespeare (New York: Routledge, 2009).

116 I will not engage here with the question of Heidegger's politics. Whether Heidegger's political conservatism and his support for National Socialism in the 1930s were personal mistakes or have deep roots in his philosophy is a point which continues to generate heated debates among Heideggerians (for a critical discussion see Slavoj Žižek, *The Ticklish Subject: The Absent Centre of Political Ontology*. London: Verso, 1999, 11–22). Yet even if the roots of Heidegger's politics are to be found in his philosophical oeuvre (as Žižek argues), it would still be possible to appropriate some of Heidegger's ideas for the progressive purposes outlined in this introduction. Dieter Thomä (in "The name on the edge of language: a complication in Heidegger's theory of language and its consequences," in *A Companion to Heidegger's* Introduction to Metaphysics, eds. Richard Polt and Gregory Fried. New Haven and London: Yale University Press, 2001, 104–5) insists on reading Heidegger's texts against Heidegger's own claims of lifelong consistency. Following this suggestion, I endeavor to use certain elements of Heidegger's oeuvre while disregarding others—and, needless to say, I reject Heidegger's politics. Such an approach allows for a productive engagement with Heidegger's thought, some aspects of which are too much related to "blood and soil" imagery to be of use in research projects like the present one, while others could effectively inform progressive thinking in the twenty-first century—see, for example, Gianni Vattimo and Santiago Zabala, *Hermeneutic Communism. From Heidegger to Marx* (New York: Columbia University Press, 2011).

117 John Gerring, *Case Study Research: Principles and Practices* (Cambridge: Cambridge University Press, 2007), 39–41.

118 Ibid., 44–5.

119 Bent Flyvbjerg, "Five misunderstandings about case-study research." *Qualitative Inquiry* 12, 2 (2006): 219–45.

120 Taylor Carman, *Merleau-Ponty* (New York: Routledge, 2008), 14.

121 Flyvbjerg, "Five misunderstandings," 223.

122 In Martin Heidegger, *Off the Beaten Track*, ed. and trans. Julian Young and Kenneth Haynes (Cambridge: Cambridge University Press, 2002).

123 In Martin Heidegger, *Poetry, Language, Thought*, trans. Albert Hofstadter (New York: Harper & Row, 1971).

124 Martin Heidegger, *The Fundamental Concepts of Metaphysics: World, Finitude, Solitude*, trans. William McNeill and Nicholas Walker (Bloomington and Indianapolis: Indiana University Press, 1995 [1929–30]).

125 Iris Marion Young, *On Female Body Experience: "Throwing Like a Girl" and Other Essays* (Oxford: Oxford University Press, 2005), 27–45.

126 Harold Garfinkel, *Studies in Ethnomethodology* (Englewood Cliffs, NJ: Prentice-Hall, 1967). The phenomenological ancestry of ethnomethodology is made more explicit in Harold Garfinkel, *Ethnomethodology's Program. Working Out the Durkheim's Aphorism*, ed. Anne W. Rawls (Oxford: Rowman & Littlefield Publishers, 2002).

127 John Law and Michel Callon, "Engineering and sociology in a military aircraft project: a network analysis of technological change." *Social Problems* 35, 3 (1988): 284–97.

128 This is testified by the persistence of gender inequalities during state socialism despite the high inclusion of women in nondomestic labor activities (Ilona Tomova, "Those who are different: between stigma and recognition," in *European Values in Bulgarian Society Today*, ed. Georgi Fotev (Sofia: St. Kliment Ohridski University Press, 2009). Also revealing in this respect are the attempts at solving the problems of difference through violence, as reflected in the forceful assimilation of Bulgarian Turks at the end of Todor Zhivkov's rule (Curtis, ed. *Bulgaria: A Country Study*. Washington: Library of Congress, 1992).

129 Tomova, "Those who are different," 120.

130 On neoliberalism and post-1989 transition see William Outhwaite, "Postcommunist capitalism and democracy: cutting the postcommunist cake." *Democratic Socialism* 1, 1 (2011): 1–23; Gareth Dale, "Introduction: The transition in Central and Eastern Europe," in *First the Transition, Then the Crash: Eastern Europe in 2000s*, ed. Gareth Dale (London: Pluto Press, 2011).

131 Center for Independent Living, *Assessment of the Assistant Services for People with Disabilities in Bulgaria* (Sofia: Center for Independent Living, 2009).

132 Center for Independent Living, *From Handicapped People to Persons with Disabilities (Disability Rights in Bulgaria: A Survey, 2001)* (Sofia: Center for Independent Living, 2002), 15.

133 Ibid.; Center for Independent Living, *Disability—A Deficit or a Survival Means (Disability Rights in Bulgaria: A Survey, 2002)* (Sofia: Center for Independent Living, 2003); and Center for Independent Living, *Equal Opportunities through Access to Social Services (Disability Rights in Bulgaria: A Survey, 2003)* (Sofia: Center for Independent Living, 2004).

134 Kapka Panayotova and Kolyu Todorov, *Integration and the Law for the Integration of People with Disabilities* (Sofia: Center for Independent Living, 2007).

135 Liliya Angelova, "The road to Mogilino: the ideology of normality and Bulgaria's abandoned children" (Sofia: Center for Independent Living, 2008); Center for Independent Living, *Equal Opportunities*; Bulgarian Helsinki Committee, *Human Rights in Bulgaria in 2010* (Sofia: Bulgarian Helsinki Committee, 2011).

136 International Disability Network, *International Disability Rights Monitor (IDRM): Regional Report of Europe, 2007* (Chicago: International Disability Network, 2007).

137 Elena L. Grigorenko, "Russian 'defectology': anticipating *Perestroika* in the field." *Journal of Learning Disabilities* 31, 2 (1998): 193–207. On the Soviet medicalization of disability see Elena Iarskaia-Smirnova, "'A girl who liked to dance': life experiences of Russian women with motor impairments," in *Gazing at Welfare, Gender and Agency in Post-socialist Countries*, eds. Maija Jäppinen, Meri Kulmala, and Aino Saarinen (Newcastle upon Tyne: Cambridge Scholars Publishing, 2011), 120.

138 Center for Independent Living, *Handicapped People*; *Disability—A Deficit*; and *Equal Opportunities*. See also Teodor Mladenov, "Institutional woes of participation: Bulgarian disabled people's organisations and policy-making." *Disability & Society* 24, 1 (2009): 33–45. The genealogy of these organizations is far from straightforward. Some, like the Union of the Deaf (www.sgbbg.com) or the Union of the Blind (ssb-bg.net), were founded well before the communists came to power in 1944, albeit under different names. Others, like the National Consumer Cooperative of the Blind (www.npksb.com), emerged during state socialist times. Yet others, like the Union of the Invalids (www.disability-bg.org) or the Bulgarian Association for Persons with Intellectual Disabilities (bapid.com), were founded after the fall of the regime in 1989. The extent to which the state socialist ideology and practice influenced the values, ideas, and activities of these organizations is not immediately obvious and requires a separate analysis.

139 Lyuben Panov and Georgi Genchev, *Assessment of the Mechanism for Allocating Subsidies from the Budget of the Republic of Bulgaria to NGOs* (Sofia: Bulgarian Center for Not-for-Profit Law, 2011).

140 This frailty of grassroots organizations is an aspect of a more general phenomenon: "The weakness of civil society, in the sense of associational life, remains a striking feature of the postcommunist world." Outhwaite, "Postcommunist capitalism," 8. Outhwaite cites Howard (*The Weakness of Civil Society in Post-Communist Europe.* Cambridge: Cambridge University Press, 2003, 13–14), who points out that "[a]lthough the breakdown or survival of democracy may not be at stake, the *quality* of post-communist democracy suffers as a result of the weakness of civil society, as post-communist citizens become increasingly alienated from the political process, while simultaneously lacking the institutional leverage that organizations might provide."

141 Len Barton, "Emancipatory research and disabled people: some observations and questions." *Educational Review* 57, 3 (2005): 320.

142 Merleau-Ponty, *Phenomenology of Perception*, 457.

143 Zali D. Gurevitch, "The other side of dialogue: on making the other strange and the experience of otherness." *American Journal of Sociology* 93, 5 (1988): 1181.

144 Lennard J. Davis, *Bending over Backwards: Disability, Dismodernism, and Other Difficult Positions* (New York: New York University Press, 2002), 164.

145 The photograph is reproduced in Teodor Mladenov, *Of People and People. Analysis of the "Assistant for Independent Living" Campaign of the Center for Independent Living—Sofia* (Sofia: Center for Independent Living—Sofia, 2004), 120.

146 See Paul S. Duckett, "What are you doing here? 'Non-disabled' people and the disability movement: a response to Fran Branfield." *Disability & Society* 13, 4 (1998): 625–6.

147 Simon Glendinning, *The Idea of Continental Philosophy: A Philosophical Chronicle* (Edinburgh: Edinburgh University Press, 2006), 30.

148 Gale Miller and Steve de Shazer, "Have you heard the latest rumor about. . .? Solution-focused therapy as a rumor." *Family Process* 37, 3 (1998): 363–77.

149 Steve de Shazer, *Putting Difference to Work* (New York: Norton, 1991) and *Words Were Originally Magic* (New York: Norton, 1994).

150 Robert C. Solomon, "Introduction," in *The Blackwell Guide to Continental Philosophy*, eds. Robert C. Solomon and David Sherman (Oxford: Blackwell, 2003), 1; and Simon Critchley, "Introduction: What is continental philosophy?" in *A Companion to Continental Philosophy*, eds. Simon Critchley and William R. Schroeder (Oxford: Blackwell, 1998), 4.

151 Glendinning, *Idea*, 6.

152 Dreyfus, *Being-in-the-World*.

153 Ludwig Wittgenstein, *Philosophical Investigations*, trans. G. E. M. Amscombe (Oxford: Basil Blackwell, 1986 [1953]).

154 John L. Austin, *How to Do Things with Words? The William James Lectures Delivered at Harvard University in 1955*, ed. J. O. Urmson (Oxford: Oxford University Press, 1962).

155 Gilbert Ryle, *The Concept of Mind* (Harmondsworth: Penguin Books, 1963 [1949]).

156 Budd L. Hall, "In from the cold? Reflections on participatory research from 1970–2005." *Convergence* 38, 1 (2005): 18–19.

157 Ibid., 19.

2

The body

This chapter articulates the presuppositions informing the understanding of the body that guides the case studies of disability-related practices in Chapters 3–8. Throughout these analyses I endeavor to maintain and promote a *weakly realist view of the body*. This means that, on the one hand, I acknowledge the reality of bodily differences—that is, their independence from the holistic, meaning-engendering contexts or worlds inhabited by humans. By "bodily differences" I mean identifiable variations in the materiality and/or functionality of the body such as presence or absence of an organ or an anatomical structure, or alterations of an organ's or an organ system's properties or ways of working and so forth. On the other hand, I insist that it is the social, political, economic, cultural, historical, and technological mediation of inhabiting a world that brings about the understanding of bodily differences as, for example, restrictions or possibilities, lacks or excesses, demands or offers. Notably, "understanding" here does not refer to cognition but to relations of disclosure that are not necessarily cognitive. One understands something when one inhabits a world in such a way so that it is possible—or necessary—to relate to something as such and such. It is this mediation of inhabiting a world that incorporates existential-ontological reductions and that is the main focus of the present investigation of disability. I use phenomenology in order to explore its mechanisms.

It might immediately be objected that one can meaningfully relate to what is independent from the mediation of inhabiting a world—or, in phenomenological terms, from being-in-the-world—only within this mediation. Nevertheless, to admit that mediation is necessary for gaining *access* to what is independent from mediation does not entail that mediation *constitutes* it. Heidegger makes this point with regard to entities studied by the natural sciences:

> To say that before Newton his laws were neither true nor false, cannot signify that before him there were no such entities as have been uncovered and pointed out by those laws. Through Newton the laws became true;

and with them, entities became accessible in themselves to Dasein. Once entities have been uncovered, they show themselves precisely as entities which beforehand already were. . . . Even the "universal validity" of truth is rooted solely in the fact that Dasein can uncover entities in themselves and free them. Only so can these entities in themselves be binding for every possible assertion—that is, for every way of pointing them out.[1]

This type of realism may be counter-intuitive but it is nevertheless defensible,[2] particularly with regard to the entities of natural sciences.[3] Yet human beings are of a qualitatively different kind than natural entities, as has been argued by Dilthey and his hermeneutic followers. Being one of them, Heidegger distinguishes humans in that they have an understanding of being, including their own being. As pointed out in the introductory chapter (Chapter 1), from such a perspective humans are by definition (self)interpreting, *hermeneutic* beings. Similarly, albeit drawing on a different philosophical tradition, Ian Hacking suggests that humans are of an "interactive kind," whereas the entities studied by the natural sciences are of an "indifferent kind."[4] This means that, unlike the latter, humans react and change in accordance with the ways in which they find themselves addressed—for example, through diagnostic categories—within the "matrix" of their contextually embedded living. Consequently, "[t]he targets of the natural sciences are stationary. Because of looping effects, the targets of the social sciences are on the move."[5]

What about the human *body* then? Is it of an indifferent or an interactive kind? What is its role in human (self)understanding?

Due to the "looping effects" highlighted by Hacking, when one attempts to gain access to human phenomena (habits, experiences, thoughts, feelings, motivations, perceptions, etc.) by exploring human bodies in their materiality, one inadvertently changes the phenomena under investigation, including the materiality of the body itself. Yet even if one accepts the radical thesis that, in the realm of the human, mediation always already constitutes that which exceeds mediation, it does not follow that such an "excess" can be reduced to mediation—it can still be conceived as *an effect that necessarily exceeds its cause*. Hence it seems possible to suspend the choice between the given and the constituted character of bodily differences while nevertheless acknowledging that bodily differences exceed mediation and have an impact on the way one inhabits a world *from out of this excess*. The meaning of this impact, though, is not independent from mediation.

Thus even though bodily differences are always already incorporated in human (self)understanding, they can still be regarded as real in the weak sense presented above. One more stipulation—in my definition of "bodily differences"

I deliberately sought to position the term outside the normal-abnormal continuum. Actually, this may well be one of the most difficult tasks of any critical and aspiringly holistic exploration of disability—to emancipate specific bodily differences from the mediation of the norm that "permits the idea of individual variation while enforcing a homogeneous standard or average."[6] Thus the norm reduces differences to deviations and undermines their ability to "make a difference," as Rod Michalko has convincingly argued.[7] In Chapter 1, I referred to this mechanism as one of "inclusive exclusion," borrowing the term from Agamben.[8]

In this chapter, I will explore the ways in which my version of weak realism with regard to the body relates to other instances of bodily realism within disability studies. Where appropriate, I will make references to relevant discussions in the chapters to come. In the concluding section I will develop further the case for weak bodily realism by revisiting the phenomenological notions of finitude, world, being-in-the-world, and lived body.

Body, realism, and disability studies

The debate about the body in disability studies has often been framed as a clash between constructionism and realism. Constructionists have accused realists of biological reductionism and traditionalism (not to mention conservatism), while realists have accused constructionists of disembodied relativism and wishful thinking (not to mention denial). The paradigmatic collision along these lines has been between the British social model theorists (e.g., Michael Oliver) and the social model's critics (e.g., Tom Shakespeare). My contention is that this clash would seem less irreconcilable and the positions of both sides more comprehensible—at least as far as the body is concerned—if it is reframed as a contest between two versions of realism, a weak one and a strong one. As already stated, in my analyses I side with the former.

Thus I tend to agree with Andrew Sayer that the metaphor of "construction" is "hopelessly misleading" and can invite an "idealist slippage."[9] Yet one should be equally careful with the metaphor of "reality," which, on its behalf, can invite an essentialist or reductionist "slippage." Accordingly, whereas the critical realism of Sayer is interested in weakening constructionism, I am interested in weakening realism. In a gesture parallel to the one distinguishing between weak and strong bodily realism, yet coming from the opposite direction, Sayer distinguishes between weak and strong social constructionism:

> In its weak form, [social constructionism] merely emphasizes the socially constructed nature of knowledge and institutions, and the way in which

knowledge often bears the marks of its social origins. In its strong form, it also claims that objects or referents of knowledge are nothing more than social constructions.[10]

What Sayer denotes as "weak social constructionism" roughly corresponds to what I refer to as "weak bodily realism," given that "knowledge" in the above formulation is not reduced to its discursive or cognitive dimensions—a point already made with regard to "understanding" in the introduction to this chapter. Having said that, I should underline that the position of weak bodily realism does not coincide with the approach of critical realism promoted by Sayer. Critical realists within disability studies tend to adopt a strongly realist view of the body, as will be argued in my discussion of Tom Shakespeare's ideas below. But let me first outline the similarities between the weak and the strong bodily realism within disability studies.

Both the weakly realist and the strongly realist disability scholars posit a relationship between three distinct elements that constitute the phenomenon of disability: (a) bodily differences, (b) mediation, and (c) restrictions of activity. As explained in Chapter 1, the present investigation is also guided by this fundamental scheme, adding two stipulations to it—first, that mediation (element b) incorporates existential-ontological reductions, and second, that restrictions of activity (element c) have an existential-ontological dimension that amounts to undermining of disabled people's existence. Indeed, when disability scholars refer to "restrictions of activity," they usually mean *to be prevented from acting* (including thinking, perceiving, feeling) in certain desired ways. Yet "restrictions of activity" can also denote *to be disciplined into acting* (thinking, perceiving, feeling) in ways that undermine important aspects of one's existence. For example, it has been argued that when disabled people strive to "pass" as nondisabled or to heroically overcome their "individual deficits," they are being disciplined into undermining their own bodies and the attendant experiences[11]; another example is desexualization, discussed extensively in Chapter 7. As far as bodily differences (element a) are concerned, disability scholars—myself included—take as their point of departure those specific bodily differences that are usually identified as *impairments* and analyze and/or criticize the social practices associated with such differences. The mediation of these practices has been referred to in various ways, but most aptly as disablism or ableism[12]; in the present work, I combine the two terms by writing "dis/ablism." Some disability scholars have also emphasized that the bodily differences usually identified as impairments can be associated with possibilities, besides restrictions.[13] The present investigation explicitly supports this argument in the chapters on media representations of inaccessibility (Chapter 6) and sexuality (Chapter 7).

How can the differences between the weakly realist and the strongly realist positions be mapped onto the three constitutive elements of disability outlined above—that is, bodily differences, mediation, and restrictions of activity? To begin with, although it is often (self)identified as "constructionist," or "social constructionist," or even "radically constructionist," the weakly realist position accepts more or less explicitly a *minimally realist view of the body*. This means that even when the body is regarded as completely dependent for its meaning on mediation, it is usually tacitly acknowledged that some bodily difference, independent from mediation, is required in order to "trigger" mediation, to make it constitute or shape this meaning. To argue that "[t]he body does not *appear* outside of the social world within which it is made manifest"[14] is not to argue that the body does not *exist* outside of the social world. When Davis writes that "the constructionist model sees disability as a social process in which no inherent meanings *attach to physical difference* other than those assigned by a community,"[15] he implicitly admits the independent reality of physical difference. Similarly, in the concluding remarks on sexuality in Chapter 7 I maintain that physicality delimits human capacities, although the bodily phenomena in question appear as limits only within a particular world.

The last point suggests that, while the weakly realist view presupposes a minimal independence of the body from the social, political, economic, historical, cultural, and technological mediation of inhabiting a world, this view tends to *reject the independence of restrictions of activity*. In other words, weak bodily realism maintains that specific bodily differences are translated into restrictions—or show up as restrictions—only when they are contextually mediated. The present work affirms this position. Its specific task is to highlight the existential-ontological aspects of mediation and the ensuing ontological undermining of disabled people's existence. Similarly to other weak bodily realists within disability studies, I regard the mediation of disability-related practices that translate bodily differences into restrictions of activity as dominated by dis/ablism—embedded, for example, in particular ways of structuring the built environment, language use, technological design, patterns of interpersonal interaction, spatiotemporal relationships, organization of services, and administration of welfare. Chapters 3–8 provide numerous examples for the workings of dis/ablism in each of these areas, while also emphasizing the ways in which these dis/ablist practices incorporate existential-ontological reductions.

In contrast, the strongly realist position maintains that some bodily differences *intrinsically* impose restrictions on human activity—intrinsically, that is, independently from any dis/ablist or non-dis/ablist mediation. Both the weakly realist and the strongly realist positions tend to acknowledge that, with regard to specific bodily differences, the social, political, economic, historical, cultural, and technological mediation is overwhelmingly dis/ablist. The weakly realist position is cautious (or hesitant, or even reluctant) in identifying bodily differences as "impairments" because it may conceive such identification as being itself an aspect of dis/ablist mediation.[16] In contrast, for the strongly realist disability scholars impairments are given *as impairments* independently of dis/ablism or any other mediation of disability-related practices. Thus besides the givenness of bodily differences, the strongly realist position accepts the givenness of intrinsic restrictions of activity ("deficits," "dysfunctions," "abnormalities") as well, while nevertheless admitting that these restrictions can be *augmented* or *multiplied* by dis/ablist mediation.

For example, a weakly realist disability scholar would maintain that stairs make the bodily difference of nonwalking—in its association with wheelchair use—to show up as intrinsically restrictive. At least such is my suggestion in the discussion of media representations of inaccessibility in Chapter 6. In contrast, a strongly realist disability scholar would assert that stairs are a failure of society to accommodate the intrinsically engendered restriction—the "deficit"—of nonwalking, conceived, again, in its association with wheelchair use. It is important to point out here that the association of nonwalking with wheelchair use in both the weakly and the strongly realist conceptualizations suggests that, strictly speaking, bodily differences are rarely—if at all—disclosed *as such* independently of their association with other entities within a world. This complicates the strongly realist thesis because it suggests that impairments are better conceived not as given, but as "assembled" (the term is often associated with the actor-network theory of Latour; its origins can be traced to Deleuze and Guattari).[17] In any case, both the weak and the strong realists within disability studies demand changes in the environment—for example, complementing stairs with ramps or lifts. In other words, both perceive unattended stairs as an architectural embodiment of dis/ablism.

Many analyses in disability studies, informed by diverse theoretical perspectives (structural-materialist, feminist, phenomenological, poststructuralist, critical realist), oscillate between the weakly realist and the strongly realist positions with regard to the body. Sometimes the difference between the two positions within a single account is undecidable. Cases of extreme antirealism or relativism are rare and can usually be exposed as tacitly presupposing some degree of realism with regard to bodily difference. As a rule, disability scholars do not accept that restrictions of activity are to be located solely within the body of the disabled individual. Even the extremely strong realists do not indulge in this type of naïve realism that is critically regarded as an instance of biological reductionism or essentialism. Below, I will illustrate these points about the shifting emphases of bodily realism within disability studies by looking at four different accounts of impairment. The first discusses the classical formulations of the British social model of disability, the second and the third present two attempts to update the social model, and the fourth rejects the social model. These examples contain notions and patterns of theorizing to which I will resort throughout Chapters 3–8. Thus they also serve to further elaborate the theoretical framework outlined in Chapter 1.

The British social model of disability

Some of the central tenets of disability studies are to be found in the classical formulations of the British social model of disability. Do these formulations adhere to the strongly or the weakly realist view of the body? The statement that grounds the British social model has been formulated in the mid-1970s by the members of the Union of the Physically Impaired Against Segregation (UPIAS), a British organization of disabled people advocating for radical change in the dominant understandings and practices concerning disability:

> we define impairment as lacking part of or all of a limb, or having a defective limb, organ or mechanism of the body; and disability as the disadvantage or restriction of activity caused by a contemporary social organisation which takes no or little account of people who have physical impairments and thus excludes them from participation in the mainstream of social activities.[18]

In this formulation, I take "impairment" to denote specific bodily difference; "disability" clearly refers to restrictions of activity; and "a contemporary social organisation which takes no or little account of people who have physical impairments and thus excludes them from participation in the mainstream of social activities" can be regarded as an apt description of the mediation of dis/ablism. According to such a reading, what the UPIAS's definition tells us is that some or probably *most* of the restrictions of activity experienced by people with specific bodily differences are mediated by dis/ablism. In other words, the dis/ablist social organization fails to take into account those bodily differences that are usually identified as impairments and this failure restricts people who are different in such ways.

To reserve the concert of "disability" for the phenomenon that emerges from the interaction between bodily differences, dis/ablist mediation, and restrictions of activity is thus not antithetical to the meaning of UPIAS's formulation. Yet does not such a reading conflate UPIAS's position with the position of the biopsychosocial approach, as advocated by the World Health Organization in its International Classification of Functioning, Disability and Health (ICF)?[19] Indeed, both UPIAS and WHO/ICF promote a relational understanding of disability, but whereas ICF adopts a strongly realist view of the body, UPIAS's position is *ambiguous*. In his review of the ICF, Rob Imrie states that "for the ICF, disability is a relational phenomenon whereby the functional limitations of impairment become disabling as a consequence of broader social and attitudinal relations."[20] A weak bodily realist would immediately point out that here bodies are inserted into the otherwise relational phenomenon of disability *too late*—that is, only after specific bodily differences are taken as intrinsically restrictive ("functionally limiting"). The weak realist would insist on questioning this "taking as," at least in the majority of cases. If ICF is dialectically relational—if it asserts that "biology and society are entwined in a dialectical relationship"[21]—then it does so only after excluding from such dialectics the restrictiveness of specific bodily differences. Thus ICF defines impairment as

> a loss or abnormality in body structure or physiological function (including mental functions). Abnormality here is used strictly to refer to a significant variation from established statistical norms (i.e. as a deviation from a population mean within measured standard norms) and should be used only in this sense.[22]

Indeed, such a definition resembles the way UPIAS defines impairment as "lacking part of or all of a limb, or having a defective limb, organ or mechanism of the body."[23] An important difference though is that, unlike ICF, UPIAS does not resort to the notion of "statistical norm." ICF presents the category of "statistical norm" as neutral and objective—in the introduction to this chapter, I pointed out that this assumption is questionable. Disability scholars such as Davis have argued that the category of the "norm" is historically contingent and is a constitutive part of networks of interrelated concepts, institutions, and practices, that is, networks of knowledge/power.[24] It has also been maintained that the "normal" body is never a brute fact, a "naked" given, but is always already mediated by technologies, language, economy, juridical regulations, cultural expectations, and so forth.[25] A weak realist would then question not only the ways in which specific bodily differences are rendered "abnormal," but also the conditions for the possibility for a body to become inconspicuous, to function smoothly, "normally." Such normality does not reside *only* within the body, it is not intrinsically given. This normal state, this smooth functioning, necessitates specific conditions; it emerges and is sustained only within a specific set of circumstances and will not emerge within another. In the same way in which it is not enough for a body to be "impaired" in order to be experienced *as impaired*, it is not enough for a body to be "normal" so that it can be experienced *as normal*. Yet the conditions for the possibility of both the former and the latter are usually too familiar to be noticed. As argued in Chapter 5, in the discussion of the Troyan Monastery case of discrimination, as well as in Chapter 6 on media representations of inaccessibility, one needs to make these conditions strange or to defamiliarize them in order to be able to address them critically.

So in its definition UPIAS avoids recourse to the questionable, from the perspective of weak bodily realism, concept of "(ab)normality." Nevertheless, rendering the bodily difference of impairment in terms of "defects" ("having a *defective* limb, organ or mechanism of the body"), as well as the general reluctance to theorize the body in sociological terms have led to accusations that UPIAS's definition and the social model that stems from it posit "a body devoid of meaning, a dysfunctional, anatomical, corporeal mass obdurate in its resistance to signification and phenomenologically dead, without intentionality or agency."[26] But while it is clear that the social model—at least in its classical formulations—takes the body as biologically given, its attitude toward the *relationship* between the bodily difference of impairment and the restrictions of activity experienced by disabled people is not straightforward.

Michael Oliver's assertion that "disablement is nothing to do with the body"[27] seems to suggest that the social model does not take the body into account in its conceptualization of disability. Yet Oliver's own definition of "disabled people" includes as one of its three constitutive components "the presence of an impairment,"[28] where "[i]mpairment is, in fact, nothing less than a description of the physical body."[29] Thus the body is actually taken into account—and could it be otherwise? The restrictions of activity that the social model criticizes emerge only when people with specific bodily differences (impairments) encounter the mediation of contexts organized in specific (dis/ablist) ways. Does this mean that the British social model, in its original formulation by UPIAS in 1976 and in its subsequent elaboration by Finkelstein in 1980 and Oliver in 1990 and 1996,[30] admits that some of the bodily differences identified as impairments are *intrinsically* restrictive? In response to criticisms that the social model disregards the limitations directly attributable to blindness, Oliver states: "the social model is not an attempt to deal with the personal restrictions of impairment but the social barriers of disability."[31] That is why issues such as pain and (chronic) illness have been resolutely avoided in the classical accounts of social model theorists—these issues have been regarded in terms of intrinsically engendered (personal, bodily, unmediated) restrictions. But this strong realism of the social model with regard to the body is not consistent and often gets weakened, for example, in analyses of everyday activities such as hand washing[32] or walking.[33] Thus Finkelstein, engaging in the aforementioned defamiliarization, argues:

> The activity, washing hands, then, in our society should not be taken as given. People with physical impairments, however, have not influenced this creation of "hand washing" and consequently *are prevented (disabled) from carrying it out, not by their personal characteristics but by the way "hand washing" was created.*[34]

The ambiguous bodily realism of the British social model of disability has made it amenable to criticisms from both camps. Strong realists within disability studies have complained that the social model does not take intrinsically engendered restrictions into account, while weak realists have complained that the social model uncritically takes some restrictions as intrinsically engendered. Both criticisms have a point. The social model has left its own conception of the body unexamined. Unexamined conceptions of the body can endanger the coherence of any methodologically holistic exploration of disability. As a consequence, the social model has disregarded a number of important questions about the relationship between bodily differences, dis/ablist mediation, and restrictions of activity. For example: How are my intrinsic restrictions recognized as such—that is, as restrictions and/or as intrinsic? How are they amplified and/or multiplied by dis/ablism? How do they contribute to—or trigger—dis/ablism? How does it happen that some bodily differences are more likely to trigger dis/ablism than others? These and similar questions have motivated attempts to update or even reject the British social model of disability. I now turn toward some of these attempts in the hope to shed additional light on the relationship between weak and strong bodily realism within disability studies.

Updating the social model

In her attempt to update the classical formulations of the British social model of disability and to address some of the questions outlined in the preceding paragraph, Carol Thomas's point of departure is the strongly realist position with regard to the body, which is subsequently weakened through contextualization. She begins by promoting:

> a non-reductionist materialist ontology of the body [that] should neither deny the "realness" of bodies and their flesh-bound variations nor

concede ground to the idea that any acknowledgement of the material reality of "the body" is tantamount to naturalising, medicalising or biologising it.[35]

Through her concept of "impairment effects," Thomas seeks to acknowledge "the *direct* or *immediate* impact that 'being impaired' can and does have in the daily lives of disabled people."[36] Is this immediate impact intrinsically restrictive? Thomas's initial response seems to be affirmative: "impairment effects refer to those restrictions of bodily activity and behaviour that are *directly attributable* to bodily variations designated 'impairments' rather than to those *imposed upon* people *because* they have designated impairments (disablism)."[37] But Thomas immediately adds a qualification, pointing out that "this simple formulation does not convey the subtleties of the bio-social processes and factors involved."[38] She then proceeds by giving an example from her own experience of an ostensibly intrinsically restrictive bodily difference—a woman missing a hand is restricted in her activity of manipulating a kettle in order to pour boiling water from it into a jug or a saucepan. As a bodily difference, missing a hand is regarded both as real and as intrinsically restrictive: "This restriction of activity is an immediate *impairment effect.*"[39] Such a restriction can then be augmented or multiplied by people occupying positions of power (parents, medical doctors) who deny to the woman access to employment or parenthood on the basis of her bodily difference. In other words, Thomas admits that the bodily (intrinsically) engendered restriction of activity can be enhanced by dis/ablism. So far, we have all the elements of the strongly realist position.

Nevertheless, a closer look at the situation urges Thomas to weaken her initial realism. It is the association of the bodily difference ("missing hand") with entities (kettle, jug, saucepan) within the context of a meaningful activity (preparing a meal) that complicates the issue. Thus restrictions that initially seemed intrinsic to the bodily difference of "missing a hand" can actually be shown to emerge when this bodily difference encounters the ableist design of paraphernalia (such as kitchen appliances), the gendered social expectations to routinely engage in specific activities (such as preparing a meal), the medicalized understandings of bodily difference, and so forth. All this makes the missing hand a "complex bio-social phenomenon."[40] At the end of her analysis, it is hard to tell whether Thomas still maintains her initial strongly realist thesis that specific bodily differences are intrinsically restrictive, or whether she has abandoned it. Her conclusion that "[t]he materiality of the body is in a dynamic interrelationship with the social and cultural context in which it is lived"[41] does not provide an answer to this question. Thomas seems to refuse to side either with the strongly or with the weakly realist positions. By resorting to the notion of "complex bio-social phenomena," she strives to keep open a conceptual space that allows freedom to oscillate between these two poles of bodily realism.

Kevin Paterson and Bill Hughes endeavor to go beyond the social model with the aid of phenomenology.[42] In this way, they embrace a weak bodily realism that is nevertheless qualified when it comes to issues such as pain. Utilizing Drew Leder's phenomenological notion of "dys-appearance," which means to appear as problematic or dys-functional[43] (see also Chapter 7), Paterson and Hughes state that

> the disablist and disabling sociospatial environment produces a vivid, but unwanted consciousness of one's impaired body. Here, the body undergoes a mode of "dysappearance" which is not biological, but social.[44]

The reality of the bodily difference of impairment is presupposed, but not as intrinsically restrictive or negative. At some points of their text Paterson and Hughes even avoid the term "impairment," referring instead to "non-conforming forms of physicality." Restrictions of activity are seen as *emerging* when such "non-conforming" bodily differences trigger dis/ablist mediation: "Exclusion from and disruption to communication is not therefore a matter of the ability of an impaired person to communicate, but about conventions and norms of communication, which are (*a priori*) hostile to non-conforming forms of physicality."[45] Here, the mediation of dis/ablism is rendered in terms of conventions of interaction that are hostile to particular bodily differences. Clearly, the ensuing restrictions of activity are not considered as intrinsic: "The 'social competence' of people with impairments is masked, not because of their carnal performance, but because the conventions and norms of 'competence' are devoid of 'their' carnal information."[46] Nevertheless, Paterson and Hughes admit that there are situations in which it is not reasonable to maintain the weakly realist position—for example, with regard to those bodily differences that bring about pain. (The same argument holds in relation to illness.) This is the reason why the two authors exclude pain from their analysis of the social and political "dys-appearance" of impairment:

> disability studies has two avenues of opportunity to develop a phenomeno-logical sociology of impairment: one which focuses on the issue of painful impairment and another which focuses on the issue of having an impair-ment which is not (biologically) painful. It is the latter avenue, which will be explored in this paper.[47]

Notably, this strongly realist position with regard to painful bodily differences is immediately weakened by pointing out that even the experience of pain is shaped by one's habitation of a world: "pain, like any other experiential mode, cannot be reduced merely to these immediate sensory qualities; rather, it is ultimately a matter of being-in-the-world."[48] Nevertheless, Paterson and Hughes explicitly restrict the scope of their analysis to those impairments that are not biologically painful—that is, to bodily differences that are not immediately identifiable as intrinsically restrictive or negative. The conclusion to be drawn from theirs and Thomas's conceptualization of the body is that neither the weak nor the strong realism of disability scholars can be easily pinned down. Moreover, it is not even desirable to insist on fixing these positions or reducing the one to the other. There will always be instances that will force strong realists to weaken their arguments about the body, as well as instances that will force weak realists to admit intrinsic restrictiveness. Importantly, both positions are interested in analyzing and/or criticizing mediation, particularly the mediation of dis/ablism. I take this common area of interest to be the defining feature of disability studies.

And yet, while I admit the equal significance of the two positions for disability studies, I do not claim that the conditions of their articulation are equal. The view that regards impairment as intrinsically restrictive is overwhelmingly dominant outside disability studies, for example in biomedical discourses on disability (as argued in the discussion of the ICF above). Furthermore, biomedical and especially popular discourses on disability are often characterized not by strong, but by naïve bodily realism, an extreme form of realism completely oblivious of mediation. In the chapters on disability assessment (Chapter 3), discrimination (Chapter 5), and sexuality (Chapter 7) I discuss examples of such an oblivion, highlighting the ways in which it incorporates the objective mode of existential-ontological reduction. Disability studies is a tiny drop in the vast sea of biomedical research on disability, not to mention the popular representations of this phenomenon. Therefore, even if within the discipline it seems justified to regard the positions of the weak and the strong bodily realism as competing on an equal footing, the more general context of contemporary knowledge/power is one of an unequally structured playing field. The supporters of weak bodily realism, especially when they venture outside the relative safety of their discipline (itself in a precarious situation due to structural factors undermining whole areas of social sciences and humanities in contemporary academia), face an additional task. This task complements the task of arguing with strong bodily realists. It consists in opening up and/or keeping open a conceptual space that provides for opportunities to question strongly realist claims. On this level, it is not a matter of finding the right arguments but rather a matter of being enabled to argue.

Rejecting the social model

Tom Shakespeare explicitly embraces the approach of critical realism in his rejection of the British social model of disability.[49] Shakespeare argues that "the social model has now become an obstacle to the further development of the disability movement and disability studies."[50] I do not agree with such a statement, although I do think that many of the conceptual presuppositions of the social model with regard to the body are in need of being clarified and/or revised. Shakespeare's analysis is consistent with the position of the strong bodily realism outlined so far. His reflections are useful for illuminating the role of the body in the phenomenon of disability, but they also raise a number of questions. I will briefly present Shakespeare's position and then address some of the concerns that arise when approaching it from the perspective of weak bodily realism.

In his critique of the social model, Shakespeare makes a number of important claims about the body.[51] My interpretation of his argument can be summarized thus: (a) Many of the bodily differences identified as "impairments" are intrinsically restrictive: "for many, impairment is not neutral, because it involves intrinsic disadvantage."[52] Nevertheless, (b) the identification of impairments is always already socially mediated: "what counts as impairment is a social judgement."[53] (c) Sometimes, mediation augments or multiplies restrictions that are otherwise intrinsically engendered: "Disabling barriers make impairment more difficult, but even in the absence of barriers impairment can be problematic."[54] Indeed, (d) sometimes it is difficult to distinguish between intrinsically engendered and mediated restrictions: "In practical terms, the inextricable interconnection of impairment and disability is demonstrated by the difficulty in understanding, in particular examples, where the distinction between the two aspects of disabled people's experience lies."[55] (e) It is nonsensical to analyze mediation and mediated restrictions without admitting the important role of intrinsically engendered restrictions: "if it wasn't for the impairment, there wouldn't be any restriction in the first place."[56] Moreover, (f) it is crucial to take intrinsically engendered restrictions into account in the analysis of disability, so that personal experience is respected: "Many respondents say that impairment is a central and structuring part of their experience."[57] Actually, (g) there are situations in which it is more important to inquire about intrinsic restrictions (e.g., utilizing statistical methods) than about their mediation or the effects of this mediation: "understanding the number of disabled people in society would seem to be important for many different areas of social policy in the real world of budgetary constraints and service planning."[58] In the final analysis, (h) changing mediation will never completely eradicate restrictions faced by disabled people because many of them are intrinsic (although some are not): "The specifics of impairment also create disadvantage which no inclusive social arrangements can mitigate."[59]

Shakespeare's critique of the social model is complex and multidimensional and its comprehensive analysis goes well beyond the scope of this chapter. In the foregoing discussion, I already corroborated some of the points made by Shakespeare—for example, point (b) about the identification of impairment; point (c) about the augmenting functions of mediation; and point (d) about the occasional indistinctiveness (undecidability) between intrinsic and extrinsic restrictiveness. Instead of assessing the other claims made by Shakespeare, here I would like to interrogate some of his supporting arguments that seem problematic from the perspective of weak bodily realism. These arguments concern *choice*, *cure*, *nature*, and *denial*.

Drawing on his strongly realist logic, Shakespeare argues that, because of their intrinsically restrictive bodily differences, "[d]isabled people have less flexibility and fewer choices than non-disabled people."[60] According to him, no mediation can change this state of affairs. Yet even if one admits that some bodily differences *intrinsically* restrict the range of available options, this should not prevent one from examining the mediation that contextualizes individual choice *in addition to* bodily difference. Granted, John depends on a wheelchair *and* public transport to go from London to Brighton, while Jim depends *only* on public transport. But probably we need to revise our understanding of (in)dependence here. A closer look[61] reveals a whole network of complementary dependencies. Besides social and technological (the transport infrastructure itself), these dependencies are also economic (access to funds for buying a ticket), cultural (know-how of railway transportation, command of English), existential (importance of the destination for the traveler, say, due to professional obligations), and so forth. The wheelchair is "in addition," but not only to an intrinsically (biologically) restricted individual. It is added to an already existing network of mediators. Every act of choosing is distributed within this network; both bodily abilities and their "lack" are parts of it. Furthermore, in an environment that is already radically altered by social practices and technologies, the degree of flexibility in choosing is in principle open to re-negotiation, even for people with severe and multiple impairments. Admitting the "real disadvantage" of impairment is not sufficient for diverting one's attention from mediation, neither for giving up attempts at re-negotiation. These points about choice and interdependence are comprehensively developed in the discussion of personal assistance in Chapter 4.

A similar point can be made on the topic of *cure*. One can eradicate restrictions of activity faced by individuals by changing ("curing") their bodies, that is, addressing individual bodily differences, instead of changing worlds, that is, addressing common structures, processes, and patterns of mediation. Yet cure does not circumvent mediation. Changing ("curing") bodies is itself distributed within networks of interconnected social, economic, political, technological, and other entities. Such networks can—and should—be studied, for example in terms of "medicalization," as is demonstrated in the analyses of disability assessment in Chapter 3 and sexuality in Chapter 7. Moreover, some medical and/or technological interventions may actually result in bolstering dis/ablist mediation even if they help to overcome restrictions of activity faced by individuals or even groups of individuals. This is the reason why disability scholars and activists—Shakespeare included—are worried, for example, about genetic testing and attendant practices.

In order to support his claim about the limits of mediation, Shakespeare resorts to the notion of *nature*: "Wheelchair users are disabled by sandy beaches and rocky mountains. . . . It is hard to blame the natural environment on social arrangements."[62] Yet who at present has an unmediated access to beaches or mountains—that is, unmediated by income distribution, transportation, built environment, tourist industry, media representations, popular culture, and so on? I agree with Shakespeare that "it would defeat the very idea of wilderness to create roads and other access facilities to unspoilt and inaccessible landscapes."[63] Indeed, it seems that something is lost when one ascends to the peak by means of a chairlift. But this only suggests that we—the lovers of wilderness, the ecologists, the mountaineers—seek to define the mountain through the difficulty of its access. And when we try to protect the mountain from technology, we do it by utilizing even more technology—social networks against bulldozers. In such cases it becomes conspicuous that the limits of mediation are themselves erected and/or enhanced *within mediation*.

And yet, for Shakespeare, too much insistence on mediation amounts to *denial*, especially when it comes to linguistic analyses: "While attention to labeling and discourse is important, there is a danger of ignoring the problematic reality of biological limitation. Linguistic distancing serves as a subtle form of denial."[64] No doubt, refusals of common sense notions about reality will always resemble denial, especially when they focus exclusively on language. Mediation is embodied and embedded. It is embodied in habits and embedded in social practices that constitute worlds—technologically (transportation, communication, surveillance), economically (income, funding, benefits), disciplinarily (fitness, dieting, rehabilitation), spatially (built environment, internal design), temporally (traditions, schedules, timetables), culturally (speech, writing, visual representations), and so forth. Thus even highly codified linguistic representations of disability—such as the UN Convention on the Rights of Persons with Disabilities—cannot circumvent the nonlinguistic aspects of mediation, as argued in Chapter 8. Nevertheless, there is something disconcerting about the attempts to dismiss critical thinking by rendering its insights in psychological terms—be it denial, projection, idealization, or something else of the sort. Besides a psychological defense mechanism of a pathological bearing, denial can also be a form of political resistance. Moreover, the ability to articulate a resolute "No!" is an important aspect of "reclaiming the voice," as suggested by the analyses in the chapters on discrimination (Chapter 5) and sexuality (Chapter 7).

The strong realism of Tom Shakespeare reminds disability scholars that the body should be taken seriously—attended to, examined, counted, treated. A weak realist would not object to this, given that the conditions that disclose the restrictiveness of those bodily differences usually identified as "impairments" are *also* attended to, examined, counted, and treated. Indeed, within particular contexts it might be nonsensical to inquire about mediation—an obvious example would be medical emergency. Nevertheless, such suspension of questioning should always be provisional, temporary, qualified. David Pfeiffer denotes this as a "philosophy of common sense with a good deal of scepticism"[65]—one accepts something as given/inevitable and moves on, but remains ready to revisit one's acceptance and/or to question its presuppositions. Among the most important tasks of weakly realist disability scholars is to keep this readiness alive (which, as already argued, can be quite difficult outside the discipline of disability studies). Otherwise, there is the risk to reduce the bodily difference of "impairment" to nothing more than a restriction and, accordingly, to foreclose any attempts at reimagining this restriction as a possibility. A weak realist would resist such a reduction, for example, by asking: "[H]ow might the experience of limit, as distasteful as it often seems, be imbued with the possibility of knowing our world differently and consequently making a different world?"[66] Without such *ontologically weakening*[67] interventions, there is also the risk of overlooking the meaningfulness of restrictions, of failing to inquire about the very recognition of specific differences *as* restrictions, of failing to explore the contexts in which a difference is translated into a restriction and the existential-ontological presuppositions underpinning such a translation. Finally, there is the risk of overlooking the contextual embeddedness of agency, to regard it as merely biologically and/or cognitively given—within the present inquiry, this last notion is explicitly challenged in the analysis of personal assistance in Chapter 3, where a distributed understanding of agency is proposed as an alternative.

I will finish this section with a more general reflection. Strong realists tend to embrace an understanding of the body *itself* as a naturally given *limit*[68] and, perhaps, as *the ultimate limit*. Critical theorists such as Thomas Tierney have argued that this understanding is historically contingent and tightly linked to the mediation of productivist/consumerist social orders.[69] According to Tierney, it is characteristic of (Western) modernity to reduce the body to a source of restrictions intrinsically imposed upon individuals.[70] In contrast, claims Tierney, in ancient Greece the body used to be regarded as a source of demands to be cared for rather than as a source of limits to be overcome. Tierney explains this difference by referring to a characteristically modern form of asceticism rooted in a ubiquitous drive toward efficiency that is mediated by modern technology:

> modernity is distinguished by the ability of the masses to free themselves from the limits of the body through the ravenous consumption of technology. The trajectory of modernity is to render everyone free not only from the limits which are imposed by the body, but even from the body itself.[71]

From such a perspective, reducing the body to a limit is seen historically as related to the increasing domination of *instrumental rationality* in modernity. Disabled people then experience the effects of a historical pattern that subjugates all humans—disabled and nondisabled alike—to the requirements of efficiency for its own sake, an efficiency detached from any consideration of substantive ends. This point is developed in Chapter 3, where I highlight the productivist underpinnings of the Bulgarian disability assessment by resorting to Heidegger's critique of modern technology. According to Tierney, who also refers to Heidegger, the progressive overcoming of the limits of the body in modernity is achieved at the price of an increasing dependency on productivist/ consumerist technological apparatuses: "these so-called 'achievements' will only be won at the cost of a greater dependency on the technological order, socialist or capitalist, which provides them."[72] Thus instead of taking care of bodily differences and the demands engendered by them, modern techno-scientific practices overwhelmingly aim at overcoming bodily restrictions that delimit productivist and/or consumerist involvement. Rather than greater freedom, this brings about greater restraint, which echoes Foucault's thesis that in modernity unfreedom results as much from restricting life as from enhancing life.[73] In such a historical situation, a mind freed from the intrinsic restrictions of its body might be technologically achievable, but such an entity would be completely dependent on productivist/consumerist technological apparatuses; moreover, its mode of being would most probably be qualitatively different from the one that we currently identify as "human."

So far, I provided a rationale for the weakly realist position, defending it from Shakespeare's criticisms. What remains to be done is to develop a more comprehensive understanding of weak bodily realism. In the concluding section of this chapter I will outline those ideas within phenomenology that could aid such an endeavor. I will specifically focus on the notions of finitude, world, being-in-the-world, and lived body, thus revisiting and building on the central phenomenological concepts presented in Chapter 1 as the theoretical framework of the present investigation.

Concluding remarks

Finitude

To say that something is *mediated* does not deny or diminish the power of that entity—for example, by reducing it to infinite displacements in the chain of signification, to playful linguistic contingencies, and so on. A category can change a life in a very material way, unimaginable from the vantage point of mere bodily materiality. The power of mediation *adds* to the power of that which enters mediation.[74] Thus when we experience bodily restrictions as overpowering, what we experience, besides perhaps the "tyranny of nature,"[75] is the overpowering force of a world, the power of a form of life. It seems that with the advance of the productivist/consumerist technological order, it becomes increasingly easier to intervene and change the bodily or material aspects of a phenomenon, whereas its sociopolitical and existential-ontological aspects become more and more elusive or "black-boxed," as science studies scholars would put it. In other words, the more we become proficient in changing bodies, the more we tend to lose our proficiency in changing worlds. This, I think, is the gist of Tierney's critique of what he identifies as the "techno-fetishism" of productivist/consumerist modernity: "the technological victory over death may indeed open up a completely new realm of order in which humans, or at least part of them, will be subjected to even greater control and regulation."[76]

This suggests that the question about human body is bound to the question about human *finitude*. Finitude can be understood negatively, as the *limits of agency* rooted in the intrinsic restrictiveness of the body. This perspective stems from strong bodily realism; it regards human body as the epitome of human frailty. Alternatively, finitude can be understood positively, as the *contextual embeddedness* of human being, including human perceiving, thinking, feeling, and acting. This perspective is akin to weak bodily realism. The differences between these two understandings of finitude are more closely explored in Chapter 6, in the section titled

"Encounters with stairs." There, I suggest that for the weak bodily realists such as Hughes, the restrictiveness of the body is not the archetype of finitude but one of its manifestations.[77] Taking this thesis a step further, one could argue that finitude is primarily not a feature of those who inhabit a world but of inhabiting itself. Therefore, finitude cannot be overcome by fixing the physical body. From this perspective, it is not that because we are bodily, we are finite; rather, it is that because we are finite (i.e., contextually embedded by being-in-the-world), our bodies can show up as intrinsically restrictive, that is, as manifestations of our finitude.

In *Being and Time*, Heidegger provides this insight with a temporal twist. There, he suggests that finitude is the basis of temporality. Temporality, on its behalf, is the horizon of any understanding of being, because being is always and necessarily understood in terms of time.[78] Thus it is only within the temporal horizon opened up by finitude that humans can have an understanding of what it means to be—that is, can encounter entities as entities: "The finitude of the human is a necessary, albeit not sufficient, condition for the unique privilege that the human has in comparison with all other living creatures—to understand *the being* of beings."[79] Existential phenomenologists assert that one can be "in" time only by pressing ahead into a finite future by way of engaging with entities and others here and now. What one does has meaning in the light of what one is oriented toward. If one's existential projects could extend indefinitely into the future, the past would not matter and one's engagement with entities and others here and now would also be irrelevant. In such a case, one's existence would be steeped in indifference or meaninglessness:

> The ecstatic unity of future, past and present is possible precisely through the finitude of the ecstasis of the future. Without it the other ecstases could not have an existential meaning. How could the past matter to Dasein, if an infinite future waited ahead?[80]

The idea that finitude is an essential feature of human being-in-the-world—rather than primarily a feature of intrinsically restricted human bodies—has profound implications for the analyses within disability studies that proceed from the presumptions of weak bodily realism. Some of these implications are explored in the case studies presented in this book, while others—such as the conjunction of disability and the temporal aspect of finitude, as well as the attendant questions concerning old age—remain unaddressed and provide a fertile ground for future phenomenological investigations of disability, as will be discussed in Chapter 9.

World and being-in-the-world

The present inquiry is guided conceptually by the notion that humans inhabit worlds. A world is not a collection of entities but a time-space where meaning obtains, a disclosive time-space, a "clearing." A world is a meaning-engendering context. To inhabit a world—to be-in-the-world—*compels* one not to be indifferent to entities, to encounter them, to identify them as such-and-such, to relate to them as meaningful. The objectified, observable, calculable, manipulable body—the body as a Cartesian "extended thing" (*res extensa*), as a container of a mind, a machine hosting a ghost[81]—is identifiable as such on the basis of this more fundamental familiarity with the world. Indeed, such familiarity is bodily, but "inhabiting a world in a bodily way" should not be conflated with "having a (physical) body within a world." On the one hand, it is impossible to understand a gesture *as a gesture* if one does not take into account the meaningful context or the situation in which it takes place. The physiology of the gesture or its mechanics cannot help with understanding it as a gesture, even less as the particular gesture it is—that is, one of welcoming, pointing, agreeing, and so forth. The reason is that "[l]ike everything else bodily, the human hand belongs so directly to human being-in-the-world that it is determined in everything it is and does by how its owner is relating to what he is at that moment encountering."[82] On the other hand, the ability to make a meaningful gesture presupposes the ability to understand *in a bodily way* (albeit implicitly, unthematically) oneself, the other, the surrounding entities, their interrelations, and the meaningful totality to which they pertain (myself, the chair, the table, my interlocutor, the room, the building, the history and purpose of our exchange, and so forth). In order for my gesture to be the gesture it is—for example, "directing someone towards something"—it needs to be part of a network of meaningful relations obtaining among me (as embodied being), my gesture, someone, something, and so on.

Such reflections help to advance weak bodily realism beyond binaries such as body versus society that have impaired conceptually the social model of disability. From this phenomenological perspective, meaning emerges out of the interrelations among humans and entities in a meaning-engendering context or world that extends from futural projections to past histories. Yet it is only after meaning has emerged that we can identify humans, entities, and their interrelations *as such*. Hence being-in-the-world is inextricably *circular*. This also means that the overcoming of the body versus society dichotomy can be achieved neither by making bodies "social," nor by making society "bodily." Both these terms need to be reconsidered and not simply re-injected into their opposites. The body that partakes in the social is not the body of the body-society dichotomy. In phenomenology, the re-conceptualization of "the body" along these lines is achieved through the notion of "lived body."

Lived body

For weak realists within disability studies, the bodily differences identifiable, for example, as "one-handedness," "blindness," or "deafness"—in other words, those bodily differences usually subsumed under the general category of "impairments"—have an impact on mediation from outside of mediation, but *the meaning* of this impact is given *within mediation*. Phenomenologically speaking, such differences are immediately incorporated into the *lived body* by being endowed with meaning in the context of one's everyday activities. Thus one-handedness can be lived, for example, as difficulty with pouring water into a jug,[83] blindness—as exclusion from social interaction,[84] and deafness—as peaceful silence in the midst of a noisy journey.[85] Other examples of the existential significance of bodily differences are presented in Chapter 6, in the discussion of media representations of inaccessibility.

Yet besides being lived, bodily differences can also be objectified. In the introduction to this chapter, I engaged in such deliberately neutralized objectification, defining "bodily difference" as "presence or absence of an organ or an anatomical structure, or alterations of an organ's or an organ system's properties or ways of working." My aim was to acknowledge the independent reality of bodily difference, which suggests that objectification gives access to entities as independent from mediation—in Heidegger's terms, it "frees" entities for "pure discovering."[86] This can be useful for scientific, administrative, or therapeutic purposes, but objectification often does more than that. Besides acknowledging an independent reality, objectification often produces existential "side effects," so to speak. It is this existential "surplus" that calls for critical scrutiny. As argued in Chapter 3, to objectify someone's bodily difference by assigning him or her 90 percent "decreased ability to work" on the basis of a missing bodily part can have detrimental existential consequences, although it makes the administration of welfare standardizable and efficient. In order to understand these detrimental consequences, one needs to question differently—not whether or how much of a bodily difference is objectively restrictive, but *how is it objectified,* and what are the existential-ontological corollaries of such a procedure. This shift of questioning is akin to Karl Mannheim's critical operation of "unmasking" that

> does not seek to refute ideas but to undermine them by exposing the function they serve. Mannheim had learned from Marxism. The notion is

that once one sees the *"extra-theoretical function"* (Mannheim's emphasis) of an idea, it will lose its "practical effectiveness." We unmask an idea not so much to "disintegrate" it as to strip it of a false appeal or authority.[87]

Within the framework of the present inquiry, there are several instances of "unmasking" that are specifically targeted at uncovering the existential-ontological aspects of bodily objectification. In Chapter 6 on media representations of inaccessibility and Chapter 7 on sexuality, these efforts are aided by the phenomenological notion of "lived body." It is the mediation of inhabiting a world that incorporates bodily differences into lived bodies. This does not make bodily differences less real but *adds to their reality* as far as the possibility of meaningfully relating to them is concerned. In other words, mediation makes bodily differences "livable." Of course, mediation is profoundly affected by bodily differences but, again, the *meaning* of this influence is not given independently of mediation. Thus it is mediation that provides access to a body in terms of objective advantages or disadvantages, certified, for example, by assigning a percentage of "decreased ability to work" (Chapter 3). Being assigned a percentage of "decreased ability to work," the body is "freed" for the administration of welfare within the order of productivism.

Moreover, phenomenologists have pointed out that to be in a bodily way "always belongs to being-in-the-world. It always co-determines being-in-the-world, openness, and the having of a world."[88] Medard Boss explains: "A human being is always 'here' with respect to some place, and human bodyhood seems to play an essential role in this 'being-here.'"[89] In what sense is it essential for a human being to be in a bodily way, to inhabit one's world bodily? A mundane example provides a clue: "I must continue to sit on the chair in a bodily manner in order to be all ears. If I wandered around the room, this would be lessened or not done at all."[90] Thus it would be hard if not impossible for me to discuss certain issues without assuming specific postures and facial expressions, making specific gestures, and so forth. The same applies to thinking. When I think without my laptop, I think differently. Similarly to the objectified body, the disembodied mind is a derivative aspect of what actually happens when thinking happens. Understanding oneself in a bodily way—as weak or strong, overweight or underweight, tall or short, walking or wheeling[91]—is a structural moment of understanding in general, that is, of the constitution of meaning, of relating to something as something. More specifically, it is a necessary component of self-understanding, of regarding oneself as an individual, a person, an "I." Perhaps this is the main reason why desexualization can be experienced as profoundly dehumanizing, as argued in Chapter 7.

To summarize, the phenomenological notions of finitude, world, being-in-the-world and lived body were explored here in view of their usefulness for the position of weak bodily realism within disability studies, whose explication was intended to clarify the theoretical presuppositions of the present investigation. These notions highlight the contextual embeddedness of human being while also acknowledging the importance of human embodiment. Thus they bolster the methodological holism underlying the weakly realist position without undermining its minimally realist understanding of the body; rather, they enhance its ability to reflectively engage with this understanding.

Notes

1 Martin Heidegger, *Being and Time*, trans. John Macquarrie and Edward Robinson (Oxford: Blackwell, 1962 [1927]), 269–70.

2 Alexandar Kanev, *Heidegger and the Philosophical Tradition* (Sofia: East-West, 2011), 140–8.

3 Hubert Dreyfus, "How Heidegger defends the possibility of a correspondence theory of truth with respect to the entities of natural science," in *Heidegger Reexamined. Vol. 2: Truth, Realism, and the History of Being*, eds. Hubert L. Dreyfus and Mark A. Wrathall (New York: Routledge, 2002). The question whether Heidegger's philosophy is "realist" or "idealist" continues to generate much debate among Heideggerians, yet its exploration exceeds the thematic confines of the present chapter. For in-depth discussions of the issue see the other entries in *Heidegger Reexamined. Vol. 2.*

4 Ian Hacking, *The Social Construction of What?* (Cambridge, MA: Harvard University Press, 1999).

5 Ibid., 108.

6 Lennard J. Davis, *Bending over Backwards: Disability, Dismodernism, and Other Difficult Positions* (New York: New York University Press, 2002), 109.

7 Rod Michalko, *The Difference that Disability Makes* (Philadelphia: Temple University Press, 2002).

8 Giorgio Agamben, *Homo Sacer: Sovereign Power and Bare Life*, trans. Daniel Heller-Roazen (Stanford, CA: Stanford University Press, 1998 [1995]).

9 Andrew Sayer, *Realism and Social Science* (London: SAGE, 2000), 92.

10 Ibid., 90.

11 Colin Cameron, "Not our problem: impairment as difference, disability as role." *The Journal of Inclusive Practice in Further and Higher Education* 3, 2 (2011): 10–24.

12 Carol Thomas, *Sociologies of Disability and Illness: Contested Ideas in Disability Studies and Medical Sociology* (Basingstoke: Palgrave Macmillan, 2007); Fiona Kumari Campbell, *Contours of Ableism: The Production of Disability and Abledness* (Basingstoke: Palgrave Macmillan, 2009).

13 See, for example, Michalko, *Difference*; John Swain and Sally French, "Towards an affirmation model of disability." *Disability & Society* 15, 4 (2000): 569–82; Tanya Titchkosky, "Disability in the news: a reconsideration of reading." *Disability & Society* 20, 6 (2005): 655–68.

14 Titchkosky, "Disability in the news," 664, emphasis added.

15 Davis, *Bending over Backwards*, 41, emphasis added.

16 See, for example, Shelley Tremain, "On the subject of impairment," in *Disability/Postmodernity: Embodying Disability Theory*, eds. Mairian Corker and Tom Shakespeare (London: Continuum, 2002).

17 Gilles Deleuze and Félix Guattari, *A Thousand Plateaus: Capitalism and Schizophrenia*, trans. Brian Massumi (London: Continuum, 2004 [1980]).

18 Union of the Physically Impaired Against Segregation, *Fundamental Principles of Disability* (London: Union of the Physically Impaired Against Segregation, 1976), n.p.

19 World Health Organization, *International Classification of Functioning, Disability and Health* (Geneva: World Health Organization, 2001).

20 Rob Imrie, "Demystifying disability: a review of the International Classification of Functioning, Disability and Health." *Sociology of Health & Illness* 26, 3 (2004): 293.

21 Ibid., 287–8.

22 World Health Organization, *International Classification*, 213.

23 Union of the Physically Impaired Against Segregation, *Fundamental Principles*, n.p.

24 Davis, *Bending over Backwards*.

25 Isabel Karpin and Roxanne Mykitiuk, "Going out on a limb: prosthetics, normalcy and disputing the therapy/enhancement distinction." *Medical Law Review* 16, 3 (2008): 413–36.

26 Bill Hughes and Kevin Paterson, "The social model of disability and the disappearing body: towards a sociology of impairment." *Disability & Society* 12, 3 (1997): 329.

27 Michael Oliver, *Understanding Disability: From Theory to Practice* (London: Macmillan, 1996), 35.

28 Ibid., 5.

29 Ibid., 35.

30 Union of the Physically Impaired Against Segregation, *Fundamental Principles*; Victor Finkelstein, *Attitudes and Disabled People: Issues for Discussion* (New York: World Rehabilitation Fund, 1980); Michael Oliver, *The Politics of Disablement* (London: Macmillan, 1990), and *Understanding Disability*.

31 Oliver, *Understanding Disability*, 38.

32 Finkelstein, *Attitudes*, 25–6.

33 Oliver, *Understanding Disability*, 95–109.

34 Finkelstein, *Attitudes*, 26, emphasis added.

35 Thomas, *Sociologies*, 135.

36 Ibid.

37 Ibid., 136.

38 Ibid.

39 Ibid.

40 Ibid., 137.

41 Ibid.

42 Kevin Paterson and Bill Hughes, "Disability studies and phenomenology: the carnal politics of everyday life." *Disability & Society* 14, 5 (1999): 597–610.

43 Drew Leder, *The Absent Body* (Chicago: The University of Chicago Press, 1990).

44 Paterson and Hughes, "Disability studies and phenomenology," 603.

45 Ibid.

46 Ibid., 607.

47 Ibid., 602.

48 Ibid., 603.

49 Tom Shakespeare, *Disability Rights and Wrongs* (New York: Routledge, 2006), 54–5.

50 Ibid., 33.

51 Ibid., 29–53.

52 Ibid., 43.

53 Ibid., 35.

54 Ibid., 43.

55 Ibid., 36.

56 Ibid., 35.

57 Ibid., 40.

58 Ibid., 32.

59 Ibid., 49.

60 Ibid., 51.

61 In this chapter, I already highlighted the importance of the "closer look" in the discussion of Thomas's analysis of intrinsic restrictiveness in her *Sociologies of Disability and Illness*. The structural-materialist presuppositions informing the British social model of disability make its proponents suspicious of analyses deployed on the micro-level. Nevertheless, it is often *only* by looking closely at the details of everyday living and interaction that one can reveal general regularities underpinning dis/ablism. The question about the relationship between micro- and macro-levels of analysis will be revisited in Chapter 9.

62 Shakespeare, *Disability Rights and Wrongs*, 45.

63 Ibid., 46.

64 Ibid., 40.

65 David Pfeiffer, "The devils are in the details: the ICIDH2 and the disability movement." *Disability & Society* 15, 7 (2000): 1082.

66 Titchkosky, "Disability in the news," 658.

67 In a different context, albeit departing from similar philosophical presuppositions, Gianni Vattimo and Santiago Zabala (*Hermeneutic Communism. From Heidegger to Marx*, New York: Columbia University Press, 2011) argue for the need to *weaken* traditional metaphysical and sociopolitical certainties through hermeneutics.

68 Bill Hughes, "Being disabled: towards a critical social ontology for disability studies." *Disability & Society* 22, 7 (2007): 676.

69 Thomas Tierney, *The Value of Convenience: A Genealogy of Technical Culture* (Albany: State University of New York Press, 1993).

70 Ibid., 38.

71 Ibid., 42.

72 Ibid., 204.

73 Michel Foucault, "Afterword: the subject and power," in *Michel Foucault: Beyond Structuralism and Hermeneutics*, eds. Hubert L. Dreyfus and Paul Rabinow (Brighton: The Harvester Press, 1982).

74 For a critical realist rendering of this thesis see Sayer, *Realism*, 91.

75 Hughes, "Being disabled," 676.

76 Tierney, *Value of Convenience*, 204.

77 Hughes, "Being disabled."

78 On this point, see also Taylor Carman, "Heidegger's concept of presence." *Inquiry: An Interdisciplinary Journal of Philosophy* 38, 4 (1995): 431–53.

79 Kanev, *Heidegger*, 177.

80 Ibid., 176.

81 Nick Crossley, *The Social Body: Habit, Identity and Desire* (London: SAGE, 2001), 38–61.

82 Medard Boss, *Existential Foundations of Medicine and Psychology*, trans. Stephen Conway and Anne Cleaves (New York and London: Jason Aronson, 1979 [1971]), 103.

83 Thomas, *Sociologies*.

84 Michalko, *Difference*.

85 This example was given by Jackie Leach Scully during a talk of hers given at King's College London in March 2011.

86 Heidegger, *Being and Time*, 414.

87 Hacking, *Social Construction*, 20.

88 Martin Heidegger, *Zollikon Seminars: Protocols, Conversations, Letters*, ed. Medard Boss, trans. Franz Mayr and Richard Askay (Evanston, IL: Northwestern University Press, 2001 [1959–69]), 97.

89 Boss, *Existential Foundations*, 105.

90 Heidegger, *Zollikon Seminars*, 96.

91 The last example is taken from Oliver, *Understanding Disability*, 99–100.

3

Disability assessment

The meaning of disability is intrinsically tied to the meaning of humanness, because picking up features that define disability presupposes deciding on the most important characteristics of being human—albeit, as a rule, in negative terms, in terms of "negative ontology,"[1] according to the mechanism of ontological privation (Chapter 1). It is in this sense that disability "acts as a mirror for society. Society is reflected in disability in terms of how society interprets disability."[2] For example, if to be disabled means to be *unable to produce*, then production is implicitly given a privileged place in defining what it means to be a human being. Existential phenomenology has shown that these decisions about the pivotal characteristics of humanness engage in a reduction of the human—whereas both phenomenology and existentialism share a "belief that what it is to be human cannot be reduced to any set of features about us (whether biological, sociological, anthropological, or logical)."[3] The point is that, in Western modernity at least, the foregrounding of certain features as *defining* humanness tends to be grounded on "substance ontology," as pointed out in Chapter 1. Consequently, such definitions abstract the human being from its lived context or world, thus covering up the human being's most basic state of being-in-the-world.[4] Explaining the meaning of the latter concept, Blattner provides the following example:

> To describe me as weighing a certain amount is (or at least, can be) to "disregard the existential state of being-in." . . . So, if we disregard a person's existentiality and treat him or her simply as a physical object, we can describe that person in terms of his or her factual determinations. In doing so, however, we are missing what makes his or her life *the life* it is. People do not just weigh *x* pounds; they live such a weight as being overweight or underweight or as being indifferent to their weight. Weight, as a way of being-in-the-world, is not an indifferent physical property.[5]

Blattner speaks here about reducing the human to a "physical object." In his later work, as reflected in the seminal essay "The question concerning technology," Heidegger argues that modernity is characterized by an increasing and totalizing reduction of humans (together with nonhuman entities) to resources.[6] Heidegger criticizes this instrumental tendency to regard everything in terms of "standing-reserve," that is, as orderable for the enhancement of the overall system's effectiveness. This chapter looks at both the objective and the instrumental modes of existential-ontological reduction, proceeding from the presumption that certain disability-related practices through which disability is understood for welfare purposes—such as the disability assessment—incorporate such reductive patterns. Consequently, one can study the procedure and outcome of the legally codified disability assessment by looking at the ways in which human beings show up in modern society as "de-worlded" entities of a particular, determinable kind.

The aim will be to analyze how modern reductive ontologies of the human underpin the sociopolitical rendering of disabled people exclusively in terms of deficient bodies and/or inefficient resources. Disability studies, in Britain at least, has been dominated by materialist approaches, epitomized by the social model of disability.[7] Indeed, as discussed in Chapter 2, the last two decades have witnessed an increasing discontent with the social model's alleged naturalization and exclusion of the body,[8] coupled with disregarding culture, meaning, and identity.[9] Yet most of these critiques have sidestepped the more general question of the *meaning of human being* and its relationship to disability. Phenomenology helps to fill this gap by providing a sound conceptual foundation for addressing the human being in a holistic manner, and consequently, for criticizing modern reductions of the human that pervade all aspects of disabled people's lives. In this chapter, the phenomenological approach will be supported by a sociologically informed analysis of the everyday working out of disability-related identities and meanings through recourse to the science and technology studies (STS) concept of "boundary object."[10] Being itself a newcomer to disability studies, this concept is particularly useful for sharpening the sociological attention to the "nuts and bolts" of identity and meaning construction.

The case study will focus on disability assessment in Bulgaria, although many of its arguments will also be valid for similar practices in other sociopolitical contexts. Chapter 1 pointed out that the Bulgarian approach to disability-related issues has been heavily influenced by the over-medicalized Soviet approach of *defectology*. Consequently, the assignment of disability status in Bulgaria has for decades been exclusively dominated by medical professionals and procedures, mimicking Russian practices in the area.[11] This over-medicalization and standardization of disability makes Bulgarian social policy particularly illustrative for exploring how certain reductions of the human dominate disabled people's lives. Such mechanisms operate in Western societies as well, but in subtler, more inconspicuous ways. For example, the UK regulations do not posit a necessary requirement to undergo special medical examination when applying for Disability Living Allowance (DLA)—and yet, additional medical information about the applicant may be collected and s/he may be asked to be examined by a health care professional. Since April 2013, the DLA has been gradually replaced by a new benefit called "Personal Independence Payment" (PIP). In comparison to DLA, PIP promises a "fair, more objective and transparent assessment of individuals"[12] through the introduction of an independent health professional to assess eligibility. Although in this way the assessment gets explicitly medicalized, the scope of this medicalization is delimited by the distinction drawn between the assessment role and the therapeutic role of the health professional: "The PIP assessor is a Health Professional (HP) with specialist training in assessing the impact of disability. The role differs from the therapeutic role of HPs in reaching a diagnosis and/or planning treatment."[13] The procedure for applying for social security disability benefits in the United States is somewhat similar, although unlike UK's DLA, these benefits are dependent on the applicant's occupational status (http://www.ssa.gov/disability/professionals/bluebook). Importantly, in both these countries no single procedure and/or document exists, which measures impairment in standardized terms and which is supposed to certify "disability status" before all support systems concerned.

In contrast, as currently practiced in Bulgaria, the medicalized disability assessment provides an all-powerful statement of crucial importance for both understanding and management of disability-related issues. Thus it can clearly illustrate how disability is produced as a function of more general reductive tendencies in modern societies, where to be a (fully) human being means to have a normatively circumscribed body capable of taking part in the process of production. I will begin my exploration with the reduction of the human to a *physical body*, analyzing the procedure followed by the medical expert commissions in charge of disability assessment in Bulgaria. This reduction is most conspicuous with regard to assessing physical and sensory impairments and is less pronounced when it comes to assessing psychiatric and/or mental impairments—therefore, I will take the former as my case example. I will further explore the reduction of the human to a *resource* by focusing on the disability assessment statement. This excludes children, for they are not regarded as economically productive and therefore in Bulgaria the assessment of their impairments is rendered not in terms of "decreased ability to work," but in terms of "decreased capacity for social adaptation," thus calling for a separate analysis. Further, the disability assessment statement will be regarded as a "boundary object" in order to analyze how the meaning of "disability" is constituted within different social worlds. I will conclude with a critique of the naturalization of disability and will rearticulate the concerns about the reduction of the human highlighted at the beginning of the chapter.

Disability assessment in Bulgaria

In Bulgaria, the medicalized disability assessment dominates all disability-related supporting structures and processes.[14] It is *only* in terms of this legally codified assessment procedure that a person can officially be recognized *as disabled*—not solely by the Bulgarian welfare state with its system of financial support and service provision, but also by the private service providers. The very definition of "person with disability" within Bulgarian legislation hinges on the outcome of the expert medical assessment.[15] A person can legitimately claim disability benefits only after being medically assessed and certified as disabled. Other types of support such as the provision of assistive technology and medical devices, personal assistance services, adaptation of the workplace, and inclusive education arrangements are also directly dependent on the assessment outcome. Official disability statistics rely heavily on the distinctions brought about by this process.[16] Finally, the disability-related social security is ultimately based on the document issued by the disability assessment commission.[17]

This dominance of the medicalized disability assessment has also been highlighted in international evaluation reports such as the *International Disability Rights Monitor*. In its 2007 issue, the report states that "[i]n countries where a purely medical disability model is used, such as Bulgaria and Armenia, the responsibility of assigning disability status is left solely to medical agencies."[18] The document also underlines that the legal definition of "disability" in Bulgaria is exclusively based on the medical assessment, which assigns to each individual a certain percentage of decreased ability to work. It criticizes this as "show[ing] the domination of the medical model of disability as opposed to the social one—the focus is on the individual's inabilities as opposed to environmental barriers."[19]

Bulgarian disability assessment incorporates two modes of reduction of the human being—to an object (a physical body) and to a resource (a productive entity). The first is mostly related to the procedure for assigning disability status, and the second to its outcome, the assessment statement. Let me begin with the former, which in Bulgaria is termed "Medical expert assessment of the ability to work" and is detailed in the Regulations for the Medical Expert Assessment of the Ability to Work (http://www.mlsp.government.bg/bg/law/

regulation/Narmedicexpertizairabotosposobnost.doc). The assessment is carried out by "territorial/national expert medical commissions," comprising exclusively of medical doctors. It is conducted in a medical setting—Article 1 of the Regulations states that "[t]he medical expert assessment of the ability to work is an inseparable part of the diagnostic-treatment and prophylactic activity of the medical treatment settings." The assessment consists of correlating a clinically determined diagnosis or functional condition of the body with certain percentage of "decreased ability to work" (Article 57). Clearly, the primary feature of the Bulgarian disability assessment is its overwhelming medicalization, understood as "expansion of medical jurisdiction" or "the power and authority of the medical profession."[20] Medicalization is "the process that occurs when a given area of human activity is defined socially as falling under the proper purview of medicine," including "any state that such a process might lead to."[21] Medicalization empowers medical experts to define issues, render certain of them problematic, and prescribe therapeutic solutions to them. This suggests that there is an intrinsic relationship between medicalization and social control: "the process of medicalization allows the medical profession to take control of an area of life that other parties, often ordinary people previously controlled."[22] Disability scholars have described this domination of the medical expertise over the lives of disabled people as the "medical model of disability."[23] It reduces disabled people to their physical bodies, rendered in biomedical terms as incomplete or flawed. Exposed to the medicalizing gaze of the experts, the human being is stripped down to its purely physical dimension, regarded at that as deficient.

This reduction to material corporeality, enforced by the assessment procedure, goes hand in hand with a second reductive operation. The outcome of the medicalized disability assessment is formulated in strictly productivist[24] terms, thus further reducing the human to a productive entity—or, in managerial jargon, a "human resource." It is the *ability to work* that is being assessed by the medical experts. This ability is expressed by a percentage, where 0 percent equals no loss, while 100 percent designates total loss. For example, a loss of an upper limb at the level of the armpit gives 75 percent decreased ability to work, while a loss of a lower limb at the level of the calf—between 50 and 60 percent.[25] Thus the human being is reduced to his/her productive capacity imagined within the framework of the routine and standardizable labor characteristic of the industrial mode of production. This implies the ethos of productivism, which "imposes both an economic and moral imperative to embrace the world of work."[26] Productivism "*reduces* people and the environment to the status of human and natural resources for economic exploitation," thus overlooking "the complex and interdependent nature of human existence."[27] It should be noted that materialist disability scholars such as Abberley, Finkelstein, and Oliver have repeatedly highlighted the close relationship between productivism and disability.[28] For example, Abberley writes:

> the "problem" of disability is why these people aren't productive, how to return them to productivity, and, if this is not seen as economically viable, how to handle their non-productivity in a manner which causes as little disruption as possible to the overriding imperative of capital accumulation and maximisation of profits.[29]

Disability shows up exclusively as a problem of productivity only against the background of an understanding of being that renders humans in terms of economically productive entities. Such an understanding is incorporated in the medicalized disability assessment, whose outcome is the assignment of a percentage of "decreased ability to work."

Linking medicalization and productivism

Bulgarian disability assessment also illustrates how *medicalization coalesces with productivism* to serve the dominant socioeconomic order. Historians of medicine have analyzed the close interlinking between medicine and the industrial mode of production in the heyday of modernity. Foucault points out that "there appeared in the nineteenth century—above all, in England—a medicine that consisted mainly in a control of the health and the bodies of the needy classes, to make them more fit for labor and less dangerous to the wealthy classes."[30] Thus "[a]t a time when medicine and its institutions were being reoriented around a deliberate concern to maintain and manage a fit and efficient industrial population, physiology and other medical sciences offered a functional understanding of health and illness which both legitimized such a reorientation and provided a technical basis for establishing standards of public provision."[31] In other words, medical science and technology provided productivism with the means to distinguish between the "lazy" and the "unproductive" and to compensate the latter, while disregarding or punishing the former. Historically speaking:

> Medical validation of physical incapacity solved the problem of malingering by circumventing the testimony of the individual. Under this confirmation scheme, the doctor sought direct communication with the body regarding its condition, eliminating the patient's ability for self-disclosure and, ultimately, for self-determination. . . . As a result, "disabled" became,

in the twentieth-century welfare state, a medicalized category by which the state could administer economic relief in a seemingly objective and equitable manner.[32]

Thomson points out that this medical-productivist administration of the economic relief follows the "logic of compensation," in which "'disabled' connotes not physiological variation, but the violation of a primary state of putative wholeness."[33] As already shown, this "state of putative wholeness" can be ascribed a value: 0 percent decreased ability to work equals a whole worker. This wholeness though should be distinguished from the *existential* wholeness, for the former is defined as physical integrity, related in biological-functional terms to economic productivity, whereas the latter—to human being-in-the-world. In the same work Thomson counterposes the "logic of compensation" to the "logic of accommodation" that "suggests that disability is simply one of many differences among people and that society should recognize this by adjusting its environment accordingly."[34] Thus compensation alleviates individual incapacity, whereas accommodation corrects structural inadequacy. The distinction between "compensation" and "accommodation" parallels the distinction drawn by Oliver between the individual and the social model of disability, where the former focuses on the individual, while the latter on the environment.[35] The tension between these two approaches within Bulgarian disability legislation will be highlighted in the next section.

Transformations of modernity and attempts at changing the *status quo*

The existential-ontological reduction of the human being to a self-enclosed, normatively circumscribed, industrially productive entity has been complicated by certain late modern developments. In the modern framework the body is regarded as fixed, as "an essence, a timeless, material thing,"[36] while production is predominantly factory-based—that is, manual, repetitive, and standardizable. In *late* modernity with its "knowledge economy"[37] both the status of the body and that of resources changes. First, in late modernity the body no longer shows up as fixed, but as *flexible*.[38] Consequently, "opportunities for biomedicalization extend beyond merely regulating and controlling what bodies can (and cannot) or should (and should not) do to also focus on assessing, shifting, reshaping, reconstituting, and ultimately transforming bodies for varying purposes, including new identities."[39] Second, late modern "human resources" are no longer understood primarily as physically, but rather as *intellectually* productive—that is, as generating and disseminating *knowledge.* Powell and Snellman point out that "[t]he key components of a knowledge economy include a greater reliance on intellectual capabilities than on physical inputs or natural resources."[40]

Bulgarian society partakes in these historical transformations. Yet the case of disability assessment is exempt from the predicaments brought about by these transformations because the country's social policy, especially in the domain of disability, has so far remained rooted in a more "traditional" version of modernity. Indeed, attempts have been made to update the Bulgarian disability legislation in line with the new sociopolitical, socioeconomic, and sociotechnical realities, as well as with a different set of values and visions. Yet these attempts have been largely unsuccessful, leaving the practices of disability assessment virtually untouched.

Recent Bulgarian legislative history has witnessed the process of setting up an alternative disability assessment procedure, which would arguably be based on expanding the meaning of human being to include the nonmedical and the nonproductivist aspects of one's existence. With the adoption of the new Law for the Integration of People with Disabilities in 2005 (http://www.mlsp.government.bg/bg/law/law/ZIHU_74_15_9_09.doc) a "social assessment" has been introduced (Article 12), ostensibly focusing on the social and not medical circumstances of the disabled individual. As currently regulated by the law, the "social assessment," among other things, is argued to evaluate "the possibilities for social integration" and to produce an "individual plan for social integration" (Article 12), including "suggestions for social inclusion" (Article 13). On its basis an "allowance for social integration" (Article 42) is provided as a certain monthly amount of money to aid integration. Yet the law explicitly *grounds* the "social assessment" on the medical assessment by stating that "[t]he social assessment is conducted *on the basis of* the medical expert assessment" (Article 12, emphasis added). The "allowance for social integration" is also explicitly made dependent on the "degree of the reduced ability to work" (Article 42), certified by the medical expert commissions. All these provisions render impotent the possibility of the social assessment to function in its own right, clearly distinct from the medical expert assessment.

Back in 2004–05 several different versions of the new disability legislation were proposed. The Center for Independent Living—Sofia (the Bulgarian disabled people's organization introduced in Chapter 1) developed and lobbied for one of the alternative bills. An attempt was made to supplement the "logic of compensation" with the "logic of accommodation"[41] and to introduce the considerations of the social model of disability within the disability policy equation—by introducing a social assessment of disability that was supposed to be *independent* of the medical one. Yet such independence was met with suspicion by the policy-makers and eventually the Parliament voted for the most conservative among the new bills, grounding as already shown the social assessment on the medical assessment. A similar scenario repeated itself in 2009–10.[42] Thus the system of institutionalized medicalization of disabled people strongly resists any substantial changes of the *status quo*. The outcome is the continuing dominance of the medicalized disability assessment, which reduces disabled people to deficient bodies and inefficient resources.

Disability assessment statement as a boundary object

The medicalized disability assessment has also a positive function to play. From a sociological point of view its statement can be regarded as a "boundary object" that consolidates the boundaries around different domains of practice, while at the same time making the interaction between them possible.[43] "Boundary object" is a concept widely utilized in the context of science and technology studies to designate a material/conceptual entity that mediates meaning and identity construction. Thus:

> Boundary objects are objects which are both plastic enough to adapt to local needs and the constraints of the several parties employing them, yet robust enough to maintain a common identity across sites. . . . These objects may be abstract or concrete. They have different meanings in different social worlds but their structure is common enough to more than one world to make them recognizable, a means of translation. The creation and management of boundary objects is a key process in developing and maintaining coherence across intersecting social worlds.[44]

In brief, boundary objects "maximize both the autonomy and communication between worlds."[45] Further, Williams *et al.* point out that boundary objects have an "anchoring," as well as a "bridging" function—they anchor actors in their local worlds or forms of life, while also bridging the gaps of incommensurability between these localities.[46] Hence a boundary object is defined through a set of binary oppositions: it is both "plastic" and "robust," maximizing "autonomy" and maximizing "communication," acting as an "anchor" and acting as a "bridge," "enabling" and "disabling," "promoting translation" and "resisting translation," and so forth.[47] Importantly, a boundary object does not reconcile or overcome the oppositions in a dialectical unity, but keeps them vital *as oppositions*. In fact, this is exactly what makes it a *boundary* object— that is, an exemplary mediator, an entity that is always in-between.

The statement of the medicalized disability assessment in Bulgaria can be regarded in a similar vein. From such a perspective, it is a boundary object, partaking in the constitution of the social worlds of medical assessment procedure, social services/welfare provision, and individual existence, while simultaneously facilitating the interaction between these three domains of practice. The analysis that follows is based on observations accumulated during my nearly 10-year professional experience in Bulgarian disability policy, and also on a review of relevant documents. It is preliminary and experimental—an attempt at thinking differently about seemingly well-known phenomena. So far, the disability assessment statement has not been regarded as a boundary object and this fresh science and technology studies perspective might stimulate fresh insights into the mechanisms of mediation that translate bodily differences into undermining of disabled people's existence.

Three social worlds

As used by Star and Griesemer, the term "social world" denotes a distinct domain of human practice in which individuals create and sustain their identities in distinct ways.[48] The notion is useful precisely for capturing this *distinctiveness* (or localness). I borrow it here in order to distinguish and analyze three domains in which the disability assessment statement plays a pivotal role in identity construction, functioning as a boundary object. These are the social worlds of the medical assessment procedure, the social/welfare work and the individual existence.

In the world of the assessment procedure, the statement about the "decreased ability to work" provides the medical professionals participating in the expert medical commissions with an opportunity to exercise their medical expertise through fixing a diagnosis and assigning a number. The socio-political space of the assessment is heavily hierarchized. The Regulations for the Medical Expert Assessment of the Ability to Work grant the experts the exceptional power to manage the lives of the individuals who seek certification, while unequivocally rendering the disabled person as "diseased." S/he cannot help but passively await the authoritative diagnostic decision of the commission, with which no negotiation is possible. Thus her or his body becomes an "object and target of power" or a "docile body,"[49] orderable and manageable in its very minute details—the list of diagnostic categories and functional conditions, correlated with percentages of "decreased ability to work" in the Annex to the Regulations for the Medical Expert Assessment, exceeds 16,000 words. The impaired body is implicated in a web of diagnostic terms and degrees of incapacity that will further regulate the individual's access to services and welfare. All these positionings and meanings are organized around the outcome of the disability assessment, expressed as a diagnosis, tied to a certain percentage of "decreased ability to work," and fixed in a document to be circulated to other disability-related sites. Besides reassuring the medical specialist's professional identity, this piece of paper stabilizes the meaning of "disability" within the confines of the expert medical discourse. As a boundary object, it renders disability in terms of medical *diagnosis*, thus circumscribing the domain of medical knowledge/power.

The world of the social/welfare work is also organized around the outcome of the assessment. In Bulgaria, the statement of the expert medical commission is required every time social services are provided to disabled people.[50] Thus the statement both controls the access to service provision and organizes its procedures. For example, at the time of writing this text there are five personal assistance schemes for disabled people in Bulgaria—four national and one municipal.[51] Different service providers are involved in these schemes, including state agencies, municipal agencies, and business and nonprofit organizations. Yet effectively transcending this diversity, *all* service providers base their "admission" decisions on the outcome of the expert medical disability assessment.[52] Thus disabled people can access personal assistance services only if certified as "appropriately" disabled (i.e., being assigned a certain percentage of "decreased ability to work") by the expert medical commissions. The world of disability service provision in Bulgaria is dominated by the medicalized disability assessment. As a consequence, social work with disabled people is often reduced to administering disability certificates—a manifestation of the often-criticized "high level of bureaucratization in the [Bulgarian] social support system."[53] Social workers exercise their disability-related expertise by correlating percentages of "decreased ability to work" with services available. Thus within the confines of the Bulgarian welfare system, the expert medical certificate stabilizes the meaning of "disability" in terms of *admission to resources*. Again, it functions as a boundary object, structuring relationships, building hierarchies, and organizing discourse and action within a distinct social world.

Finally, the disabled person's individual existence is also at stake in the disability assessment. Subjected to the already described double reduction, the person undergoing the medical assessment procedure is constituted *both* as a deficient human body *and* an inefficient human resource. At that, the more deficient and incapable the body-resource, the more open the access to support services and financial benefits. The twofold function of the boundary object—to be simultaneously *enabling* and *disabling* with regard to social action[54]—is clearly evident here. As a boundary object, the statement of the medicalized disability assessment *enables* people's access to welfare resource, while at the same time consolidating their status as *disabled* by fixing (anchoring) their corporeal "deficiency" and productive "incapacity" through assigning a medically determined percentage of "decreased ability for work." Such a subject position breeds passivity and acquiescence, but it also provides access to social services and financial benefits. The medicalized disability assessment is rarely (if at all) informative about the actual life circumstances and capacities of the person. Indeed, as Hahn has pointed out, "[i]n an environment designed to meet the needs of disabled individuals, traditional assumptions about their capacities and productivity embedded in the 'functional-limitations' model of disability probably could no longer be sustained."[55] Nevertheless, the medicalized assessment implicates the disabled individual within a system of power/knowledge that effectively incapacitates, while also being productive—it produces identities and enables action in terms of consuming welfare resources. Foucault highlights this productive capacity of modern power, which "incites, it induces, it seduces, it makes easier or more difficult."[56] In this respect, the medicalized disability assessment might be regarded as a paradigmatic instance of the exercise of biopower. Through its mediation a privative mode of being emerges. As a boundary object, the assessment organizes individual lives around *deficiency* and *access to welfare resources*.

To summarize, the medicalized disability assessment statement means different things for different groups of people within their different social worlds. In the world of the medical assessment procedure it means *expertise and medical diagnosis*. In the world of social work and welfare provision it means *administration and admission*. Finally, in the world of individual existence it means *deficiency and access to resources*. Thus in all these different and divergent social worlds the assessment functions as a boundary object—it draws the boundaries of meaning, distinguishing and distributing priorities, stakes, and modes of being. Through the assessment some become experts, others administrators and gatekeepers, yet others deficient body-resources and social assistance/welfare receivers. No wonder that it has been difficult to change or displace this boundary object, as the case with the already mentioned Bulgarian disability legislation testifies.

The administrative and the sociopolitical: Coordination, standardization, and naturalization

The disability assessment statement not only partakes in the construction of local meanings and identities, but also facilitates the interaction between these localities. Thus the medical domain of the disability assessment is connected to the social domain of the service provision through a document certifying the percentage of "decreased ability to work." This boundary object effectively crosses the gap between the medical and the welfare social worlds, building a bridge of coordination. It also relates the domains of the medical and the welfare to the domain of the individual existence, attaching people's lives and identities to medical diagnoses, percentages of inability, and inputs of social/welfare assistance. Thus a network of associations between sites and agencies can be traced, constituting what is commonly regarded as "disability." The coherence of this network relies on the mediation of boundary objects such as the assessment statement that are circulated in a very *material* way among its "nodes." Bruno Latour points out that the social can be stabilized only through the recruitment of the nonsocial, the "inert," the material.[57] Thus certain nonhuman entities can be regarded as "agents," actively partaking in the construction of meaning and the performance of intentional, human action. The medicalized disability assessment statement is an example of such nonhuman mediator, effectively binding together sites, people, meanings, actions, and resources.

The more standardized this mediation, the more effective the "government of disability."[58] Consequently, the statement of the expert medical commission functions as a special type of boundary object—a *standard*, allowing for manageability, efficiency, accountability, and comparability. The point is that "standards can enable heterogeneous systems of people and things to interact and combine across time and space."[59] In the case of the medicalized disability assessment the standard comprises a common unit used to measure "disability," much like temperature is commonly expressed in degrees centigrade (except in the United States and a few other countries). The common unit of "disability" in Bulgaria is the percentage of "decreased ability to work." Being assigned this number, people become orderable on a *single* scale. Such homogenization makes their comparison and management within the system of the welfare provision possible; it makes distribution of resources and accountability feasible. Finally, it enhances the overall effectiveness of the networked localities by avoiding repetition and reducing uncertainty associated with face-to-face human interaction.

Notably, all these arguments regarding the utility of standardization are of an instrumental nature and tend to leave out such considerations as human diversity, freedom, and self-determination. Thus functional-administrative concerns overshadow sociopolitical ones. Furthermore, with its routine and widespread application, the standard of the medicalized disability assessment gets *naturalized*, covering up its social origins. In similar terms, Smart et al. analyze a nationwide process of standardization in the context of race/ethnicity.[60] They describe how UK biobanks have uncritically adopted the UK Census classification of ethnicity, driven by the need for coordination and stabilization of action.[61] The "dark side" of this unreflexive utilization of the Census classification is the erosion of "the epistemological status of its categories as socio-political constructs,"[62] which opens up bleak prospects for the human being. The authors remind the reader that "[t]he history of racial science shows the potential for socio-political constructs of population groupings to be transformed into innate, immutable and natural categories, with dire social consequences."[63] The standard produced by the expert medical disability assessment and "materialized" in the form of the assessment statement also tends to naturalize the otherwise socially constituted, highly contested, and ambiguous category of disability.[64] Consequently, it becomes a matter of *common sense* to regard disabled people as deficient bodies and/ or incapable resources.

Concluding remarks

Disability scholars and activists have resisted the medical-productivist reduction of disabled people to (deficient) bodies and/or (inefficient) resources with bold statements such as "disability is beautiful,"[65] but most notably by decoupling body and society through the development of the social model of disability. In Bulgaria, the latter has been embraced by disability advocates as a general framework for informing progressive social policy changes, thus functioning as what Shakespeare and Watson have termed the "ideological litmus test of disability politics."[66] Yet the social model's exclusively materialist focus on the structures and processes oppressing disabled people, albeit strategically relevant, is insufficiently worked out in ontological terms, as argued in Chapter 2. The reduction of disabled people to deficient bodies and incapable resources is rooted in general existential-ontological tendencies that concern disabled as well as nondisabled people, their lived bodies, and nonhuman entities as well.

Phenomenologists such as Heidegger have argued that such reductive tendencies underlie the whole history of the Western civilization that has been dominated by fascination with detached self-presence.[67] In Chapter 1, the genealogy of this metaphysics of presence was traced to the idea that *being* is ultimately some kind of substance that occurs in space and endures through time. The existential-ontological reduction of the human to a physical body can be regarded as an instance of this general hegemony of the metaphysics of presence. It amounts to a de-worlded understanding of human being, whose basic state is by no means disconnected and self-present but involved and engaged, contextually embedded being-in-the-world. Humans are much more than discrete bodies occupying physical space, but tradition has tended to reduce them to detached, objective, self-present entities, and medicalization is a modern epitome of this tendency. Indeed, one can attribute to humans object-like properties or "state-characteristics,"[68] but with this one obliterates their basic ontological state of being-in-the-world. In his later work Heidegger has also tackled the question concerning the reduction of human beings to productive resources.[69] He has analyzed the technological "enframing" (Gestell), which "does not simply endanger man in his relationship to himself and to everything that is [but also] banishes man into that kind of revealing which is an ordering."[70] This "ordering" is a tendency to regard everything, including human beings, in terms of resources or "standing-reserve" (Bestand),[71] utilizable for the enhancement of the overall system's effectiveness.

From such a perspective, the reduction of disabled people to deficient bodies and inefficient resources illuminated by the analysis of the Bulgarian disability assessment can be regarded as a limit-case of more general reductive tendencies inherent in modernity. It is *because* human beings tend to be regarded exclusively as detached objects and/or utilizable resources *that* disabled people can be rendered exclusively in terms of *flawed* objects and *un*utilizable resources. The mechanism of ontological privation, outlined in Chapter 1, is fully at work here—against the background of objectified and instrumentalized understandings of the human being, certain humans inadvertently show up as *ontologically lacking*. In the present case study, this existential-ontological analysis was supplemented by an inquiry into the mediation of the disability assessment statement conceptualized as a "boundary object" that shapes and stabilizes the practices of assessing disability for welfare purposes. Therefore, if in social policy terms this chapter argues for de-medicalization of disability assessment and for decoupling of its methodology from productivist considerations, in methodological terms it shows how the mediation of disability-related practices can be explored in view of its significance for the understanding of the human being.

Notes

1   Fiona Kumari Campbell, "Legislating disability: negative ontologies and the government of legal identities," in *Foucault and the Government of Disability*, ed. Shelley Tremain (Ann Arbor: The University of Michigan Press, 2005).

2   Rod Michalko, *The Difference that Disability Makes* (Philadelphia: Temple University Press, 2002), 168.

3   Mark A. Wrathall and Hubert L. Dreyfus, "A brief introduction to phenomenology and existentialism," in *A Companion to Phenomenology and Existentialism*, eds. Hubert L. Dreyfus and Mark A. Wrathall (Oxford: Blackwell, 2006), 5.

4 Martin Heidegger, *Being and Time*, trans. John Macquarrie and Edward Robinson (Oxford: Blackwell, 1962 [1927]), 78.

5 William Blattner, *Heidegger's* Being and Time: *A Reader's Guide* (London: Continuum, 2006), 44–5.

6 Martin Heidegger, *The Question Concerning Technology, and Other Essays*, trans. William Lovitt (New York: Harper & Row, 1977).

7 Carol Thomas, "Disability theory: key ideas, issues and thinkers," in *Disability Studies Today*, eds. Colin Barnes, Mike Oliver, and Len Barton (Cambridge: Polity Press, 2002).

8 Liz Crow, "Renewing the social model of disability," *Coalition News*, July (1992); Tom Shakespeare and Nicholas Watson, "The social model of disability: an outdated ideology," in *Research in Social Science and Disability, Vol. 2: Exploring Theories and Expanding Methodologies*, eds. Sharon N. Barnartt and Barbara M. Altman (Stamford, CT: JAI Press, 2001).

9 For example, Shakespeare ("Cultural representation of disabled people: dustbins for disavowal?" *Disability & Society* 9, 3 (1994): 283) argues that the social model theorists' materialist focus on societal structures results in the tendency "to bracket . . . questions of culture, representation and meaning." When issues of meaning are addressed by the adherents of the social model, they are regarded as secondary to and derivative of material/economic structure. This suggests a determinist position that "privileges the material level of explanation, and does not give much explanatory space or autonomy to the realm of culture and meaning" (Ibid., 289). In contrast, Shakespeare insists that culture/meaning has an autonomous role in the constitution of disability and should be addressed in its own right: "the role of culture and meaning is crucial, autonomous and inescapable" (Ibid.).

10 Susan Leigh Star and James R. Griesemer, "Institutional ecology, 'translations' and boundary objects: amateurs and professionals in Berkeley's Museum of Vertebrate Zoology, 1907–39." *Social Studies of Science* 19, 3 (1989): 387–420.

11 International Disability Network, *International Disability Rights Monitor (IDRM): Regional Report of Europe, 2007* (Chicago: International Disability Network, 2007), compare pp. 65–6 and 360–1.

12 Department for Work and Pensions, "Differences and similarities between Disability Living Allowance (DLA) and PIP," in *Personal Independence Payment: Fact Sheet Pack (Version 4.0: October 2013)* (London: Department for Work and Pensions, 2013), 3.

13 Department for Work and Pensions, *PIP Assessment Guide* (London: Department for Work and Pensions, 2013), 8.

14 Kapka Panayotova and Kolyu Todorov, *Integration and the Law for the Integration of People with Disabilities* (Sofia: Center for Independent Living, 2007), 11.

15 Law for the Integration of People with Disabilities, Additional Provisions, paragraph 1, http://www.mlsp.government.bg/bg/law/law/ZIHU_74_15_9_09.doc, accessed September 27, 2013.

16 Center for Independent Living, *From Handicapped People to Persons with Disabilities (Disability Rights in Bulgaria: A Survey, 2001)* (Sofia: Center for Independent Living, 2002), 8.

17 Social Security Code, chapter VI, section II, http://www.mlsp.government.bg/bg/law/law/KSO.doc, accessed September 27, 2013.

18 International Disability Network, *International Disability Rights Monitor (IDRM): Regional Report of Europe, 2007* (Chicago: International Disability Network, 2007), x.

19 Ibid., 65.

20 Peter Conrad, "The shifting engines of medicalisation." *Journal of Health and Social Behavior* 46, 1 (2005): 4.

21 Soren Holm, "The medicalization of reproduction—a 30 year retrospective," in *Reprogen-Ethics and the Future of Gender*, ed. Frida Simonstein (London & New York: Springer, 2009), 33.

22 Ibid.

23 Thomas, "Disability theory," 40.

24 On productivism in modern society see Anthony Giddens, *Beyond Left and Right: The Future of Radical Politics* (Cambridge: Polity Press, 1994), 175ff.

25 See the Regulations for the Medical Expert Assessment of the Ability to Work, Annex 1, http://www.mlsp.government.bg/bg/law/regulation/Narmedicexpertizairabotosposobnost.doc, accessed September 27, 2013.

26 Damon Anderson, "Productivism, vocational and professional education, and the ecological question." *Vocations and Learning* 1, 2 (2008): 110. Anderson draws on Giddens, *Beyond Left and Right*.

27 Ibid., 120.

28 Paul Abberley, "The concept of oppression and the development of a social theory of disability." *Disability, Handicap & Society* 2, 1 (1987): 5–19; Victor Finkelstein, *Attitudes and Disabled People: Issues for Discussion* (New York: World Rehabilitation Fund, 1980); Michael Oliver, *The Politics of Disablement* (London: Macmillan, 1990).

29 Abberley, "The concept of oppression," 15–16.

30 Michel Foucault, "The birth of social medicine," in *Power. Essential Works of Foucault, 1954–1984*, ed. James D. Faubion, trans. Robert Hurley and others (New York: The New York Press, 2000 [1974]), 155.

31 Steve Sturdy and Roger Cooter, "Science, scientific management and the transformation of medicine in Britain c. 1870–1950." *History of Science* 36, 114 (1998): 28.

32 Rosemarie Garland Thomson, *Extraordinary Bodies: Figuring Physical Disability in American Culture and Literature* (New York: Columbia University Press, 1997), 50.

33 Ibid., 49.

34 Ibid.

35 Michael Oliver, *Understanding Disability: From Theory to Practice* (London: Macmillan, 1996), 32.

36 Bill Hughes, "Medicalized bodies," in *The Body, Culture and Society*, eds. Philip Hancock, Bill Hughes, Elizabeth Jagger, Kevin Paterson, Rachel Russel, Emmanuelle Tulle-Winton, and Melissa Tyler (Buckingham: Open University Press, 2000), 12.

37 Walter W. Powell and Kaisa Snellman, "The knowledge economy." *Annual Review of Sociology* 30, 1 (2004): 199–220.

38 Hughes, "Medicalized bodies," 13.

39 Adele Clarke, Janet K. Shim, Laura Mamo, Jennifer R. Fosket, and Jennifer R. Fishman, "Biomedicalization: technoscientific transformations of health, illness, and U. S. biomedicine." *American Sociological Review* 68, 2 (2003): 181.

40 Powell and Snellman, "The knowledge economy," 201. The transition to "knowledge economy," enhanced by globalization, is especially problematic for people with intellectual impairments: "This shift clearly holds risk and disadvantage for people with intellectual disability in the labour market who once might have been able to take their place as largely unskilled manual workers but who are less likely to possess the social and cognitive skills required for employment in the new service and information economy." Leanne Dowse, "'Some people are never going to be able to do that.' Challenges for people with intellectual disability in the 21st century." *Disability & Society* 24, 5 (2009): 573.

41 Thomson, *Extraordinary Bodies*, 49.

42 More information is available at www.cil.bg/Новини/114.html, accessed September 27, 2013.

43 Star and Griesemer, "Institutional ecology."

44 Ibid., 393.

45 Ibid., 404.

46 Clare Williams, Steven P. Wainwright, Kathryn Ehrich, and Mike Michael, "Human embryos as boundary objects? Some reflections on the biomedical worlds of embryonic stem cells and pre-implantation genetic diagnosis." *New Genetics and Society* 27, 1 (2008): 16.

47 See Star and Griesemer, "Institutional ecology"; Williams et al., "Human embryos"; Joan H. Fujimura, "Crafting science: standardized packages, boundary objects and 'translations'," in *Science as Practice and Culture*, ed. Andrew Pickering (Chicago: University of Chicago Press, 1992).

48 Star and Griesemer, "Institutional ecology," 388.

49 Michel Foucault, *Discipline and Punish: The Birth of the Prison*, trans. Alan Sheridan (London: Penguin, 1991 [1975]), 136.

50 Regulations for the Implementation of the Law for Social Assistance, Article 40, http://www.mlsp.government.bg/bg/law/law/ZSP_15_9_09.rtf, accessed September 27, 2013.

51 Center for Independent Living, *Assessment of the Assistant Services for People with Disabilities in Bulgaria* (Sofia: Center for Independent Living, 2009).

52 Ibid.

53 Platform "Social Policies," *White Paper: Basic Principles of Effective Support for Vulnerable Social Groups in Bulgaria trough Social Services* (Sofia: Platform "Social Policies," 2009), 18.

54 Williams et al., "Human embryos," 15.

55 Harlan Hahn, "Can disability be beautiful?" in *Perspectives on Disability. Text and Readings on Disability*, ed. Mark Nagler (Palo Alto, CA: Health Markets Research, 1990), 554.

56 Michel Foucault, "Afterword: the subject and power," in *Michel Foucault: Beyond Structuralism and Hermeneutics*, eds. Hubert L. Dreyfus and Paul Rabinow (Brighton: The Harvester Press, 1982), 220.

57 Bruno Latour, *Reassembling the Social: An Introduction to Actor-Network-Theory* (Oxford: Oxford University Press, 2005). It should be underlined that from the perspective of actor-network theory, although important for the stabilization of social practices, material durability is itself constituted within practices. Thus after pointing out that "a relatively stable network is one embodied in and performed by a range of durable materials,"

the actor-network theorist John Law is eager to add that "durability is yet
another relational effect, not something given in the nature of things. If
materials behave in durable ways then this too is an interactional effect"
(John Law, "Notes on the theory of the actor network: ordering, strategy,
and heterogeneity." *Systems Practice* 5, 4 (1992): 387). In the case of
the disability assessment statement, it is clear that all of its constitutive
elements are conventional and/or made—starting from the paper on which
it is written, going through the medical diagnosis, and ending with the
percentage of the "decreased ability to work." It is also possible to further
trace the networks sustaining each of these elements, which would involve
an investigation of the papermaking industry, the international health care
institutions, the labor market, and so forth.

58 Shelley Tremain (ed.), *Foucault and the Government of Disability* (Ann Arbor:
The University of Michigan Press, 2005).

59 Andrew Smart, Richard Tutton, Paul Martin, George T. H. Ellison, and Richard
Ashcroft, "The standardization of race and ethnicity in biomedical science
editorials and UK biobanks." *Social Studies of Science* 38, 3 (2008): 409.

60 Ibid.

61 Ibid., 416.

62 Ibid., 417.

63 Ibid., 418.

64 On this ambiguity see Thomson, *Extraordinary Bodies*, 13–15.

65 Hahn, "Can disability be beautiful?"; Susan Peters, "Is there a disability
culture? A syncretisation of three possible world views." *Disability & Society*
15, 4 (2000): 583–601.

66 Shakespeare and Watson, "The social model," 10.

67 Heidegger, *Being and Time*.

68 William Blattner, "Existence and self-understanding in *Being and Time*."
Philosophy and Phenomenological Research 56, 1 (1996): 97–110.

69 Heidegger, *Question Concerning Technology*.

70 Ibid., 27.

71 Ibid., 17–18.

4

Personal assistance

In October 2010 disabled people from all over Bulgaria took part in an event called *Freedom March*. Held in the capital for a second consecutive year, the public action was conducted under the slogan "Adopt a law for personal assistance and grant us freedom!" The event was inspired by another rally—the *Freedom Drive*, organized biannually in Strasbourg by the European Network on Independent Living (www.enil.eu), an international disabled people's organization advocating for independent living. Among the main messages addressed to politicians and the general public in both the Bulgarian *Freedom March* and the European *Freedom Drive* is the claim that personal assistance is an essential condition for disabled people's freedom. Hence it should be recognized as a human right and be provided for by the state.

These advocacy efforts of disabled Europeans demand the relocation of welfare resources—most notably from institutionalized and/or professionalized care toward direct payments (also referred to as "cash benefits").[1] But their stake is more than economic redistribution. Descending from the disability activism of the 1970s, they demand cultural *recognition* as insistently as they demand economic redistribution—a feature that characterizes new social movements in general.[2] Consequently, economic or welfare rationality alone cannot provide adequate means for understanding disabled people's claims for freedom and independence—neither can it ground them. To this end, questions of *having* need to be put in context by attending to questions of *being*. As already suggested in the preceding chapters, such reasoning leads to exploring the existential-ontological aspects of disability. What is called for is an inquiry into the very understanding of human being that underpins disability advocates' demands for redistribution.

The results of such an inquiry are not immediately given or obvious. Understandings of our being permeate our actions but remain transparent and invisible, like the air we breathe. As Heidegger points out, "that which is closest" to us in our everyday living—to wit, our own *being*—is also "that which is farthest" in terms of its *meaning*.³ Charles Guignon explains:

> In Heidegger's view, many of the most pressing problems in the contemporary world arise because of the tacit understanding of Being that pervades and guides our thought and practices. We tend to see the world as a collection of objects on hand for our knowing and manipulation, and we even begin to see ourselves as "human resources" to be mobilized in the project of mastering the earth. This narrowed down and unreflective stance toward things governs our relations to all aspects of the earth, but it itself remains unnoticed.⁴

As pointed out in Chapter 1, from the perspective of existential phenomenology to be a human being or "Dasein" is to be "thrown" into an understanding of being, including an understanding of one's own being: "Dasein is the entity whose being is always at issue in what it does, that is, the entity who always has an understanding of itself, and whose self-understanding is constitutive of its 'being-so,' its being what or who it is."⁵ Crudely put, I always and necessarily experience myself as in being (*that* I am), but I usually do not explicitly consider the meaning of this experience (as *what kind of entity* I am). In experiencing myself, do I understand myself as a self-determining, self-governing, autonomous entity—as a "thinking thing," a subject? Or do I understand myself as a delimited, fixed, physical entity—as a body, an object, an "extended thing"? Or do I understand myself as a useful entity, a "human resource"? Or do I understand myself as part of a greater whole, as always already extending toward things and others in my surroundings—in phenomenological vocabulary, as being-in-the-world?

Importantly, the understanding of our being is not stored in unconscious belief systems, but is embodied in what we do.⁶ In other words, "our social practices embody an ontology."⁷ Chapter 3 capitalized on this insight by exploring the ontology incorporated in the medicalized disability assessment as currently practiced in Bulgaria. The case study presented there followed the methodological injunction of phenomenology to look at the activities in which people are immediately involved in order to highlight the more general existential-ontological patterns of human living. In the words of Merleau-Ponty, phenomenology "puts essences back into existence, and does not expect to arrive at an understanding of man and the world from any starting point other than that of their 'facticity'."⁸ This basic phenomenological principle provides the methodological guideline for the analysis presented in this chapter as well.

Both the European *Freedom Drive* and the Bulgarian *Freedom March* mentioned above demanded personal assistance. For the advocates of disabled people's rights this disability-related practice is absolutely pivotal.[9] Its crucial importance has also been recognized in international documents such as the UN Standard Rules on the Equalization of Opportunities for Persons with Disabilities (Rule 4) and the UN Convention on the Rights of Persons with Disabilities (Article 19). The significance of personal assistance for disability equality can be compared to the significance of rational debate for deliberative democracy—that is, personal assistance is a major condition for the possibility of disability equality just like rational debate is a major condition for the possibility of deliberative democracy. Consequently, the best way to explore the understanding of human being underpinning not only the recent advocacy efforts mentioned above but also a great deal of disability activism over the past forty years is to study those statements and demands of disability advocates that concern the organization and provision of personal assistance.[10]

Hence the question which I would like to address in this chapter: What understanding of human being is incorporated in the practice of personal assistance as promoted by the independent living advocates? My attempt to articulate an answer will be complemented by an exploration of those existential-ontological meanings that are being challenged by the advocates. My point of departure is the observation that a significant degree of consensus exists among independent living advocates on the particularities of the "ideal" mechanism for the provision of personal assistance. Consequently, advocacy efforts such as the Bulgarian *Freedom March* and the European *Freedom Drive* are as much for principles as for practices—or, rather, these instances of advocacy clearly exemplify how principles are always and necessarily embodied in practices. Actually, more often than not the fight is *not* over ideas but over the particularities of the practices that translate ideas into realities of everyday living. Looking at personal assistance schemes and their effects on disabled people's lives and self-understanding, one cannot help the persistent feeling that both god and the devil are in the details—a feeling that motivates a phenomenological concern for the irreducible facticity of essences.

Proceeding from these presumptions, this chapter will make a phenomenologically informed contribution to the long-standing debates within disability studies over the ideological underpinnings of independent living, direct payments, and personal assistance in particular.[11] These debates have focused on the tension between individualist and collectivist approaches to disability equality. I will argue that even in their plainly individualist suggestions, independent living advocates presuppose a distributed, relational understanding of human being commensurate with the phenomenological notion of being-in-the-world. The policy corollary will be that it is imperative to promote and support disabled people's self-organizing if individually designed independent living solutions are to succeed.

The European Center for Excellence in Personal Assistance project

As already noted, many independent living advocates, including the participants in the Bulgarian *Freedom March* and the European *Freedom Drive*, share an understanding of the best way to organize personal assistance. In 2004 such consensus was authoritatively articulated in a document titled "Model national personal assistance policy."[12] It was an outcome of an international project for exploring and promoting best practices in personal assistance for disabled people called *The European Center for Excellence in Personal Assistance* (ECEPA). The project's website describes ECEPA as:

> an initiative of major Centers for Independent Living in Europe and their respective networks consisting of grassroot groups of disabled people, most of whom are users of personal assistance, with a long experience of helping each other move out or keep out of residential institutions. (www.ecepa.org/mission/index.htm)

The project included disabled people's organizations from nine European countries: Germany, Sweden, Finland, Norway, Ireland, Austria, Italy, Greece, and Switzerland.[13] Unlike traditional social policy, whose development is dominated by experts, the ECEPA project was designed as a "bottom-up" initiative, an instance of policy-making in which practice and personal experience preceded theory and impersonal generalizations. It was coordinated by Adolf Ratzka—an internationally renowned independent living activist and author, one of the pioneers of the independent living movement in Europe. The movement itself was initiated by disabled Americans, who set up the first personal assistance schemes as early as in the 1970s by establishing a network of Centers for Independent Living in the United States.[14] In the 1980s, Ratzka "imported" these ideas and practices into Sweden and founded the Stockholm Cooperative for Independent Living (www.stil.se)—the first European user-led cooperative for personal assistance.[15] It provided disabled people with the opportunity to live independently outside residential institutions by hiring their own personal assistants. Subsequently, the practices developed and tested in the Stockholm Cooperative served as the model for the Swedish Personal Assistance Act of 1994. This legislation has been regarded by disability activists and analysts as a "gold standard" in the area of personal assistance.[16] It had a significant impact on the ECEPA model as well.

   In the next sections, I will explore the description of the model, compiled and edited by Ratzka himself.[17] It meticulously outlines each and every detail of an "ideally" organized personal assistance, as envisioned by European independent living advocates—themselves users of personal assistance. I will argue that the ECEPA model exemplifies a description of a social policy practice that is sensitive not only to the material and psychophysiological exigencies of being disabled in present-day Western society (which it undeniably addresses), but also to the ways in which the practice defines people who engage with it in their very being. Hence it is a phenomenologically promising description, one which is attentive to the existential-ontological implications of the support mechanism it promotes.

From autonomy to interdependence

According to the ECEPA model, an ideal policy for personal assistance will make it possible for disabled people "to live in the community, as equal and fully participating citizens."[18] The mechanism is contrasted with more traditional, top-down, professionalized social policy solutions (or lack thereof) that make people totally dependent on charity, on their families of origin, or exclude them in residential institutions. Accordingly, the model regards the full human being in terms of "self-determination" and "full citizenship."[19] It grounds this status in the possibility of exercising choice and control. Yet such choice and control are not primarily concerned with the ordinary everyday activities that people perform, say, when deciding what subject to study at university or which channel to watch on television. Rather, the choice and control promoted by the ECEPA model *in the first place* are of a higher order—they are concerned with the support one needs in order to exercise choice and to have control in the ordinary sense. Thus the properly organized personal assistance allows disabled people "to choose their preferred degree of personal control over service delivery according to their needs, capabilities, current life circumstances, preferences and aspirations."[20]

In more concrete terms, the service user is empowered to choose and control "who is to work [as his/her assistant], with which tasks, at which times, where and how."[21] This is provided for through a complicated system of interrelated measures that specifies how a disabled person's needs assessment, direct payments and accountability should be organized. The system comprises many subtle details, for example: insistence on decoupling eligibility criteria from medical diagnosis (a point which chimes with the discussion of disability assessment in Chapter 3), as well as income; requirement to cover personal assistance needs in all areas of living, including assistance inside and outside home, at school, at work, during leisure time, etc.; requirement to express assistance needs in assistance hours rather than in terms of specific services needed; requirement to have one central funding source on the national level instead of many dispersed local funding bodies; requirement to cover all assistance-associated costs and not only the assistant(s)'s wage(s); and so forth.[22] Each and every one of these elements is crucial for the functioning of the scheme as a whole, notwithstanding that the emphasis is often put on the principle that disabled people should receive cash benefits (direct payments) instead of services in kind.[23] Yet this principle should not be treated in isolation from the other measures suggested by the model, neither should the scheme be reduced to a financial transaction between a "funding body" and a "service user."

In order to understand the ECEPA model and by extension personal assistance as promoted by the independent living advocates, one needs a different ground. As suggested at the beginning of this chapter, such a ground might be secured by phenomenology, considering its attention to the meaning of being as incorporated in social practices. Thus from a phenomenological perspective the whole system of interrelated measures, summarized in the preceding paragraph, incorporates a specific understanding of what it means to be a (fully) human being. Such an understanding hinges on the opportunity to have choice and exercise control over the assistance one receives in order to go about one's everyday living.[24] Accordingly, *to be fully human does not mean to cope without assistance*. Thus on the homepage of the Independent Living Institute (www.independentliving.org), a nonprofit organization of disabled people chaired by Adolf Ratzka, one reads that: "Independent Living does not mean that we want to do everything by ourselves and do not need anybody or that we want to live in isolation." This point implies a shift of meaning with significant social and political consequences because it radically changes the conventional understanding of *independence*. Instead of *autonomy*, it now means a particular type of *interdependence*.

Putting the shift in context

The shift of the meaning of "independence," urged by the independent living advocates, shatters deep existential-ontological and sociopolitical intuitions inherited from the European Enlightenment. An example will make the point clear. The Kantian distinction between the private and the public spheres hangs on the principle that "the individuals comprising the public are endowed with a rational will which is independent of all empirically existing institutions and experience."[25] In his widely discussed article "An answer to the question: 'What is Enlightenment?'" Kant defines Enlightenment as the moment in history in which humans become "mature," that is, autonomous in their use of reason.[26] Importantly in the context of the present discussion, Kant uses the metaphor of "walking alone" to illustrate his idea of autonomy.[27] Kant stipulates that "maturity" would be considered dangerous and difficult by the "entire fair sex" which is bound to private use of reason, inherently restricted by obligation, convention, prejudice, and so forth. In another of his important political writings Kant also declares that in order to be a full citizen, that is, to have the right to co-legislate, the person "must be his *own master* (*sui iuris*) and must have some *property* (which can include any skill, trade, fine art, or science) to support himself."[28] At that "[t]he domestic servant, the shop assistant, the labourer, or even the barber, are merely labourers (*operarii*), not *artists* (*artifices*, in the wider sense) or members of the state, and are thus unqualified to be citizens."[29]

This Kantian logic suggests that humanity is at its best when it is abstracted from all particularities of historically contingent institutions, including formal and/or informal support systems. The corollary is that

> Kant openly excludes women, children and salaried workers from the public sphere because of their supposed lack of autonomy. In his estimation they are emotionally and economically dependent, which means that if allowed to participate in public affairs, they are likely to embrace a politics of irrational need rather than a juridical politics of freedom and rational cognition. If this happens, law is deprived of its epistemological dimension at the same time that the transcendence of natural and mechanical necessity is forfeited.[30]

Such reasoning would similarly exclude disabled people from the public sphere, for they are by definition implicated in various formal and informal systems of support. Actually, such exclusion has been exposed and criticized by many disability scholars and advocates as a historical fact.[31] The ECEPA model challenges the very logic on which this exclusion is based, together with its attendant disembodied and disembedded Kantian view of the subject.[32] Through a carefully devised scheme for user-led and user-centered support, the ECEPA model suggests in a very material and practical way that independence is not a matter of autonomy but of a *particular type of inter-dependence*. On this reading, one *can* be dependent and fully human, that is, "endowed with rational will" and entitled to participate in the public sphere. Moreover, one is always already interdependent, and the attainment of "fully human" status is contingent upon modifying or structuring this foundational interdependence in a certain way. This is the important phenomenological lesson to be drawn from the ECEPA model.

It is enough to think about the myriad ways in which present-day people are implicated in support systems ranging from transportation through telecommunication to health care and other public services in order to see the plausibility of such a claim. Using the activity of washing hands as an example, Finkelstein puts it thus: "The fact that an able-bodied person requires a wash-basin, tap, plumbing and so on, as well as an army of people to plan, build and maintain the water works so that he or she can wash indicates that *dependency is not unique to disabled people.*"[33] Let me have recourse again to phenomenological vocabulary and grammar borrowed from Heidegger's analysis of equipmental failure in order to explicate the point.[34] Proximally and for the most part, the infrastructural networks in which we are implicated remain transparent and therefore hidden from us. They become conspicuous, obtrusive, or obstinate in situations of breakdown, for example when the public transport workers go on strike. In such moments we feel vulnerable, fragile, exposed. We become anxious—yet, as will be argued in the case study of media representations in Chapter 6, such anxiety is profoundly illuminating because it reveals a truth about our way of being. When support networks cease to be user-centered, our foundational interdependence announces itself anew.

Self-driven customers?

Notwithstanding this focus on interdependence though, it might be argued that the ECEPA model still presupposes detached, individualized, autonomous decision-making. It seems that the liberal individual—the heir of the autonomous Kantian subject of the Enlightenment[35]—is more or less tacitly posed as a condition for any nonoppressive interdependence. The reason is the stipulation that *only a sovereign subject can choose and be in control of his/her assistance*—and, by implication, of his/her existence. From such a perspective, the ECEPA model, indeed, shifts the traditional meaning of independence from autonomy to interdependence, but only by grounding this interdependence in an even more robust form of autonomy—that of the sovereign subject. Hence personal assistance might be said to deconstruct the view of the *body* as a detached entity by exposing and normalizing the ways in which its materiality is *distributed*[36] within networks of assistive practices. Yet critics would retort that the price for such deconstruction is further consolidation of the autonomy of the *mind.* Philosophically speaking, such a move reasserts the Cartesian mind-body dualism, discussed in Chapter 1, and with it the Kantian prioritization of the rational, sovereign, universally legislating subject. In other words, the subjective mode of existential-ontological reduction seems fully at work here.

Is this the case? Does the ECEPA model really suggest that only a sovereign subject can choose and be in control? In order to answer this question, one needs to pay attention to the precise ways in which the model uses the notions of "choice" and "control." And indeed, it seems that Ratzka's description deploys these ideas in exclusively liberal-individualist vein. The ECEPA model envisions disabled people as "assistance users with purchasing power which, in turn, creates a market for assistance services"[37] and states that, "[s]imply put, 'personal assistance' means the user is customer or boss."[38] These ideas are emphatically re-emphasized in a footnote proclaiming that "[c]ash payments create a market with competing providers and *turn users into customers who have a choice and can demand quality*."[39] Obviously, such claims render disabled people in terms of self-driven consumers who sovereignly wield the power to buy. They are rooted in the neoliberal belief in unleashing free-market forces that are allegedly going to eliminate monopolies and improve the diversity and quality of services provided.[40] Disability scholars, especially those working in the area of intellectual impairments, have been strongly critical of this paradigm.[41]

Yet I will argue that there are aspects of the ECEPA model that complicate and even undermine this liberal-individualist logic with its attendant reduction of the human being to a self-sufficient, detached, rationally calculating subject. On a practical level, that is, in terms of organization of personal assistance, the model in fact presupposes a decentered, distributed understanding of choice and control that corresponds to the phenomenological understanding of human being as being-in-the-world. The reason is that, in order to be "sovereign" and "independent," the choice and control exercised by disabled people over their assistance need to be supported *themselves* by a certain infrastructure. In the next section, I will draw its outline, highlighting those elements of the ECEPA model which most directly concern the infrastructure supporting the user's decision-making.

Choice and control revisited

Let me begin with the more conspicuous ones, related to children and people with mental impairments. A stringent liberal-individualist logic would suggest that it is not possible for such individuals to be "customers" or "bosses" in the strict sense because of their lack of capacity for sovereign decision-making. Yet the ECEPA model explicitly refuses to exclude from its purview those who are deemed incapable to choose and control their assistance *on their own*. Instead, it stipulates that children and cognitively or psychosocially impaired users "might need support from third persons with [the] functions [of customers or bosses]."[42] Hence the model admits that others might be involved in one's decision-making without that compromising the basic tenets of the scheme—that is, the notions of choice and control. Moreover, it suggests not only that choice and control can be distributed through delegation to third persons, but also that such distribution should be financially acknowledged and supported by the scheme:

> Citizens who, despite appropriate information, counseling and other support, are unable to select and evaluate services or to employ their assistants themselves can also benefit from the policy provided that they receive the support from third persons such as a legal representative, family member or other person close to them. The costs of such support need to be covered by the policy, if necessary, by higher payments for the average assistance hour.[43]

A crucial question remains, though: Does the ECEPA model apply its distributed understanding of decision-making to other categories of users besides children and intellectually or psychosocially impaired people? In other words, does it admit that the assistance-related choices of (allegedly) sovereign decision-makers are also in some ways socially and materially distributed? An answer has already been prompted by the above quote that presupposes the availability of "information, counseling and other support" prior to more conspicuous forms of distribution such as delegation of decision-making power to third persons. For one thing, the model suggests that the activities of choice and control require the mastering of specific skills. It envisions that by using the personal assistance scheme people can "try assistance solutions with varying degrees of user responsibility and, step by step, at their own pace, . . . *develop the skills required to take on more control over their services*."[44] But skills are acquired through socialization, which highlights the need to contextualize the roles of "customer" or "boss" even in cases where the conventional sovereignty of decision-making is not at stake.

This last point is also suggested by those elements of the ECEPA model that concern peer support. Generally speaking, self-help has long been recognized as a major pillar of the disability movement.[45] In his analysis of "direct payment" schemes in the United Kingdom, Colin Barnes states it clearly:

> From the outset it was recognized by the disabled people's organizations that for disabled people to use direct payments effectively they need

appropriate support. This may include help with advertising, recruitment, wages, management skills, employment law, etc. Indeed, many disabled people have never been employed themselves and so the idea of employing personal assistants is often especially daunting. Such services were pioneered by CIL-type organizations during the 1980s and 1990s.[46]

The ECEPA model also envisions peer support as pivotal for the functioning of any personal assistance scheme. Thus when the disabled person's assistance needs are being assessed, an opportunity is provided for him/her to be supported by an individual of his/her choice.[47] More generally, "[i]n all contacts with the funding agency's staff regarding needs assessment, appeals or other administrative issues assistance users can utilize the counsel and support of third persons of their choice, in particular, other personal assistance users."[48] Peer support is also considered essential in information, training, and advocacy activities related to the use of personal assistance.[49] Finally, among the costs that should be covered by the scheme are those of "training and support of assistance users . . . if deemed necessary by the user."[50]

My conclusion is that the ECEPA model, at least implicitly, promotes an understanding of human being that matches the phenomenological notion of being-in-the-world. From such a perspective, to be fully human does not mean to be autonomous in any material and/or ideal sense. Neither the objectively delimited "healthy" body nor the subjectively delimited "sovereign" mind can serve as ultimate existential-ontological reference points for proposing social policy solutions to disability-related problems. One needs a much more contextualized or relational understanding of human being in order to combine economic redistribution with cultural recognition in the quest for social justice.[51] Without being determinable, free choice and subject-centered control are nevertheless *mediated* by choice-facilitating practices in which humans engage in their being-in-the-world. This might seem puzzling, but only if we stick to an understanding of "independence" as "autonomy" in the liberal-individualist way. On the other hand, if we understand "independence" as a *particular type of interdependence* (as suggested above), the empuzzlement dissolves. I will revisit this point in my concluding remarks.

Collective action for legislative change

Personal assistance is related to interdependence in yet another sense. This is the sense of collective public action for social change, which characterizes social movements in general, no matter whether "old" or "new."[52] As I mentioned earlier, personal assistance of the type described by Ratzka emerged in the 1970s out of the self-organizing of disabled people in their quest for independence.[53] The independent living movement, first in the United States and then in Europe, has made it possible for disabled people to claim control over their own lives not only through an economic redistribution of welfare resources but also through a certain "pedagogy of the oppressed"[54]—that is, disabled people taught each other how to manage their own assistance, thus gaining insights into new possibilities of being. Developing a network of user-led Centers for Independent Living, the movement has provided ongoing support in the form of peer education and counseling for disabled people who wanted to live differently. It has also served as a watchdog of personal assistance policies, constantly monitoring and assessing their complicity with models such as the ECEPA one, developed by assistance users themselves. Thus over the years the personal assistance scheme has retained strong connections with certain ways of being and acting together, as a community. Let me recount a recent example of such a collective action. Similar to the account in the preceding chapter, the one provided below draws not only on a review of existing documents, but also on my own observations and experiences gained over the years of engagement with the independent living movement in Bulgaria.

The Bulgarian *Freedom March* of 2010, mentioned at the beginning of this chapter, demanded the adoption of a law for personal assistance. The public action, organized in Sofia for a second consecutive year, was in support of a new bill developed by the advocates themselves. So far, a number of similar attempts for legislative innovation have repeatedly encountered strong resistance from the social policy establishment.[55] Notably, such innovations were significantly hindered by the big "nationally representative" organizations of and for disabled people that have for a long time been co-opted by the authorities.[56] In addition, the government agency for social assistance (www. asp.government.bg) announced in 2010 its own program for "individual budgets"—heir of a number of similar governmental "care" programs for disabled people, implemented since 2002. Their availability has always been a strong argument against any claims for change: "We already provide what you demand!" Yet what the government institutions have provided has consistently been very different both in its details and in its principles from the personal assistance scheme proposed by the *Freedom March* participants.[57] In sum, the failed attempts in the domain of "rational deliberation" re-emphasized the need for direct action and on October 21, 2010, disabled Bulgarians took to the streets of Sofia.

The march was organized by the Center for Independent Living—Sofia. According to the organization's website (www.cil.bg), the public action was supported by disabled people from all over the country, the number of participants exceeding 100. Another Bulgarian website for disability activism (www.lichna-pomosht.org) publicized photographs from the march, as well as videos from its media coverage. Unsurprisingly, both these internet sources depict and interpret the event in markedly activist-collectivist terms. The reports stress the quantity of people gathered and the strength of their collective will for change:

> The memorable date was 21 October 2010—memorable because of the significantly greater number of people who were not afraid of the mild but annoying drizzle and bravely stated their firm will to seek responsibility from the Bulgarian MPs for the lack of personal assistance regulated by a law. Over 100 disabled people from Burgas, Kazanlak, Novi pazar, Simeonovgrad, Sofia, Stara Zagora and probably from many other places came in front of the Council of Ministers,[58]

The number of people is "significantly greater," they are "over 100"; they come from numerous towns and cities, some of them enumerated, but "many other" implied; they are "not afraid" and "bravely" state their "firm will"—it is hard to overlook the vocabulary and grammar of collective emancipatory struggle. A distributed, communal mode of being is summoned as a ground on which to build the claims for individual liberation. The advocates also emphasize that the personal assistance bill they propose is a joint product, rooted in the common experience of everyday disability-related hardships: "We wrote it [the bill], devoting time and care—we, the people who need it."[59] These references to collective subjectivity are vital ingredients of the demand for progressive legislative change voiced by the disabled Bulgarians, especially given the context of the over-medicalized and highly paternalistic system of Bulgarian disability policy (see Chapter 3). Such acknowledgment does not mean an endorsement of identity politics because the collective subject summoned by the Bulgarian *Freedom March* is not homogeneous. Or rather, the emphasis is more on collectivity than on subjectivity. In any case, it seems obvious that the concerted action of many is needed in order to bring about the legislative conditions for the independent living of each and every one in particular.

Collective action after legislative change

What is less obvious is that such a collective mode of being does not automatically become obsolete when legislative changes supporting individual emancipation take place. Quite the contrary! Looking at disability activism in Britain just before the passing of the Disability Discrimination Act 1995, Barnes and Oliver warn that the adoption of antidiscrimination legislation in the disability area should not be regarded as an end in itself, but as a means.[60] In itself, it is not enough. Rather, "civil rights will only be achieved through the adequate funding of the nationwide network of organizations controlled and run by disabled people themselves."[61] Eleven years later, Oliver and Barnes reiterate this concern about the ground-laying role of the disability movement, this time sounding a more pessimistic note:

> since the turn of the millennium we have witnessed the growing professiona-lisation of disability rights and the wilful decimation of organisations controlled and run by disabled people at the local and national level by successive government policies despite rhetoric to the contrary. As a result we no longer have a strong and powerful disabled people's movement and the struggle to improve disabled people's life chances has taken a step backwards.[62]

The corollary is that without collective action and thought in the domain of civil society, the success of civil rights legislation is questionable, to say the least—a point that will be further developed in Chapter 8 with regard to the UN Convention on the Rights of Persons with Disabilities and its interpretation. The same applies to any actual or proposed legislation for personal assistance for independent living. The impending permanent closure of the Independent Living Fund in the United Kingdom will put this claim to a painful practical test, but I would like to substantiate it here with a recent example from Bulgaria. It is related to the personal assistance scheme funded and managed by the Sofia Municipality. The ordinance for its provision was adopted in 2007, after years of advocacy and lobbying on behalf of the independent living activists in the capital. Finally, on July 26, 2007, the Municipal Council passed the local bill. The legislation had been developed by the disability advocates themselves and was strongly influenced by the ECEPA model analyzed above. Thus in 2007 disabled inhabitants of the Bulgarian capital started benefiting from personal assistance, which approximated the "gold standard" in the area. Yet before long—in January 2008—the ordinance was clandestinely amended, and shortly after, in November 2008, it was amended again. The changes prompted the Center for Independent Living—Sofia to evaluate the provision of the service by the municipal authorities. In 2009 the organization submitted to the Municipal Council in Sofia an evaluation report, written in partnership with the Department of Sociology at the Sofia University.[63] The report strongly criticized the current enforcement of the scheme by the municipal authorities.

The document was hailed by some of the municipal councilors but largely disregarded by the municipal administration. Eventually, in 2010, 45 disabled people, most of them personal assistance users, signed a protest letter addressed to the Ombudsman of the Republic of Bulgaria. In this document the claimants state that during the initial phase of its enforcement the municipal ordinance on personal assistance "helped a lot of disabled people to start living a more dignified and independent life." "Unfortunately," they continue, "during the further implementation of the ordinance a lot of problems emerged and Sofia Municipality, instead of improving the lives of the disabled people, embarked on their blatant harassment."[64]

Thus a hard-won legislative battle evolved into a set of skewed practices, in some cases turning the initial ideas on their heads. The evaluation report and the protest letter cited above did not produce any (immediate) effects. Nevertheless, these collective and public efforts at social policy critique highlighted issues that would otherwise remain deeply hidden from the general public. Both the report and the letter bristle with details. They explain how seemingly small changes in the regulation and provision of personal assistance have resulted in huge deviations from the independent living framework, originally underpinning the legislation. As I have already shown in my discussion of the ECEPA model, the details of the personal assistance policy shelter gods and devils alike. It seems that only conceptually and organizationally strong disabled people's collectives can keep gods happy and devils at bay, as will also be argued in the discussion of the UN Convention in Chapter 8. The backbone of personal assistance is disabled people's self-organizing—both before as well as *after* the appropriate legislation takes place. Colin Barnes has stated that in order to have a working "direct payments" scheme in the United Kingdom, what is needed is "to develop and support a nationwide network of locally based user-controlled organizations providing services for local direct payment users."[65] Similar considerations have been put forward by Morris, Roulstone and Morgan, Stainton and Boyce, and others.[66] Some disability scholars have also argued for the development of politically "stronger and more unified action for greater resources and input into resource distribution"[67] on behalf of the recipients of direct payments. The Bulgarian case described here corroborates these suggestions.

Concluding remarks

For the past 40 years, the independent living advocates have been fighting for certain practices that are meant to enable disabled people's choice and control over important aspects of their lives. Among these practices, personal assistance stands out as pivotal. Although financially based on the mechanism of "direct payments" (or "cash benefits"), it should not be reduced to financial transactions taking place among institutions and individuals—neither should choice and control be reduced to self-driven actions of autonomous decision-makers, with their self-explanatory consumer preferences. As described in "ideal" models such as the ECEPA one, personal assistance comprises a patterned network of interrelated activities, involving needs assessment procedures, intricate funding and accountability arrangements, appeal options and, importantly, peer training, support and counseling. From a phenomenological point of view, such a network incorporates a particular understanding of human being. I have argued that such an understanding is better articulated through notions like interdependence and distribution (of embodied action and/or decision-making) than through the liberal framework of individual autonomy. To refer to interdependence and distribution is to thematize being-in-the-world.

Nevertheless, tension between autonomy and interdependence/distribution characterizes the independent living movement *from the inside*. The clash within the movement between the liberal-individualist and the structural-collectivist frameworks has long ago been identified and commented on.[68] It would be all too easy (or naïve) to dismiss the ECEPA model's recourse to notions such as "customer" or "boss" as mere rhetorical devices or as instances of purely strategic appropriation of liberal-individualist language and grammar. Still they *do have* a strategic function—to wit, to challenge traditional forms of "care" that significantly restrict disabled people's possibilities, understood not only in the material, but also in the existential-ontological sense, as possibilities of being. Merleau-Ponty points out that "in any case freedom modifies [history] only by taking up the meaning which history *was offering* at the moment in question, and by a kind of unobtrusive assimilation."[69] Similarly, the ECEPA model takes up and assimilates the meanings offered by the currently dominant neoliberal individualism in order to fight the traditional reduction of disabled people to passive objects of care interventions. Such a strategy is characteristic of the independent living movement in general; its advocacy for consumer sovereignty and self-reliance has made it prone to critiques of favoring "only a relatively small section of the disabled population: notably, young intellectually able, middle class white males."[70] A careful exploration of "ideal" schemes for personal assistance for independent living such as the ECEPA one, though, shows that they devise a system of measures that effectively contextualizes and distributes the sovereignty and autonomy of individual action and decision-making. Both strategies—the liberal-individualist and the structural-collectivist one—need to be taken into account. The crucial point is to understand the former in the context of the latter and not *vice versa*.

Translated into policy terms, this means that it is imperative to promote and support disabled people's self-organizing, both with regard to peer support as well as with regard to collective watchdog and advocacy activities. In the second part of this chapter I tried to develop this suggestion by showing that the very fight for the practice of personal assistance, with its characteristic forms, visions, language, etc., incorporates an understanding of the human being as interdependent, distributed and contextually embedded—that is, as being-in-the-world. This hints at the intrinsic relationship between the two major social practices explored in this chapter—the *practice of personal assistance* and the *practice of its collective vindication* in the public sphere. From such a perspective, there can be no personal assistance for independent living without the collective action of self-organized personal assistance users. The reasons for this are complex and I will return to their discussion in Chapters 7 and 8. I will finish this chapter with some preliminary stipulations.

Freedom, understood in terms of "independence," is possible only on the basis of a shared world—as Merleau-Ponty puts it: "Nothing determines me from outside, not because nothing acts upon me, but, on the contrary, because I am from the start outside myself and open to the world."[71] It is the shared world in which people are always already implicated that provides them with the means to individualize themselves. Yet another condition for independence is the possibility to reflexively engage with the world of one's being—for "if one is not free to adjust the limits of freedom, citizenship is a trap and one can be considered to be free in prison."[72] It is impossible to be "internally" free without being "externally" free. From this perspective, an individualized human being needs to have access to the infrastructures mediating his/her individualization. Such access should allow continuous readjustment of these infrastructures themselves, which can never be fixed once and for all but require constant problematization and re-enactment. A condition for this is the possibility of acting collectively in public[73]—only such collective activity can keep the infrastructures mediating one's individualization open for access, problematization and readjustment.

Notes

1 Adolf Ratzka, "Model national personal assistance policy," a project of the European Center for Excellence in Personal Assistance (ECEPA), 2004, 5.

2 Pamela Fisher, "Experiential knowledge challenges 'normality' and individualized citizenship: towards 'another way of being'." *Disability & Society* 22, 3 (2007): 283–98; Mike Oliver and Gerry Zarb, "The politics of disability: a new approach." *Disability, Handicap & Society* 4, 3 (1989): 221–39.

3 Martin Heidegger, *Being and Time*, trans. John Macquarrie and Edward Robinson (Oxford: Blackwell, 1962 [1927]), 36.

4 Charles Guignon, "Being as appearing: retrieving the Greek experience of Phusis," in *A Companion to Heidegger's* Introduction to Metaphysics, eds. Richard Polt and Gregory Fried (New Haven and London: Yale University Press, 2001), 35.

5 William Blattner, "Existence and self-understanding in *Being and Time*." *Philosophy and Phenomenological Research* 56, 1 (1996): 98.

6 Hubert L. Dreyfus, *Being-in-the-World: A Commentary on Heidegger's* Being and Time, *Division I* (Cambridge, MA: MIT Press, 1991), 16–23.

7 Ibid., 16.

8 Maurice Merleau-Ponty, *Phenomenology of Perception*, trans. Colin Smith (New York: Routledge, 2002 [1945]), vii; see also Mark A. Wrathall, "Existential phenomenology," in *A Companion to Phenomenology and Existentialism*, eds. Hubert L. Dreyfus and Mark A. Wrathall (Oxford: Blackwell, 2006).

9 Ratzka, "Model," 2; see also Helen Spandler, "Friend or foe? Towards a critical assessment of direct payments." *Critical Social Policy* 24, 2 (2004): 192–3.

10 Colin Barnes, "Direct payments and their future: an ethical concern?" *Ethics & Social Welfare* 1, 3 (2007): 348–50.

11 See, for example, Colin Barnes, "Independent Living, politics and implications" (Leeds: Centre for Disability Studies, 2004); Charlotte Pearson, "Money talks? Competing discourses in the implementation of direct payments." *Critical Social Policy* 20, 4 (2000): 459–77; Alan Roulstone and Hannah Morgan, "Neo-liberal individualism or self-directed support: are we all speaking the same language on modernising adult social care?" *Social Policy & Society* 8, 3 (2009): 333–45; Spandler, "Friend or foe?"; Gareth H. Williams, "The movement for Independent Living: an evaluation and critique." *Social Science & Medicine* 17, 15 (1983): 1003–10.

12 Ratzka, "Model."

13 Ibid., 1.

14 Barnes, "Direct payments"; Gerben DeJong, "Independent Living: from social movement to analytic paradigm." *Archives of Physical Medicine and Rehabilitation* 60, 10 (1979): 435–46.

15 Adolf Ratzka, "The Swedish Personal Assistance Act of 1994" (Stockholm: The Independent Living Institute, 2004).

16 Peter Anderberg, "ANED country report on the implementation of policies supporting independent living for disabled people. Report on Sweden" (Academic Network of European Disability experts, 2009), 2.

17 Ratzka, "Model."

18 Ibid., 1.

19 Ibid., 2.

20 Ibid., 3.

21 Ibid.

22 Ibid., 4–7.

23 Ibid., 5.

24 See Jenny Morris, "Independent living and community care: a disempowering framework." *Disability & Society* 19, 5 (2004): 427–9; Tim Stainton and Steve Boyce, "'I have got my life back': users' experience of direct payments." *Disability & Society* 19, 5 (2004): 449.

25 Darrow Schecter, *The Critique of Instrumental Reason from Weber to Habermas* (London: Continuum, 2010), 190.

26 Immanuel Kant, "An answer to the question: 'What is Enlightenment?'" in *Kant: Political Writings*. 2nd edn, ed. Hans S. Reiss, trans. H. B. Nisbet (Cambridge: Cambridge University Press, 1991 [1784]), 54.

27 Ibid. On the cultural politics of "walking" metaphors see Michael Oliver, *Understanding Disability: From Theory to Practice* (London: Macmillan, 1996), 95–109.

28 Immanuel Kant, "On the common saying: 'This may be true in theory, but it does not apply in practice,'" in *Kant: Political Writings*. 2nd edn, ed. Hans S. Reiss, trans. H. B. Nisbet (Cambridge: Cambridge University Press, 1991 [1793]), 78.

29 Ibid., footnote, original emphasis.

30 Schecter, *Critique*, 191; see also Andreas Brenner, "The lived-body and the dignity of human beings," in *A Companion to Phenomenology and Existentialism*, eds. Hubert L. Dreyfus and Mark A. Wrathall (Oxford: Blackwell, 2006).

31 See, for example, Len Barton, "The struggle for citizenship: the case of disabled people." *Disability & Society* 8, 3 (1993): 235–48; Peter Beresford and Jane Campbell, "Disabled people, service users, user involvement and representation." *Disability & Society* 9, 3 (1993): 315–25; Helen Meekosha and Leanne Dowse, "Enabling citizenship: gender, disability and citizenship in Australia." *Feminist Review* 57, 1 (1997): 49–72.

32 For a critique of Kantian subjectivity from a Heideggerian perspective see Béatrice Han-Pile, "Early Heidegger's appropriation of Kant," in *A Companion to Heidegger*, eds. Hubert L. Dreyfus and Mark A. Wrathall (Oxford: Blackwell, 2005), 89–90.

33 Victor Finkelstein, *Attitudes and Disabled People: Issues for Discussion* (New York: World Rehabilitation Fund, 1980), 25, original emphasis.

34 Heidegger, *Being and Time*, 102–7.

35 Michael J. Sandel, *Liberalism and the Limits of Justice* (Cambridge: Cambridge University Press, 1998 [1982]); Darrow Schecter, "Liberalisms and the limits of knowledge and freedom: on the epistemological and social bases of negative liberty." *History of European Ideas* 33, 2 (2007): 195–211.

36 I borrow the notion of "distribution" from the work of actor-network theorists within disability studies such as Ingunn Moser ("Disability and the promises of technology: technology, subjectivity and embodiment within an order of the normal." *Information, Communication & Society* 9, 3 (2006): 384), who points out that "agency is not a capability or property that belongs inherently in particular and bounded human bodies. Agency is always mediated. People are not actors, they are enabled to act in and by the practices and relations in which they are located, and they become actors because agency is distributed and attributed." Moser also underlines that such "distributedness" of agency remains black-boxed for nondisabled people: "with standardized abled actors, this distribution, the arrangements and even the bodies tend to move into the background and become invisible. With disabled actors, however, the heterogeneous materiality and embodiment is much more present and visible" (Ibid., 384). This point chimes with Heidegger's analysis of "equipmental failure," outlined in the preceding paragraph.

37 Ratzka, "Model," 2.

38 Ibid., 3.

39 Ibid., 5, n. 12, emphasis added.

40 On the significance of market discourse and consumerism for direct payment schemes see Pearson, "Money talks," and Spandler, "Friend or foe."

41 Leanne Dowse, "'Some people are never going to be able to do that': Challenges for people with intellectual disability in the 21st century." *Disability & Society* 24, 5 (2009): 571–84.

42 Ratzka, "Model," 3.

43 Ibid., n. 4.

44 Ibid., n. 3, emphasis added.

45 Oliver and Zarb, "The politics of disability," 230.

46 Barnes, "Direct payments," 352.

47 Ratzka, "Model," 4.

48 Ibid., 5.

49 Ibid., 4, nn. 8 and 18.

50 Ibid., 7.

51 Nancy Fraser, *Justice Interruptus: Critical Reflections on the "Postsocialist" Condition* (New York: Routledge, 1997).

52 Neil Stammers, "Social movements and the social construction of human rights." *Human Rights Quarterly* 21, 4 (1999): 984–5.

53 Gerben DeJong, Andrew I. Batavia, and Louise B. McKnew, "The independent living model of personal assistance in national long-term-care policy." *Generations: Journal of the American Society on Aging* 16, 1 (1992): 89–95.

54 Paulo Freire, *Pedagogy of the Oppressed*, trans. Myra B. Ramos (London: Continuum, 2006 [1968]).

55 Vera Dakova, *For Functionaries and People, Part 1* (Sofia: Center for Independent Living, 2004). For more recent developments see www.lichna-pomosht.org, accessed September 27, 2013.

56 Teodor Mladenov, "Institutional woes of participation: Bulgarian disabled people's organisations and policy-making." *Disability & Society* 24, 1 (2009): 33–45.

57 For a critical overview see Center for Independent Living, *Assessment of the Assistant Services for People with Disabilities in Bulgaria* (Sofia: Center for Independent Living, 2009).

58 Center for Independent Living—Sofia, website, news section, www.cil.bg/Новини/126.html, accessed September 27, 2013.

59 Ibid., www.cil.bg/Новини/117.html, accessed September 27, 2013.

60 Colin Barnes and Mike Oliver, "Disability rights: rhetoric and reality in the UK." *Disability & Society* 10, 1 (1995): 111–16.

61 Ibid., 115.

62 Mike Oliver and Colin Barnes, "Disability politics and the disability movement in Britain: where did it all go wrong?" *Coalition*, August (2006), n.p.

63 Center for Independent Living, *Assessment of the "Assistant for Independent Living" Service* (Sofia: Center for Independent Living, 2009).

64 The letter is available at www.cil.bg/userfiles/media/do_ombudsmana.doc, accessed September 27, 2013.

65 Barnes, "Direct payments," 353.

66 Morris, "Independent living," 438–9; Roulstone and Morgan, "Neo-liberal individualism"; Stainton and Boyce, "I have got my life back," 444–5.

67 Spandler, "Friend or foe," 204.

68 Williams, "The movement for Independent Living." For more recent discussions see David Gibbs, "Public policy and organisations of disabled people," text of a seminar presentation (Leeds: Centre for Disability Studies, 2005), and Roulstone and Morgan, "Neo-liberal individualism."

69 Maurice Merleau-Ponty, *Phenomenology of Perception*, trans. Colin Smith (New York: Routledge, 2002 [1945]), 523.

70 Barnes, "Independent Living," 8.

71 Merleau-Ponty, *Phenomenology of Perception*, 530.

72 Schecter, *Critique*, 227.

73 In the twentieth century social and political thought, this insight has been most comprehensively articulated by Jürgen Habermas, who has provided its historical, sociological and philosophical justification in his seminal work *The Structural Transformation of the Public Sphere*, trans. Thomas Burger with the assistance of Frederick Lawrence (Cambridge, MA: The MIT Press, 1993 [1962]).

5

Discrimination

On October 5, 2010, the Bulgarian Commission for Protection against Discrimination found the hegumen of the Troyan Monastery guilty of harassment on the basis of disability.[1] Referring to the provisions of the Bulgarian Law for Protection against Discrimination, the Commission defined the hegumen's actions as unlawful and penalized him with a fine of BGN 250 (EUR 128). In addition, it stated that the monastery had violated the Law for Protection against Discrimination by failing to make its architectural environment accessible for disabled people. The Commission prescribed that the hegumen should take the necessary actions in order to ensure the accessibility of the monastery. The incident in question happened 2 years earlier, on July 19, 2008. The story is recounted in the Commission's decision (number 259, issued on November 23, 2010)[2]:

The claimant is a person with disability with 100% invalidity entitled to assistance, who uses a wheelchair. He reports that from 18 till 25 July he participated in a Program for Youth Exchange between Bulgaria and Finland. On 19 July 2008 the Bulgarian-Finnish group visited the Troyan Monastery. They requested for someone to tell them about and show them around the monastery and a young priest responded. While he was narrating the history of the monastery to the group, he was interrupted by an elder man in cassock, with a beard, who was carrying a wooden stick in his hand. The claimant argues that the elder man in the cassock "slapped through the feet and rudely growled out to the young priest: 'Out you go, you have no business with these. You have other things to do.'" Then the young man apologized and left the group, while the elderly man urged everybody with a broad gesture of his hands to leave and went inside the premises of the monastery. The claimant points out that after this rude interruption and unequivocal expulsion of the group he nevertheless decided to continue and to enter inside in order to pray before the miraculous icon, for which he was helped by his mother who accompanied him. While he was praying, the same elderly monk showed up and, clattering with his stick, told his mother: "The bikes out! Quick, quick, quick. Get the one with that bike out of here," while pointing nervously with his hand towards the exit. Kichashki later found out that this is the hegumen of the monastery Teodosiy. He [Kichashki] points out that at this moment the group's interpreter Yanina joined them. She asked why the monastery is not adapted for people with disabilities, to which question the hegumen responded with anger and shouts: "What do you want, huh? To adapt, no way! This is a cultural heritage building, such [referring to the disabled people] do not even have the right to enter here! Petition the Council of Ministers, the Parliament, whoever you want. I will adapt nothing for you here!" With these words and clattering frequently with his stick, the hegumen chased them out. The claimant shares that this made him feel insulted, defiled, and affected because according to him this was the last place to expect such manifestations of cruelty. Kichashki's mother turned to the hegumen with the words: "Excuse me, I'm very sorry, but I would have been very happy if my son had entered with a bicycle, as you said, and if you had chased him out because of that—and not with a wheelchair, which according to you is a sin." The claimant also asked him: "Is it that according to you I am a sinner because I am on a wheelchair?! Do I not have the right to pray before an icon?!" At that moment the hegumen looked at him for the first time, clearly displaying his indignation, and stated: "Well, obviously you pay for others' sins, since you are like this." Then he insisted again: "C'mon, everybody out. Out, out, out. Off, there is no place for you here. It is written on the door outside. There is an interdiction for such like you. C'mon, off!" The hegumen hurried to exit together with some of the visitors in order to show them the interdiction that did not exist. He refused to disclose his name and position. The claimant states that all the visitors were shocked by this event.

The incident can easily be interpreted as a case of religiously motivated intolerance leading to blatant discrimination on the basis of disability. First, the hegumen seems to display fervent adherence to a one-sided interpretation of the Bible by regarding disability exclusively in terms of "a punishment meted out by God."[3] Such an interpretation is not fortuitous—as Shakespeare puts it, "[i]f original sin, through the transgression of Eve, is concretized in the flesh of woman, then the flesh of disabled people has historically, and within Judaeo-Christian theology especially, represented divine punishment for ancestral transgression."[4] Second, the conduct of the hegumen, corroborated by numerous witnesses including the "young priest," is institutionally recognized as harassment on the basis of disability by the Bulgarian Commission for

Protection against Discrimination; consequently, due sanctions are imposed.[5] I take both these readings of the event—the theological and the juridical one—as legitimate. Understanding the hegumen's motivation in terms of his own interpretation of holy texts and sanctioning his actions by penalizing him with a fine and prescribing accessibility within the framework of the modern antidiscrimination legislation are indispensable for making sense of the event and taking a stand on it. I also consider the penalty and the prescription imposed by the Commission as just, albeit incommensurable with the harm inflicted. Nevertheless, this theological and juridical approach to interpreting the incident seems too narrow. It tends to individualize the problem, focusing on the attitudes and activities of a single person (the hegumen). This might suggest that the incident is an isolated event, an accident, an exception, a fortuitous and atypical excess of inhospitality. Such inhospitality could appear to be grounded in prejudices that allegedly have long ago loosened their grip on the collective consciousness of advanced and secularized liberal societies.

I would like to propose the possibility of interpreting the event differently, building on the phenomenological approach developed in the previous chapters, by advancing further the methodological guideline about the facticity of essences.[6] The point is that, even in its extreme manifestations, the existential-ontological reduction of disabled people to flawed bodies and their concomitant exclusion from the domain of the human draws on the mundane, the everyday, the ordinary. Such a reduction recruits familiar spatial and temporal relationships, along whose axes selves, others and nonhuman entities are distributed and thus assigned a value. This is one of the reasons why the "violence of disablism"[7] is (still) ubiquitous—it is grounded in that which is closest, thereby remaining invisible and immutable. By uncovering the ways in which the excesses of dis/ablism (the term is defined in Chapter 1) are rooted in the mundane and the taken-for-granted, phenomenology allows going *beyond* the theological and the juridical readings of the event in the Troyan Monastery. The value of this approach is not in generating new knowledge, but in highlighting what we already know, for phenomenology is primarily "a work of 'explication,' 'elucidation,' or 'description' of something we, in some way, already understand, or with which we are already, in some way, familiar but which, for some reason, we cannot get into clear focus for ourselves without more ado."[8]

Moreover, the phenomenological defamiliarization of the familiar bears its own transformative potential. The methodological holism of the phenomenological approach suggests that there is something beyond the individual and/or the juridical that needs to be addressed so that violence—physical as well as symbolic—can be exposed and challenged. Phenomenology's concern with the meaning of being—and the meaning of human being in particular—links the events of everyday living to certain existential-ontological patterns that transcend them. The failure to recognize and address these ubiquitous but ghostly patterns explains the limited success of many attempts. to overcome the detrimental effects of power through purely juridical means. These detrimental effects are experienced by disabled people as exclusion, oppression and violence, as was the case in the Troyan Monastery. What made this incident possible, besides the exclusionist mindset of an enraged servant of the church?

A phenomenological approach to space and time

In *Being and Time* Heidegger insists on exploring space and time in existential-ontological terms—ontological, because related to being (*Sein*), and existential, because concerning the specifically human way of being, that is, Dasein conceived as being-in-the-world. This insight provides an important interpretive clue by suggesting that human existence is *intrinsically* spatio-temporal. On the one hand, humans understand themselves through certain distribution of selves, others and nonhuman entities in space and time. Spatially, I am here, you are there, or both of us are in, while they (the "others") are out. Temporally, I continue certain tradition, you interrupt it with novelty, or both of us share a heritage, while they (the "others") threaten its permanence with change. These spatial and temporal proximities and distances, permanence and transience make me *who* I am, provide me with the possibility to be someone vis-à-vis "you" and "them" (the "others"). On the other hand, a certain organization of space and time itself calls for a specific positioning of self and others. Spatially, this place is accessible for me, it lets me in, you too, but not them; temporally, this history accommodates me, it narrates my identity in positive terms, probably yours, but not theirs. Boundaries are embedded in space, inscribed in time; people are thrown into assemblages of entrances and exits, walls and doors, thresholds and leeways, past axioms and futural question marks. These assemblages have the power to grant human status to some, while relegating others to the domain of the nonhuman. They embody understandings of human being—that is, they incorporate certain assumptions of what it means to be human.[9] The spatio-temporal assemblages are welded together by social practices such as disability-based discrimination, as was the case in the Troyan Monastery, or the already explored disability assessment (Chapter 3) and personal assistance (Chapter 4). Yet while in the preceding chapters the spatial and temporal significance of disability-related practices remained unthematized, this chapter will explicitly focus on the spatio-temporal aspects of the Troyan Monastery event.

To this end, phenomenology is helpful because it invites us to suspend our ordinary understanding of space and time as extrinsic to the core of our existence. This received understanding renders space and time either in realist terms, as empty vessels filled up with our bodily (objective) and/or mental (subjective) presence, or in idealist/Kantian terms, as *a priori* intuitions, that is, ideal forms of consciousness given, again, independently of any worldly being. In contrast, phenomenology has asserted that neither empirical reality nor transcendental ideality escape the mediation of being-in-the-world. Accordingly, space and time are regarded as horizons of understanding that shape and are shaped by inhabiting a world. As Heidegger puts it, "Dasein's spatiality is not to be defined by citing the position at which some corporeal Thing is present-at-hand"[10]; and, with regard to temporality, "Dasein does not fill up a track or stretch 'of life'—one which is somehow present-at-hand— with the phases of its momentary actualities."[11] In methodological terms, the suspension of these received spatio-temporal notions stems from Husserl's *epoché*—or "bracketing" of what is identified by Husserl as the "natural attitude," that is, the common, everyday way of thinking and acting, "in which we all live and from which we thus start when we bring about the philosophical transformation of our viewpoint."[12] It is characteristic of this "natural attitude" to posit Cartesian thinking subjects over and against extended objects—as Leder points out, "Cartesianism . . . is by now so firmly entrenched in our culture that it is difficult to think outside of its parameters."[13] Husserl's *epoché* suspends the assumption of objects, retaining only the subjective consciousness and its content as a proper phenomenon for study, which, in a way, preserves the core of Cartesianism, albeit by way of a Kantian revision. Heidegger, on the other hand, goes beyond the subject/object distinction by focusing on being-in-the-world, the involved and engaged way of existing within a meaning-engendering context, among already meaningful entities and others, that is ontologically more "primordial" than the subject and its consciousness. Notwithstanding these differences between their positions, both Husserl and Heidegger invite us to suspend or "bracket" our taken-for-granted notions of space, time and our place within them, among entities.

Such an approach makes it possible to show that even in the most extreme instances of dis/ablism there are common, everyday spatio-temporal relations, too familiar to be ordinarily noticed. In what follows, I will highlight these relations in the Troyan Monastery incident, as recounted by Petar Kichashki and recorded in the decision of the Bulgarian Commission for Protection against Discrimination. The juridical representation of the event has the advantage over other instances of its depiction[14] of being institutionally sanctioned as true. In addition, Kichashki's testimony, as recorded in the Commission's decision, had obvious real-life, material consequences, since on its basis a financial penalty and an obligation to change the built environment were imposed. Therefore, I take it as a truthful and influential account. Moreover, its representation of exclusion goes way beyond its juridical character and purpose. Hence if in terms of content I am interested in highlighting the mundane dimension of an excessive event, in terms of form I embark on highlighting the existential-ontological dimension of a juridical representation. This, I hope, will strengthen my argument about the ubiquity of the mechanisms I explore.

Objectification

The first thing of interest in the excerpt from the Commission's decision presented above is that the hegumen strives to avoid any immediate contact with the disabled people who nevertheless are *there with him*. Instead of directly addressing them, he speaks to others *about them*. These others—the young priest, the mother, the interpreter—are approached as "proxies" for the visitors in wheelchairs. Among disability scholars and activists such a pattern of interaction has long ago been identified as the "does he take sugar syndrome."[15] In it, disabled people are excluded from social interchange by people addressing their companions (friends, assistants, relatives) in their stead. Thus it is these companions who are expected to make decisions and take action on behalf of the disabled person. Indeed, "does (s)he take sugar" usually signifies benevolent intention, whereas the attitude of the hegumen is inimical; nevertheless, the pattern is the same.

From a phenomenological point of view, the result is objectification of the other. Heidegger points out that "any entity is either a '*who*' (existence) or a '*what*' (presence-at-hand in the broadest sense)."[16] In "speaking about" someone in his or her presence, I relate to him/her in terms of a "what," not a "who." Thus I tend toward reducing the other to an object-like entity, an entity "present-at-hand" (*vorhanden*), that is available for manipulation, an entity that can be submitted to external forces—kept in place or removed, shown or concealed, described or disregarded. This effect of objectification is greatly enhanced when the other is willing to communicate but is nevertheless denied the opportunity to do so. In such cases the reductive operation silences the person, deprives him or her of voice and therefore of agency. It neutralizes the other, makes him/her "docile."[17] Thus the "does (s)he take sugar" way of relating incorporates an objectifying pattern of existential-ontological reduction similar to the one characteristic of medicalization that was discussed in the case of disability assessment in Chapter 3.

The hegumen reduces disabled people to objects by *speaking about* them instead of *speaking to* them in their presence. He speaks about them with others, who on their behalf are in direct contact with the disabled visitors. Thus the hegumen tells the young priest that he has "no business with these" (enhancing his message with a physical assault); he commands the mother to get the "bikes" and "the one with that bicycle out of here"; he retorts to the interpreter that "such do not even have the right to enter here." The mediation of these "proxies"—the priest, the mother, the interpreter—allows the hegumen to keep a safe distance from the people in wheelchairs. To this end, his speech is also cleansed from all the particularities of those who are spoken about—it is easier to keep distance from objectified others if they are anonymous and generalized. All this results in an "ontological invalidation"[18] of disabled people—they are negated in their very being; their existence gets undermined.

Notably, this strategy works until the hegumen is compelled to *speak to* them by being addressed by one of the visitors in the wheelchairs, that is, by being *spoken to*. It is this event that triggers the accusation of sinfulness. The hegumen cannot keep the objectifying distance any longer; the other breaks out of his/her imposed passivity and impersonal generality and demands recognition. This makes the hegumen to resort to other tactics—the invocation of divine providence. His suggestion is that it is not something secular, this-worldly which is wrong with the disabled people, but something transcendent, other-worldly. The attempt to re-inscribe the other in the domain of passive, docile objectivity appeals to a transcendent order: "obviously you pay for others' sins, since you are like this."

What is the meaning of the demonstrative pronoun ("like *this*") used by the hegumen in this explanation of disability? Stripped from all particularities, the demonstrative bears the full weight of dis/ablism, for it identifies Kichashki's bodily difference as inherently negative, "ontologically intolerable."[19] At the same time, it betrays anxiety in the face of that which comes with such a dangerous difference. For as an "extraordinary body," the impaired body *demands* accommodation, while resisting assimilation.[20] It will soon become clear that this is a major concern for the hegumen and a major source of his inhospitality. From such a perspective, the impaired body is "nonconformity incarnate"[21]—a feature which no normative regime can tolerate. It is resistive in its very materiality, because it defies control, command, normalization.[22]

But there is something else besides the embodied nonconformity of the wheelchair users' physical presence that epitomizes the resistance against the normative and exclusionary order instituted by the hegumen—it is Kichashki's resolute action. His entering of the church despite the "rude interruption and unequivocal expulsion of the group" anticipates the whole chain of events to follow, culminating not only with the Commission's decision, but also going beyond it to include the media reports of the incident, my writing and your reading about it, and so forth. Thus Kichashki's action can be regarded in phenomenological terms as *world-disclosing*, that is, as setting up a whole new context that changes the meaning of past and present events while also opening up possibilities for the happening of previously unforeseen (and even unthinkable) future ones. With his action, Kichashki resists victimization, refusing to internalize the blame for the violence perpetuated by the external conditions (i.e., inaccessible environment) and the hegumen's conduct. He also reclaims agency that has been forfeited by being "spoken about." And, as will be explained in more detail below, Kichashki's action challenges a certain distribution of human beings in space; and it also lays claim to a particular past, thus bringing about new possibilities for the future. In this way, Kichashki's entering of the church opens up a "clearing" (*Lichtung*)[23] in which all subsequent utterances and actions will show up in terms of exclusion and its interrogation. Whatever happens next will either solidify exclusion or challenge it. Accordingly, Kichashki's action sets the stage for a series of subsequent problematizations—one being articulated by the interpreter who inquires about the inaccessibility of the monastery, another assuming a juridical form in the decision of the Commission for Protection against Discrimination, yet another being formulated in this very moment of my writing about the event. The framework of these problematizations is lucidly pinpointed by Kichashki himself, as recorded in the Commission's decision:

> Kichashki points out that he is a law student in New Bulgarian University, *he does not perceive himself as a second class person and he cannot allow such treatment of himself and other people* in this situation on behalf of the hegumen of the Troyan Monastery. The claimant deems that he has been subjected to discrimination on the basis of disability. (emphasis added)

I now turn toward those aspects of the situation that were (more or less inconspicuously) challenged within the framework of refusing to be treated as a "second class person"—the new "clearing" opened up by Kichashki's resolute action. I will focus on the distribution of humans in space and time, that is, on those spatial and temporal relations implicated in the dis/ablist practices perpetuated by the hegumen that undermine disabled people in their very being. Notably, their familiarity makes them too obvious to be immediately noticed.

Space

From a critical phenomenological perspective, the distance instituted by the hegumen between himself and the disabled visitors can best be grasped in existential-ontological terms. He affirms one way of being human, while denying another. *I* (implies the hegumen) am a human being; *you*—the priest, the mother, the interpreter—are most probably too (for I speak to you); but *these*—such like "the one with that bike"—are certainly not. Therefore, they can only be *spoken about*, not *spoken to*.

This affirmation/denial of humanness shapes space. It orders spatiality along a series of topological dichotomies such as in/out, inside/outside, here/there, entering/leaving, entrance/exit, accessible (adapted)/inaccessible (not adapted). Let me italicize the words indicating these topological binaries in the excerpt from the Commission's decision cited above. "*Out* you go," growls the hegumen to the young priest, then urges the group "to *leave*" and goes "*inside* the premises." But Kichashki also decides to "*enter inside*." The hegumen reappears, commanding everybody to get "*out of here*," pointing "towards the *exit*." Asked why "the monastery is *not adapted* for people with disabilities," he retorts that "such do not even have the right to *enter here*. . . . I will *adapt nothing* for you *here*!" The visitors are "chased . . . *out*" again. The mother complains, Kichashki himself asks for an explanation. The hegumen vociferously reiterates: "everybody *out*. *Out, out, out*. Off, there is *no place* for you *here*. It is written on the door *outside*." Thus bodies are distributed within a strategically divided space. Some remain "in," others are pushed "out." With this, humanness is distributed too. Those who are expelled from the *proximity* of the "inside"—those for whom "there is no place . . . here," "such like you"—are denied the possibility of being fully human. For "to have a place" means also to be recognized as a human being, and *vice versa*.

On the other hand, the affirmation/denial of humanness enacted by the hegumen is itself ordered by the apparatus of physical space. The shape and distribution of planes, boundaries and ways of passage exert their own performativity. Being adapted for some and not adapted for others, the built environment embodies a norm, a tacit statement about what it means to be a human being.[24] The space itself *speaks to* some, while *speaking about* others; it addresses some in their being-in-the-world, while reducing others to their presence-at-hand. Space matters, as will be argued more emphatically in the analysis of media representations of inaccessibility in Chapter 6. That is why the question about the architectural adaptation of the monastery for disabled people is taken by the hegumen as challenging a higher (divine, transcendent) order. For him, this is not a technical but an existential-ontological issue.

It is a matter of knowing *who* you are and *what* you are not, of being able to recognize good from bad, right from wrong. All these issues are embedded in the space inhabited.

The proper *space of disability* according to the transcendent order invoked by the hegumen is "out" (in Bulgarian: *van*)—that is, the externality, the periphery, the margins of humanness, within a neutralizing distance safeguarded by architectural boundaries, interdictions and reportive utterances ("speaking about"). As Rod Michalko puts it, "[d]isability is not welcome in our homes and we see it as a threat to the structure of our homeland."[25] What, then, is the proper *time of disability* according to this logic? Is there a temporal counterpart to the spatial distribution of humans according to the in/out pattern of exclusion?

Time

The clash between the visitors from the Youth Exchange Program and the hegumen is prefigured by the brief collision between the hegumen and the young priest. Both these encounters happen against the background of a more general tension. Its poles can be provisionally subsumed under the opposing temporal categories of "the new" and "the old." These categories are not rooted in biological age, although age-specific characteristics might be recruited to express the distinction, as is the case in counterposing the "young priest" to the "elder man." The ageist connotations of this and other similar temporal binaries set up in the Commission's decision should not distract from what I take to be their *primary* significance—to manifest the contest over a particular rendering of time and its existential-ontological implications. The following analysis also demonstrates that these binary oppositions are inherently unstable, intrinsically unsustainable.

The Commission's decision recounts the event in such a way that "the new" is framed as the domain of what is coming (the future), which implies *change*. In contrast, "the old" is bound up with what is gone (the past), understood as *permanence*. Both are enacted in the present, where the former is associated with admission, permission and desire to adapt, whereas the latter—with expulsion, interdiction and refusal to adapt. This dichotomy has its institutional expression too. The hegumen relegates the claims for accessibility voiced by the visitors to specific political institutions. He mentions the Council of Ministers and the Parliament, although it will actually be the Commission for Protection against Discrimination that will be "petitioned." His remark suits his overall authoritarian demeanor. On the other hand, he perceives himself as a custodian of "cultural heritage," which is embedded in the building and the institution of the Troyan Monastery: "To adapt, no way! This is a cultural heritage building, such [referring to the disabled people] do not even have the right to enter here! Petition the Council of Ministers, the Parliament, whoever you want. I will adapt nothing for you here!"

On such a reading, the hegumen resists the change which comes with "the new," while safeguarding the permanence of "the old." That is, he clings to the past of tradition and is suspicious toward the future of novelty. For him, disabled *young* people (with their "bicycles") are part of an unwelcome coming that challenges tradition. The demand for architectural accessibility is a major expression of this threat. Tradition is embedded in the built environment of the monastery—therefore, any change in this environment might be taken as challenging tradition itself. On the other hand, the visitors are represented as prioritizing "the new" and questioning "the old." They insist on changes in the attitudes, behaviors and the environment. Hence the hegumen enacts in the present the permanence of the past, while the visitors enact the change-ability of the future. All these temporal binaries can be summarized as follows:

"the old"	"the new"
the "elder man" (the hegumen)	visitors from the Youth Exchange Program; the "young priest"
past, understood as permanence	future, understood as change
expulsion, interdiction, refusal to adapt	admission, permission, desire to adapt
tradition, "cultural heritage," Troyan Monastery	Council of Ministers, Parliament, Commission against Discrimination

Most importantly, though, the incident is a contest over the *boundary* separating these two series of opposing terms. The boundary is put into question by the young priest and the visitors; the hegumen reacts by trying to reinforce the boundary, thus engaging in what science and technology studies scholars have termed "boundary-work"[26]—an activity of constructing a social boundary in order to enhance one's status and authority.[27] The young priest is friendly toward the visitors, but he is also part of the monastery and its "cultural heritage." He knows its history and obeys its hierarchy. The visitors demand accessibility, that is, environmental change, but they are also willing to get in contact with the "permanence" of tradition (actually, this is the reason why they demand accessibility in the first place). They request for someone to tell them the story of the monastery. It is this narration that is interrupted by the hegumen—violently, relentlessly, "slapping" the narrator "through the feet" with the wooden stick. The physical intensity with which the historical narration is disrupted suggests that the hegumen does not merely interrupt storytelling, but *denies access to the past.* Later, when put under pressure by Kichashki's resolute action and the problematizations that follow, the hegumen will admit the possibility of such an access, but only in negative terms, in terms of "sin." Within this logic, the only possibility for disabled people to be included in the domain of the past and tradition is through a kind of *inclusive exclusion*—a mechanism that has already been outlined in Chapter 1 as rooted in ontological privation. Disabled people are granted recognition, but only as privative versions of able-bodied people, in terms of *lack*—which, in the eyes of the hegumen, is a lack of grace.

The temporal distinctions outlined here overlap with the spatial ones highlighted in the preceding section. Keeping outside certain spatial interiority (one of *proximity*) is coextensive with keeping outside certain temporal interiority (one of *permanence*). Both incorporate denial of human status. With the very act of entering the "inside" of the monastery building, disabled people and their companions also demand access to the "inside" of the monastery's past. But this building and this past are domains over which the hegumen asserts domination. He needs this domination in order to safeguard a particular existential-ontological order, sustaining at that his own identity and authority. The alterity that comes with disability makes the hegumen existentially anxious. Alterity decenters the self, delimits its power. It is *the* antidote to enclosure. The "other" is exteriority *par excellence*, s/he radically resists the power of the self to comprehend, possess, control, dominate: "The strangeness of the Other, his irreducibility to the I, to my thoughts and my possessions, is precisely accomplished as a calling into question of my spontaneity."[28]

On the other hand, for the disabled people to challenge the spatio-temporal boundary upheld by the hegumen is a matter of gaining human status. It is a matter of not being treated as "second class persons," as Kichashki has aptly put it—hence the resoluteness of his entering the church in order to pray before the "miraculous icon." This point suggests that the spatial and temporal relations highlighted so far are also mediated by nonhuman entities—the wheelchairs, the stick, the door and the icon. Similarly to the disability assessment statement explored in Chapter 3, these entities are the tangible components of the disability-related practices that incorporate existential-ontological reductions and that translate the bodily differences of "impairments" into undermining of disabled people's existence. Below, I will focus on the spatial and temporal significance of these nonhuman entities, and accordingly—on their relation to the spatio-temporal boundary-work of the hegumen.

Nonhuman entities

Letting some humans in while keeping others out is related to the constitution and maintenance of identity and authority. Accordingly, the control over the boundary around the spatio-temporal interiority is pivotal and often infused with conflicts and contestations—or even, as the present case study suggests, with symbolic and/or physical violence. Different nonhuman entities partake in this process.

First, the *wheelchairs*—it seems that the hegumen misnames them as "bicycles" strategically. The misnomer injects his effort to deny spatio-temporal access to disabled people with certain legitimacy by obliterating the difference between assistive and nonassistive technology. The twisted syllogism suggests that (1) if wheelchairs are similar to bicycles, and (2) it is forbidden to enter a church with a bicycle, then (3) it should be forbidden to enter the church with wheelchairs as well. At least this is the way Kichashki's mother reads the hegumen's logic. Accordingly, she insists on the difference, thus challenging the hegumen's boundary-work: "I would have been very happy if my son had entered with a bicycle, as you said, and if you had chased him out because of that—and not with a wheelchair, which according to you is a sin."

Second, in his constitution of the boundary the hegumen uses his *stick* for assault, intimidation or as an authority-enhancing prop. The three Bulgarian words with which the stick is designated in the excerpt—*prachka, toiaga, sopa*—connote such aggressive usage since in Bulgarian they are strongly associated with punishment and assault, especially the words *toiaga* and *sopa*. Yet it is at least conceivable that the stick can also be utilized as a *cane*—that is, as a mobility aid, especially considering the advanced age of the hegumen. Indeed, the corresponding Bulgarian word *bastun* does not figure in the Commission's decision. Yet at some point in their testimony the two candle-sellers (mentioned in an endnote above) note that "the hegumen sometimes walks with a small stick, on which he leans when climbing the stairs in the monastery." From this perspective, the stick implies ambiguity, mediating both power and vulnerability. In the first case it facilitates exclusion; in the second it enlists the hegumen among those to be excluded. Thus it is also a reminder that it is actually able-bodiedness and not impairment that is temporary and transitory.[29] As such an ambivalent piece of equipment, the stick is yet another nonhuman entity that both enhances (when used for assault or intimidation) and challenges (when considered as a walking aid) the boundary-work undertaken by the hegumen.

Third, the *door*. Its ambiguity is related to its double function of allowing access when open and of denying access when closed or locked and/or when there is an interdiction inscribed on it. The door in the Commission's decision is even more ambiguous, since the alleged interdiction written on it is actually nonexistent: "Off, there is no place for you here. It is written on the door outside. . . . The hegumen hurried to exit together with some of the visitors in order to show them *the interdiction that did not exist*" (emphasis added).

Finally, the *miraculous icon*. The one referred to here is the "Three-Handed Virgin" (in Bulgarian: *Troeruchitsa)*—an important image within the Eastern Orthodox tradition.[30] According to the legend, the eighth-century Christian Saint John of Damascus lost his hand as a punishment for his defense of holy images during the First Byzantine Iconoclasm. He subsequently prayed devotedly before the icon of Virgin Mary and his hand got miraculously restored. In gratitude, he attached a third, silver hand to the icon, which thereafter became known and reproduced as the "Three-Handed Virgin." This story makes the "miraculous icon" in the Troyan Monastery a symbol of restored able-bodiedness. Yet it is also a representation of corporeal difference because, outside the interpretive framework imposed by the legend, one can easily perceive Mary to be depicted as *having* three hands. But icons are also ambiguous from a more general perspective, functioning as exemplary "boundary objects"—a term already introduced in Chapter 3 in order to explain the way in which the disability assessment statement partakes in both the constitution and bridging of social boundaries. As far as icons are concerned, they can be regarded as maintaining the boundary between the secular and the religious spaces, distinguishing the latter as places of worship, prayer and meditation. Yet on the other hand, they also facilitate the interaction between these two domains. They bridge the gap between the "this-worldly" and the "other-worldly." Within the tradition of the Bulgarian Orthodox Church, a preferred way for a secular person to gain access to the religious domain is through the mediation of icons. Thus icons are often sold as souvenirs on stalls in the vicinities of the Bulgarian monasteries (the Troyan Monastery included); people buy and display them in their homes; secular painters draw their own versions of icons; rich collectors store originals in their estates; and so forth.

In sum, the paraphernalia figuring in the Commission's decision contribute both to the *consolidation* and to the *undermining* of the boundary around the spatio-temporal interiority of proximity and permanence, sustained by the hegumen in his boundary-work. Expressing thus an "agency" of their own, these nonhuman mediators resist full appropriation, defy ultimate control. Latour points out that "[m]ediators transform, translate, distort, and modify the meaning or the elements they are supposed to carry."[31] Similarly, the wheelchairs, the stick, the door and the miraculous icon figuring in the account of the Troyan Monastery event modify the boundary-work they are supposed to carry.

Concluding remarks

To recapitulate, on July 19, 2008, the hegumen of the Troyan Monastery expelled a group of disabled visitors from the cloister. The explicitness of this action provided good grounds for the Bulgarian Commission for Protection against Discrimination to judge it unlawful, to penalize the defendant and to prescribe environmental corrections. In this chapter, I tried to complement this juridical understanding of the incident—as recounted in the Commission's decision—with a phenomenological clarification of the mechanisms implicitly at work in it. Compared with the crudeness of the hegumen's unlawful conduct, these mechanisms are much milder; compared with its exclusivity, they are much more mundane; compared with its conspicuousness, they are rather clandestine; compared with its extraordinariness, they are all too familiar; finally, compared with its origins in individual intention and reasoning, they are highly impersonal. Being a case of outright dis/ablism, the event in the Troyan Monastery is nevertheless saturated with familiar, common, everyday ways of thinking and acting.

These mechanisms include the objectification of disabled people by "speaking about" them instead of "speaking to" them; as well as the attendant reduction of disabled people to their bodies rendered as inherently deficient, which, when translated into the hegumen's language, means inherently sin-full: "obviously you pay for others' sins, since you are like this." In disability studies, objectification has been analyzed in terms of the "does s/he take sugar" interaction,[32] while the rendering of disabled people's bodies as inherently deficient has been said to manifest the understanding of disability as "ontologically intolerable"[33]; both have been regarded as ubiquitous in contemporary society. On a more general level, a spatio-temporal distribution of human beings according to a rigid interiority/exteriority logic is also at work in the incident. This spatio-temporal distribution is informed by an understanding of space that prioritizes proximity and by an understanding of time that prioritizes permanence. Finally, the interiority/exteriority division, on its behalf, is sustained by a highly contested boundary-work in which different nonhuman entities are recruited as mediators. Boundary-work has been extensively studied in the context of science and technology studies, forming the core of its "anti-essentialist approach to understanding authority."[34]

Importantly, each and every one of these mechanisms contains the seeds of its own collapse. "Speaking about" presupposes "speaking to"—in terms of the speech act theory, "there is no cut-and-dried reportive utterance. Some 'primary' performative value is always presupposed in it."[35] Or, in the words of Emmanuel Levinas, "[t]he knowledge that absorbs the Other is forthwith situated within the discourse I address to him."[36] Further, being "inherently negative," the impaired body is also "nonconformity incarnate"[37]—it resists assimilation and demands accommodation. Most importantly, the domain of "here"—that is, of *proximity*—can never be completely closed; it requires and reaches toward the domain of "yonder" at the very moment of its constitution.[38] As Medard Boss puts it, "[a]t any given moment my 'here' is defined by the 'there' of the beings at which I as an open realm of perception dwelling in an open, free time-space—am dwelling, encountering them where they are."[39] Similarly, the time of the "past" can never be irreversibly "gone" and cannot for that reason guarantee *permanence*. Human past always already reaches toward human future in order to constitute itself as "past," as Heidegger's analysis of existential temporality suggests.[40] Thus, phenomenologically speaking, human space and time—that is, the space and the time of the world inhabited by human beings—are inherently decentered or, in Heidegger's terms, *ecstatic*.[41] This feature is discernible in the instances of boundary-work highlighted above. As shown in the penultimate section of this chapter, the nonhuman entities recruited in such efforts at boundary-work themselves transform and therefore problematize what they are supposed to mediate.

Such an analysis suggests that dis/ablism and the attendant disability-related practices more generally are inherently unstable, problematic, self-denying. They cannot succeed completely or permanently in translating the bodily differences of impairments into undermining of disabled people's being. Still, on the other hand, they are widespread because they are rooted in what is closest, most common, everyday and taken-for-granted. This familiarity makes them inconspicuous too. Hence they need to be highlighted—and the phenomenological *epoché*, by suspending our "natural attitude," facilitates such an analysis. That way, what is familiar becomes *uncanny*; its spatio-temporal grip on thought and imagination gets loosened. The notions of defamiliarization and uncanniness are key for phenomenological thinking and will be further explained and applied in the next case study presented in Chapter 6. I would like to close this chapter by reminding that the analysis presented here was deployed in a space opened up by Petar Kichashki's resolute action. If there is any worth in this study, it builds upon such resoluteness that has dared to challenge dis/ablism in the midst of its exclusionist fury.

Notes

1 The hegumen (in Bulgarian: *igumen*) is the head of an Eastern Orthodox monastery, the Catholic equivalent being the abbot. The Troyan Monastery or the Monastery of the Dormition of the Most Holy Mother of God (in Bulgarian: *Troyanski manastir 'Uspenie Bogorodichno'*) is one of the largest monasteries in Bulgaria. It was founded in the sixteenth century and is located in the central-northern part of the country.

2 The excerpt from the decision that is cited in the text is based on the testimony of Petar Kichashki, the claimant. The original document is in Bulgarian and is available on the internet at http://cil.bg/userfiles/media/RESHENIE259_10_PR110_09.pdf, accessed September 27, 2013. The present translation is mine, with my glosses in square brackets.

3 David L. Braddock and Susan L. Parish, "An institutional history of disability," in *Handbook of Disability Studies*, eds. Gary L. Albrecht, Katherine D. Seelman, and Michael Bury (London: SAGE, 2001), 14. See also Margrit Shildrick, "The disabled body, genealogy and undecidability." *Cultural Studies* 19, 6 (2005): 759–60.

4 Tom Shakespeare, "Cultural representation of disabled people: dustbins for disavowal?" *Disability & Society* 9, 3 (1994): 292.

5 Elsewhere in the Commission's decision the hegumen refuses the allegations, defining them as "untrue" and "tendentious." He admits to have expulsed the disabled visitors, but justifies his actions with the stipulation that the visitors were "disturbing the order in the church." The Commission discards this statement as lacking in evidence. Two of the monastery employees (candle-sellers) who witnessed the incident support the hegumen's version of the story. The Commission discards their testimonies too as "subjective and markedly interested, since the candle-sellers are financially dependent on the defendant and therefore they are not to be trusted."

6 Maurice Merleau-Ponty, *Phenomenology of Perception*, trans. Colin Smith (New York: Routledge, 2002 [1945]), vii.

7 Dan Goodley and Katherine Runswick-Cole, "The violence of disablism." *Sociology of Health & Illness* 33, 4 (2011): 602–17.

8 Simon Glendinning, "What is phenomenology?" *Think*, (Summer 2004).

9 Rod Michalko recounts asking his students "to 'walk' around the university with an 'eye' to 'see' the type of person the architecture and artifice of the university intended and expected to have show up" (*The Difference that Disability Makes*. Philadelphia: Temple University Press, 2002, 173).

10 Martin Heidegger, *Being and Time*, trans. John Macquarrie and Edward Robinson (Oxford: Blackwell, 1962 [1927]), 142.

11 Ibid., 426.

12 Edmund Husserl, *The Basic Problems of Phenomenology: From the Lectures, Winter Semester, 1910–1911*, trans. Ingo Farin and James G. Hart (Dordrecht: Springer, 2006 [1910–11]), 2.

13 Drew Leder, "A tale of two bodies: the Cartesian corpse and the lived body," in *Body and Flesh: A Philosophical Reader*, ed. Donn Welton (Oxford: Blackwell, 1998), 122.

14 For example, in Bulgarian media reports. A particularly revealing transcript from a radio interview with the hegumen, conducted soon after the incident, can be found here: http://dariknews.bg/view_article.php?article_id=286579, accessed September 27, 2013. A TV interview with Petar Kichashki can be found here: http://www.btv.bg/shows/shouto-na-slavi/videos/video/1439744218-Kak_jiveyat_horata_s_uvrejdaniya_v_Bulgaria.html, accessed September 27, 2013.

15 Simon Brisenden, "Young, gifted and disabled: entering the employment market." *Disability, Handicap & Society* 4, 3 (1989): 217–20.

16 Heidegger, *Being and Time*, 71.

17 Michel Foucault, *Discipline and Punish: The Birth of the Prison*, trans. Alan Sheridan (London: Penguin, 1991 [1975]).

18 Goodley and Runswick-Cole, "Violence," 7.

19 Fiona Kumari Campbell, *Contours of Ableism: The Production of Disability and Abledness* (Basingstoke: Palgrave Macmillan, 2009).

20 Rosemarie Garland Thomson, *Extraordinary Bodies: Figuring Physical Disability in American Culture and Literature* (New York: Columbia University Press, 1997), 130.

21 Ibid.

22 Dan Goodley, "Becoming rhizomatic parents: Deleuze, Guattari and disabled babies." *Disability & Society* 22, 2 (2007): 154.

23 Heidegger, *Being and Time*, 171.

24 Kevin Paterson and Bill Hughes, "Disability studies and phenomenology: the carnal politics of everyday life." *Disability & Society* 14, 5 (1999): 597–610.

25 Michalko, *Difference*, 18. The theme of the *home* and, accordingly, the *unhomely/uncanny* will be looked at in the next chapter.

26 Thomas F. Gieryn, "Boundary-work and the demarcation of science from non-science: strains and interests in professional ideologies of scientists." *American Sociological Review* 48, 6 (1983): 781–95.

27 Ibid., 782.

28 Emmanuel Levinas, *Totality and Infinity: An Essay on Exteriority*, trans. Alphonso Lingis (The Hague: Martinus Nijhoff Publishers, 1979 [1961]), 43.

29 Tom Shakespeare and Nicholas Watson, "The social model of disability: an outdated ideology," in *Research in Social Science and Disability, Vol. 2: Exploring Theories and Expanding Methodologies*, eds. Sharon N. Barnartt and Barbara M. Altman (Stamford, CT: JAI Press, 2001).

30 The icon is presented in Alfredo Tradigo, *Icons and Saints of the Eastern Orthodox Church: A Guide to Imagery*, trans. Stephen Sartarelli (Los Angeles: Getty Publications, 2006).

31 Bruno Latour, *Reassembling the Social: An Introduction to Actor-Network-Theory* (Oxford: Oxford University Press, 2005), 39.

32 Brisenden, "Young, gifted and disabled."

33 Campbell, *Contours of Ableism*.

34 Sergio Sismondo, *An Introduction to Science and Technology Studies* (Oxford: Blackwell, 2004), 30.

35 Jacques Derrida, *The Politics of Friendship*, trans. George Collins (London: Verso, 2005 [1994]), 214.

36 Levinas, *Totality and Infinity*, 195.

37 Thomson, *Extraordinary Bodies*, 130.

38 Heidegger, *Being and Time*, 142.
39 Medard Boss, *Existential Foundations of Medicine and Psychology*, trans. Stephen Conway and Anne Cleaves (New York and London: Jason Aronson, 1979 [1971]), 105.
40 Heidegger, *Being and Time*, 373.
41 Ibid., 377.

6

Media representations of inaccessibility

A mother assists her son, a wheelchair user, on his way to school in a Sofia neighborhood. There is a staircase at the exit of the block of flats they live in. The woman takes pains to let the wheelchair down as smoothly as possible. Nevertheless, a banging noise indicates the concussions accompanying each step. The couple reaches the sidewalk and moves on. Soon they need to descend again, this time to the street. "Oh, this one here is dreadful, it is like Everest, it is just incredible," exclaims the mother, while struggling to gently lower the wheelchair down the sidewalk curb. More obstacles lay ahead.[1]

A young man bumps with the front wheels of his electric wheelchair against an uncut curb at the entrance to the Sofia City Library. His forward movement is interrupted and he is forced to stop. Motionless in front of the obstacle, he reflects on his situation: "Now, this curb, the 10 centimeter one, is for me the ceiling. Without a ramp or some other way, this, for me, is a wall—the Berlin Wall is this." A six-step staircase awaits him after the curb, impeding further his access to the library. More obstacles lay ahead.[2]

A woman drives her electric wheelchair parallel to the first step of an imposing flight of stairs in one of the Sofia Metro underground railway stations. She reaches the end, turns around and comes back, approaching the metal rails mounted directly upon the stairs at its other end. The rails are steep, narrow and slippery—it is impossible for her to use them in order to go up. Her comment: "These are stations that are taboo for me—they do not figure in my thoughts at all." More obstacles lay ahead.[3]

These three vignettes translate in writing highlights from media reports featured on the Bulgarian television in 2011. The topic is inaccessibility. The reports expose environmental restrictions faced by disabled people in their everyday living. More precisely, the audience is shown individuals who are impeded by external, built obstacles in their efforts to engage in meaningful activities that involve wheelchair-mediated action. The message is consistent with the social model of disability—the major problems encountered by disabled people are caused by environmental inadequacy and not by their individual impairments. Below, I will explore the form and content of this message more closely, not only utilizing but also going beyond the framework of the British social model. Within this framework, disability is defined as "all the things that impose restrictions on disabled people; ranging from individual prejudice to institutional discrimination, from inaccessible public buildings to unusable transport systems, from segregated education to excluding work arrangements."[4] I would like to complement this understanding with the idea that disability also opens up possibilities for "a way of perceiving that awakens new perceptions."[5] As Rod Michalko eloquently puts it, "[t]he door to the arcane buried deeply in the ordinary is what is open to disability."[6]

The idea that disability discloses a deep truth about the human way of being that is covered up by convention, habit or familiarity builds on arguments developed in the preceding chapters. In Chapter 3, disability assessment discloses how the system of modern welfare reproduces an impoverished understanding of human being rooted in the metaphysics of presence; in Chapter 4, personal assistance for independent living discloses how inter-dependence grounds independence; and in Chapter 5, resistance to dis/ablism discloses how space and time shape and are shaped by inhabiting a shared everyday world. In this chapter, I will develop further this theme of existential-ontological disclosure by exploring media representations of inaccessibility. My methodological presumption is that a reflection on the *form* of the media message will eventually expand the understanding of its *content*. Such point of departure is intended as a way of entering the "hermeneutic circle"[7] and not as an argument about the priority of either "form" or "content." It also means that my investigation will be circular—taking as its clue the (explicit) "what" of the media message, it will explore its (implicit) "how" in order to gain insight into its (implicit) "what else." In a nutshell: as far as the "what" of the message is concerned, Bulgarian media expose *environmental restrictions* faced by disabled people in their everyday activities; in terms of "how" the media (unwittingly) engage in *defamiliarization*; finally, in terms of "what else" they (unwittingly again) disclose the *uncanniness* of human beings in general. The notions of "defamiliarization" and "uncanniness" will be clarified in the next section; for now, suffice it to say that I will constantly go back and forth among these three levels of analysis. In this, I will continue to be guided by the key phenomenological insight that has guided the investigation so far— that the meaning of disability is inseparable from the meaning of human being in general.

Two more stipulations are needed before proceeding with the analysis. First, I am myself not a wheelchair user and therefore I am not claiming any *experiential* knowledge of this practice. What I propose is primarily an investigation of media representations and not of wheelchair users' experiences. Nevertheless, these experiences are somehow reflected in these representations, they inform them and are in turn shaped by them. So, occasionally, I may cross the boundary between "representations" and "experiences." When this is the case, I should concede the final word or the "epistemic privilege"[8] to those who *are* experienced—that is, wheelchair users themselves. Second, the study in this chapter focuses on representations of obstacles faced by people who use wheelchairs for moving about. Nevertheless, most of its arguments would apply to other types of technologically mediated human action and, accordingly, to (representations of) other types of bodily differences as well. The reason is that, albeit departing from the particularity of a specific "impairment" (to wit, the one related to nonwalking), the analysis nevertheless touches upon issues concerning not only disability and its representations as such, but also the human being in general. As already pointed out, it is impossible to say something about the meaning of disability without simultaneously saying something about the meaning of human being.

That said, I can now turn toward the notions of "defamiliarization" and "uncanniness" that will consequently guide the in-depth exploration of eight media reports featured in the period May 5, 2011 to August 5, 2011 on five leading Bulgarian television channels.[9] Most of these reports were made in response to a public action of disabled people who protested against inaccessibility in Sofia. The action was held on May 5, 2011 on the streets of the Bulgarian capital, which explains the concentration of the reports in May and June. The link between making a statement and collective public action has already been highlighted in the chapter on personal assistance (Chapter 4), and Chapter 5 emphasized the importance of resolute action for opening up new spaces of meaning. Recalling these arguments, I acknowledge from the outset that without the resoluteness of the protesters neither media representations nor analyses like the present one would have ever come into existence.

Defamiliarization and uncanniness

The term "defamiliarization" (in Russian: *ostranenie*) comes from literary criticism. It was introduced a century ago by the Russian formalist Victor Shklovsky in his seminal essay "Art as technique," first published in 1917.[10] The idea is that in order to (re)gain a genuine perception of the world, one needs to detach oneself from the automatic, publicly sustained, habitual manner of perceiving it. "Habitualization devours works, clothes, furniture, one's wife, and the fear of war," writes Shklovsky.[11] Art fights this tendency by *making strange what is familiar*. Thus it interrupts everyday automatisms and enables people to (re)gain perceptual access to essential but forgotten aspects of themselves and their worlds. One of Shklovsky's examples is Leo Tolstoy's story "Kholstomer." There, human relations are seen through the eyes of a horse, which defamiliarizes the institution of private property, illuminating its conventional and contingent character.[12]

Phenomenology amplifies the significance of defamiliarization, extending it beyond perception and art toward human existence in general. From such a perspective, defamiliarization is a major condition for (re)gaining access not only to our deeper perceptions, but also to our basic state of being, that is, being-in-the-world. Thus Heidegger argues that one needs to experience the world as uncanny (*unheimlich*, which also means "unhomely") in order to be freed from the internalized and automatized clichés of the publicly accepted norms of conduct, thought and perception—or what Heidegger calls "the 'they'" (*das Man*).[13] This experience of "uncanniness" comes with the mood of anxiety (*Angst*), which is a profoundly illuminating affective state of Dasein. Later, in his lecture series *The Fundamental Concepts of Metaphysics* given in 1929–30, Heidegger makes the same points with regard to the mood of boredom (*Langeweile*).[14] Similar to existential anxiety, profound boredom can be a liberating experience: "[b]y stripping *Dasein* of its inauthentic reliance on *das Man*, and by disrupting the everyday absorption in the world of its concern, [profound boredom] brings *Dasein* face to face with itself as a free entity that ultimately, and on its own, must define itself as someone in particular."[15]

But rather than a free-floating subjective freedom, what both existential anxiety and profound boredom ultimately reveal is that the only way to define oneself is through engaging with entities and others within the world. Similar to Husserl's *epoché* discussed in Chapter 5, these moods defamiliarize the world as given in the "natural attitude," thus revealing a deeper existential-ontological truth. Yet there are significant differences in the positions of the two philosophers on what exactly is revealed when one suspends the "natural attitude":

> what is revealed in anxiety is precisely the opposite of what is revealed in Husserl's transcendental reduction. While both reductions isolate Dasein as a "solus ipse," and both reveal to the natural attitude that takes intelligibility for granted that intelligibility must be produced, Husserl's reduction reveals the transcendental ego as *the absolute source of all intelligibility*, while anxiety reveals Dasein as *dependent upon a public system of significance* that it did *not produce*.[16]

The mood of anxiety accompanies the experience of "uncanniness" that reveals to Dasein its basic structure by defamiliarizing received meanings. Before Heidegger, the intrinsic relationship between uncanniness, anxiety and the estrangement from the familiar had been influentially elaborated by Sigmund Freud.[17] But Freud studied these phenomena in individual-psychological terms, whereas Heidegger provided an existential-ontological perspective. The latter argued that the experience of uncanniness wrests us from the tranquilizing numbness of everyday automatisms we are socialized into, although ordinarily we tend to "flee" from it:

> When in falling we flee *into* the "at-home" of publicness, we flee *in the face of* the "not-at-home"; that is, we flee in the face of the uncanniness which lies in Dasein—in Dasein as thrown Being-in-the-world, which has been delivered over to itself in its Being. This uncanniness pursues Dasein constantly, and is a threat to its everyday lostness in the "they," though not explicitly.[18]

"Fleeing" from uncanniness is motivated by its disorienting, unsettling character given in the basic mood of anxiety. For example, in his essay "The uncanny valley" the Japanese roboticist Masahiro Mori advises engineers to avoid making their robots too human-like.[19] The reason is that this might lead the people interacting with these humanoid machines to a "fall" into what Mori calls the "uncanny valley"—a state of uneasiness, anxiety, even aversion. Yet from the phenomenological perspective outlined above, such a "fall" is caused not by a *lack of likeness* (in what is otherwise similar) but by *hyper-likeness*—the humanoid robot causes anxiety because it resembles me more than I am immediately ready to admit. (Note that in this sense Mori's "fall" is opposite to Heidegger's "falling" as used in the block quotation above.) In other words, the real source of anxiety is the fact that at some point the human-machine hybrid becomes a truer representation of me than the one I adhere to in my everyday living.

This insight has been persuasively articulated by the feminist Donna Haraway.[20] For her, a human being is more like a "cyborg," constituted by both natural (given) as well as artificial (made) elements, than a purely organic entity or a "healthy person," as Mori puts it. In other words, one is *constitutively* embedded in networks of nonhuman entities, assistive technologies and infrastructures of support—a point already made in all the preceding chapters. Nevertheless, one tends to "flee" from the awareness of this basic human condition, for it causes anxiety. Therefore, the "uncanny valley" is where one gets back to one's basic state of being—it is the human being-in-the-world that is uncanny. This does not invalidate Mori's conclusions—it just emphasizes that the uncanny, brought about through defamiliarization, harbors deep existential-ontological insights. Mori is right—if one wants to avoid anxiety, one is better advised to stay away from the "uncanny valley." But what about people who bump into uncanniness on an everyday basis in their encounters with the built environment?

Encounters with stairs

What happens when a wheelchair user encounters a staircase? The tension between the traditional architectural solution (staircase) and the technologically mediated (through the wheelchair) human action (of overcoming spatial distances) *invites* defamiliarization. In making sense of what thus happens, one can either accept this invitation or decline it. In the first case, one brings about defamiliarization by illuminating the strangeness of the otherwise taken-for-granted, familiar architectural elements like flights of stairs. In the second case, one obscures defamiliarization by focusing on the nonwalking ("impaired") body, whose strangeness (i.e. "abnormality") is usually taken for granted anyway.

The last point suggests that, paradoxically, the familiarity of the impaired body consists in taking its "strangeness" for granted—the impaired body is *familiar as strange*. Consequently, an attempt at defamiliarizing the body that departs from its "abnormal" variants will require a procedure opposite to the one that defamiliarizes the familiar environment. What is needed is to highlight familiarity, not strangeness. In other words, one needs to show that the "strange" body has always already been more familiar than the "familiar" one; yet people have tended to disavow this more fundamental familiarity because of the anxiety it produces—a mechanism already alluded to with regard to Mori's humanoid robots. Within disability studies, such an approach has been implied in the work of Tom Shakespeare and Nicholas Watson, who have argued that "*we are all impaired*. Impairment is not the core component of disability . . ., it is the inherent nature of humanity."[21] Yet to underline the originary familiarity of the strange body might backfire in unwittingly reaffirming the taken-for-granted negativity of strangeness. Thus Shakespeare and Watson have been criticized for "universaliz[ing] ontological lack and attribut[ing] deficit to us all."[22] As an alternative, Bill Hughes has proposed to depart not from "abnormal" corporeality but from the "normal" one in the attempt to defamiliarize the body. Thus instead of normalizing and/ or universalizing impairment as Shakespeare and Watson have done, Hughes has chosen to make the familiar body of the nonimpaired people strange in the first place: "It is . . . the normative, invulnerable body of disablist modernity that is the problem."[23] In other words: "[t]he problem rests with the normative body that does not want to be reminded of its own vulnerability or to admit that abjection and death is its fate."[24] The concluding section of Chapter 2 elaborated on this point by arguing that human frailty is ultimately grounded in the irreducible finitude of being-in-the-world.

In brief, Shakespeare and Watson seek to defamiliarize the body by departing from the *materially given deficiency* of the impaired body and highlighting its *familiarity*—"we are all impaired." Alternatively, Hughes seeks to defamiliarize the body by departing from the *culturally made completeness* of the nonimpaired body and highlighting its *strangeness*—it is the norm of the "invulnerable body" that is the problem. In Chapter 2, the first approach was linked to the position of "strong bodily realism," while the second, to that of "weak bodily realism." In terms of defamiliarization though, the two approaches coincide because *both defamiliarize corporeality*—the first by highlighting the (disavowed) familiarity of "deficiency," the second by highlighting the (disavowed) strangeness of "completeness." Importantly, the possibility for defamiliarizing the body has been opened up by defamiliarizing the environing world in the first place. In British disability studies, the latter was brought about by the development of the social model of disability during the 1980s and 1990s.[25] Elsewhere, other versions of the same explanatory mechanism have achieved similar results.[26] They have prepared the ground for defamiliarizing the body, as exemplified by the aforementioned and many other attempts to "bring the body back" into disability studies during the 1990s and the 2000s.[27]

So what happens when a wheelchair user encounters a staircase? Such an event invites defamiliarization. The media representations of inaccessibility, featured in 2011 on several major Bulgarian TV channels, accept this invitation. They do so by eliciting the strangeness of the otherwise familiar architectural environment. This does not mean that they completely bracket the question concerning the body/impairment though. Yet unlike disability scholars of the last two decades, Bulgarian media "bring the body in" without defamiliarizing it. Thus they repeatedly reassure the audience about the taken-for-granted strangeness of "deficient" bodies, and with it about the audience's all too familiar fantasies of "carnal normalcy," as Hughes puts it.[28] And this is not surprising, considering the hegemony of the traditional understanding of disability in Bulgaria, as highlighted in Chapter 3 with regard to medicalization and productivism, and as will also be argued in the following Chapter 7 with regard to issues of gender and patriarchy. Nevertheless, the media representations explored here do not simply reassert corporeal clichés but simultaneously transcend them.

Bodies and human activity

In the reports on inaccessibility studied here, the Bulgarian media engage in a double process of illuminating the impaired body in its taken-for-granted strangeness (i.e. "abnormality"), while transcending this traditional corporeal representation by defamiliarizing the familiar environment. Bodies *do* feature in these media materials, and when the camera focuses on bodily parts the image often slides into representing impairment in terms of lack, weakness and impotence. It is as if in such cases the cameraman cannot resist the clichés of misfortune attached to what is usually taken for granted as "deficient" corporeality. Consequently, we are presented with familiar shots of strange ("abnormal") organs, informed by the traditional view of disability— medicalized, individualized and suggesting "personal tragedy."[29] For example, hands are shown *in their inability* to manipulate, legs *in their inability* to move the body.[30] Sometimes the camera juxtaposes, in two consecutive shots, the agility of walking feet to the stillness of the body "bound" to a wheelchair.[31] Such images have their verbal counterparts—time and again, disabled people are referred to as "invalids" (in Bulgarian: *invalidi*—see Chapter 1)[32]; medical diagnoses such as "muscular dystrophy" or "microcephaly" are used to introduce personalities[33]; journalists appeal to mutual support and "public tolerance" for solutions to inaccessibility issues[34]; and so forth.

At the same time, however, the overall focus of the media reports is not on *bodies*, nor on *bodily action*, but on *acting people* with their wider concerns, wishes and projects. Therefore, the aforementioned instances of representing corporeal "deficiencies" should be put into perspective. For, overall, media representations of inaccessibility featured recently on the Bulgarian television highlight bodily organs such as hands, legs and feet not as discrete entities but *as elements of technologically mediated human activity*. Thus if we are shown a close-up of a hand, it eventually turns out to be a hand that controls the joystick steering the wheelchair toward going into the next room of an office building.[35] Similarly, if we are shown a close-up of feet, these are feet resting on the wheelchair's footrests just above the front wheels of the wheelchair bumping into obstacles on the person's way toward the city library.[36]

Such an approach reverses the traditional direction of disability-related questioning by going from the external toward the internal or from the context toward the entity.[37] It is the very *direction* of investigation that makes a difference here. This difference is consistent with the phenomenological insights concerning the "lived body." In explaining the meaning of this concept in Chapters 1 and 2, I pointed out that, phenomenologically speaking, the body and its organs are better understood within meaningful human activity rather than as discrete, occurrent entities. Consequently, it is the practical engagement with entities and others within the meaningful context of a world that needs to be interrogated in order to understand the body. As Merleau-Ponty puts it: "[t]he body is the vehicle of being in the world, and having a body is, for a living creature, to be intervolved in a definite environment, to identify oneself with certain projects and be continually committed to them."[38] Thus one needs to understand the "projects" that involve walking in order to be able to understand what "legs" mean. Conversely, one understands leg-less-ness only by understanding restrictions in walking, which presupposes proficiency in its cultural meaning or in the wider existential projects that incorporate walking.[39] It is in this sense that "[w]e are not able to 'see' because we have eyes; rather, we can only have eyes because, according to our basic nature, we are beings who can see."[40] In other words, the *meaning* of the organ called "eye" comes from the practices of seeing in which the eye takes part, and not the other way round. We can "have eyes" because we are able to inhabit *a world of seeing* where "having eyes" makes sense.[41]

To recapitulate, if the media reports explored here represent "deficient" bodies, this is nevertheless done *in the wider context of meaningful human activity*. First, such reading is suggested by the frequent use of action words— examples include recurring verbs of physical movement such as "go out," "overcome," "walk," "go down," "leave," "cross," "move," "walk round," "come up," "reach" and so forth. Second, bodies' engagement in practices is depicted as technologically mediated. Thus whenever a corporeal deficit is illuminated, its "deficiency" is subsequently shifted from the plane of corporeality to the plane of technology. Consequently, what shows up is not so much a bodily, but rather a *technological deficiency*—for example, the inability of *the wheelchair* to climb stairs. In one of the media reports the journalist asks: "How will *you* go through?," to which the person, a wheelchair user, replies: "Well, *for the wheelchair*—it is impossible *for it* to go through."[42] Another example is: "In such a wheelchair the best you can do is injure your child"[43]—the "deficiency" of the given (body) is overshadowed by the "deficiency" of the made (technology).

Nevertheless, third, the overall focus of media reports is not on individual deficiency—be it corporeal or related to assistive technology—but on the environmental one. It is the inadequacy of the architectural environment that illuminates the inadequacy of the mobility aid and not the other way round. The headings of the media reports strongly suggest such a reading. Two examples will suffice: "Sofia—a capital of obstacles for people with disabilities,"[44] and "The way to school—mission impossible for a mother of a child with cerebral palsy."[45] The point of departure is the environing world in its restrictive character—Sofia as "a capital of obstacles," or "the way to school" as "mission impossible." If we take a closer look at the second example, we will notice that: the child is defined through his medical diagnosis, which illuminates his "deficient" corporeality; yet the attention is actually focused on his mother, who acts as the boy's personal assistant, thus complementing the functionality of his mobility aid (as the report itself suggests); and ultimately, all this happens within the general framework of pursuing a meaningful human activity—attending school.

Human activity and self-definition

Phenomenology can help to clarify further this argument. The point is that every dealing with a piece of equipment (such as a staircase) takes place within a hierarchy of involvements that goes up to taking a stand on what it means to be as a human being. Heidegger unpacks the different layers of this structure, underlining their interconnectedness:

> The "for-the-sake-of-which" signifies an "in-order-to"; this in turn, a "towards-this"; the latter, an "in-which" of letting something be involved, and that in turn, the "with-which" of an involvement. These relationships are bound up with one another as a primordial totality; they are what they

are as this signifying [Be-deuten] in which Dasein gives itself beforehand its Being-in-the-world as something to be understood.[46]

For example, I am *in* the underground railway station, facing the elevator *with which* I am able to reach the surface, *in order to* go to the office, being oriented *toward* coordinating the activities of the project personnel, *for the sake of* being a reliable project manager.[47] The point is that the handling of equipment is implicated in taking a stand on *who* one is—as explained in Chapter 1, every activity of Dasein implies understanding of Dasein's own being, because to be Dasein is to be "thrown" into relating, understanding and self-understanding. It follows that if I cannot use the elevator, this is likely to have a negative impact on all the layers of the involvement structure, going up to my self-understanding as a competent project manager and, ultimately, as a full human being. Human dignity itself is at stake in such situations, as strongly suggested in a media report about the refusal of a wheelchair user to be pulled up the stairs in a Sofia Metro station[48]—a resolute action bearing resemblance to that of Petar Kichashki discussed in Chapter 5. The woman was going home after work. When she reached her neighborhood station, she found out that the elevator had broken during the day. She was offered manual help, but she refused, declaring: "I am not a sack of potatoes." The woman insisted for the elevator to be repaired and was determined to wait until after midnight for this to be done.

Thus in the media reports explored here the existential significance of the environing world is highlighted by showing how inaccessibility (of sidewalks, exists/entrances, platforms, etc.) makes it extremely hard for disabled people to be diligent workers, good parents, excelling students, active citizens—and, ultimately, full human beings. That is why the difficulties experienced by the wheelchair users and their assistants and denoted as "hard physical labor," "inconceivable efforts," "everyday hardships" and so forth resonate with existential-ontological meaning. When a mother is shown *struggling* with the combined *weight* of her son and his wheelchair, while taking him down the staircase at the exit of their home,[49] her *physical* effort shines in the light of the *existential* effort to be a good mother of an assiduous student. For a wheelchair user, a curb in front of the library is "the Berlin Wall"[50]—similar to the actual wall that used to divide the German capital, the uncut curb does not simply interrupt spatial displacement, it *interrupts a way of being.* An underground railway station can be perceived as "taboo"[51] because its inaccessibility prohibits not only physical but also *symbolic* presence.

It is usually the case that this constitutive embeddedness of humans in their environing worlds remains *hidden* because it is too close, thus being covered up by habit or automatism. Heidegger uses the example of the street as "equipment for walking" in order to highlight this usual inconspicuousness:

> One feels the touch of it at every step as one walks; it is seemingly the closest and Realest of all that is ready-to-hand, and it slides itself, as it were, along certain portions of one's body—the soles of one's feet. And yet it is farther remote than the acquaintance whom one encounters "on the street" at a "remoteness" ["Entfernung"] of twenty paces when one is taking such a walk.[52]

Typically, the street resides in the background of familiarity—that is why it is "remote," despite being "the closest." The same point can be made with regard to a flight of stairs—until the familiarity is *broken* by the use of a wheelchair. Such an event invites defamiliarization and the attendant experience of uncanniness. In it, "[t]he context of equipment is lit up, not as something never seen before, but as a totality constantly sighted beforehand in circumspection. With this totality, however, the world announces itself."[53] In other words, the use of a wheelchair in the context of an inaccessible environment opens up the possibility to interrupt familiarity and thus to illuminate the environing world as a "totality" in which human self-definition is implicated. Such a totality can then show up as always already encountered *before* encountering any single entity *in it*—including ourselves as discrete, corporeally circumscribed, naturally given (and not artificially made) individuals.

Illuminating the strangeness of the familiar

Defamiliarization is brought about within the media representations explored here by focusing on taken-for-granted details of our environing world. First, details are visually emphasized. Media reports highlight different elements of inaccessibility impeding wheelchair users. Through repeated close-ups, attention is drawn to wheels meeting obstacles on the disabled person's way—curbs, stairs,[54] steep ramps, the gap between the train and the platform edge,[55] displaced shaft covers, misplaced sidewalk pegs,[56] and so forth. Thus details of the environing world are singled out and their power to exclude is exposed. They are decontextualized, which makes them strange—but not *too* strange, for their familiarity is immediately reasserted through recontextualization with the next wide shot of the whole structure, the building or the transport vehicle. This e-strangement (in Russian: *o-stranenie*) of what is familiar is also enhanced by the point of view—details are often shot from an unusual perspective, as though seen by the wheelchair itself. That way, the eyes of the audience see from the perspective of the wheels or the footrests of the mobility aid.

Second, environing details are verbally highlighted. Elements of inaccessibility are spoken about, discussed, criticized, calculated. In one of the reports, the journalist takes out a roll-up tape-measure in order to determine the elevation of a trolley-bus floor above the ground—it turns out to be 30 cm.[57] Details are described as "dreadful" or "incredible," they are compared with Everest[58] or the Berlin Wall.[59] Such comments elicit "disharmony" in what is usually taken as a "harmonious context"[60]—curbs and flights of stairs become "abnormal," they do not fit any more and they *disturb* the order of movement instead of facilitating it. Taking the usual place of the impaired body, it is the environing details that are subjected to diagnosing and enlisted for corrective interventions. It is no longer the nonwalking body but the dysfunctional elevator that is identified as "vulnerable."[61]

Third, details are temporally emphasized—their perception is prolonged. In media reports of inaccessibility the camera tends to linger over elements of our surroundings that most people systematically disregard. Such a way of representing forces the audience to stop and remain *there* for a while— *there* where it ordinarily just passes by.[62] Remember the young man who approaches the Sofia City Library: "His forward movement is interrupted and he is forced to stop. Motionless in front of the obstacle, he reflects on his situation"[63] The camera follows such interruptions, coming to a halt in front of obstacles, fixing the audience's attention on them. Again, an environing detail takes the place usually reserved for the impairment. It becomes the object of an otherwise dis/ablist gaze.[64] Consequently, bits and pieces of our everyday world are stared at—attentively, insistently, disapprovingly. The camera does violence—yet not by objectifying subjects, but by *objectifying objects*. Visual representations "speak about" environing details in the way in which disabled persons are usually "spoken about" (see Chapter 5).

Fourth, details are shown in a holistic perspective. Media reports illuminate totalities—complex networks of heterogeneous entities. The point is that "when something is partly accessible, it is [actually] not accessible" because "there is a *whole totality of measures* that have to be implemented."[65] It is not enough to cut a curb or to install a ramp. For example, a woman assists her son, pushing his wheelchair out of an elevator at the exit of an underground railway station. There she stops, explaining:

> I found myself on the other side of the road, which I cannot cross, because there is a fence blocking the way. And now I will go down with the elevator again and will have to climb those stairs in order to proceed in the desired direction.[66]

When there is no coordination among different architectural elements, no accessibility ensues. Moreover, details tend to efface each other. The purchase of an electric wheelchair is subsidized by the Bulgarian state every 10 years. Yet:

> in order to retain it for ten years, to be able to use it for ten years, I need very good driving conditions. And with these high curbs it will very easily break down as early as during the first year. Now my dread is how to preserve it for a longer period.[67]

In summary, media reports of inaccessibility defamiliarize taken-for-granted environing details through visual, verbal, temporal and perspectival means. Visually, details are stared at; verbally, they are being hyperbolized, labeled, diagnosed; temporally, they are made to stay longer, to linger in the field of perception; perspectively, they are shown from a holistic point of view—the audience's attention is switched from the figure to its constitutive background.[68]

Concluding remarks

In this chapter, I addressed two interrelated questions. First, how is the Bulgarian media message about environmental restrictions faced by disabled people constituted; what are the tactics employed in its articulation, what makes it work? Second, in *thus* illuminating restrictions, what else gets illuminated? In other words, what do such media representations (unwittingly) tell us *in addition to* the truth about the external, "manmade" constitution of disabled people's problems? As in the previous chapters, I resorted to phenomenology—complemented here with concepts borrowed from literary criticism—in order to go beyond the British social model of disability while retaining a relationship with its core tenets.

If such an analysis is critical, it is critical in a peculiar sense—it explains a mechanism of critique that is already happening. With the aim to strengthen this mechanism, to add to its momentum, I explained in terms of "defamiliarization" the tactics of representing inaccessibility employed by the Bulgarian media. These defamiliarizing representations illuminate the power of the closest items of our everyday environment (e.g., stair or curbs) over the lives of people who use wheelchairs for getting about. Yet there is an (unintended) consequence of rendering strange these otherwise familiar architectural details. Analyses of literary representations of disability have highlighted the potential of disability to disrupt taken-for-granted normative orders, bringing about the anxious experience of "aesthetic nervousness."[69] In literature:

> the impairment is often taken to be the physical manifestation of the exact opposite of order, thus forcing a revaluation of that impulse [towards order], and indeed, of what it means to be human in a world governed by radical contingency.[70]

Similarly, in media representations of inaccessibility, the defamiliarization of the entities that constitute our everyday, taken-for-granted world says something about the condition of being human in general. Phenomenologically speaking, it is our existential-ontological *finitude* that shows up in such cases. Understood positively, "finitude" refers to the contextual embeddedness of human being, as has already been pointed out in Chapter 2. Facing our contextual embeddedness brings about anxiety. We enter the "uncanny valley," where being human is revealed as decentered, extending beyond the taken-for-granted closure of its "objective" body and/or "subjective" mind. The statement reiterates an argument from the preceding chapters—that the familiar incorporates existential-ontological reductions. These reductions inhere in the building blocks of our homes.

When one enters the unhomely regions of the "uncanny valley," one is reminded that one's existential projects are always already integrated in the world one inhabits—I cannot be a diligent worker unless a space is opened up for people like me to be *as workers*. Thus when a wheelchair user encounters inaccessibility, she or he simultaneously encounters a *whole world* with its values, norms and expectations.[71] Three decades ago Victor Finkelstein made this point with regard to the activity of washing hands.[72] Similarly, the activity of walking is also "created" and not given. *A whole world is there*, surrounding it, making it possible, sustaining it and investing it with meaning and value. More recently, Campbell has pointed out in her critique of ablism that "there is no such thing as a purely human—*we are always* combined with nonhumans wherein the environment is mediated through a layer of technologies."[73] This also means that "the 'essence' of being human lies in our fundamental reliance on appendages, prosthesis and that which is 'outside' ourselves."[74] Usually, however, this "fundamental reliance" remains invisible because it is all too familiar to be noticed. In his analysis of disabled people's experience of their homes, Imrie cites a respondent who puts it thus: "the detail was very minute and you couldn't see it, but it was very major to me."[75]

In the case of the media reports of inaccessibility explored here, it was the presence of the (usually absent) disabled Bulgarians on the streets of Sofia that *interrupted the invisibility* of the environing world. The experience of uncanniness—the feeling of being not-at-home at the very heart of one's home, at the edge of the staircase or on the brink of the sidewalk curb— comes with the detachment from the clichés that make up what we regard as "home."[76] Such detachment reveals that our homes have a profound power over our lives—what we regard as "home" comprises myriad minute details that interact with our selves through the medium of our lived bodies. Each and every one of these minute details incorporates prescriptions on how to act, what to value, whom to be. Making our familiar world strange makes us unhomely, thus bringing about anxiety. Yet it also engenders the possibility for liberation from the iron grip of our habitual homes that are capable of devouring human lives. Here lie the price and promise of following the wheels of a wheelchair through the uncanny valley.

Defamiliarization enables us to see how our habits of constructing our world cause suffering. When defamiliarized, these habits and these constructions become uncanny. The "homely" world is illuminated in its oppressive artificiality. What we have taken as natural and/or given elements of our closest environment turns out to be conventional and contingent, like private property for Tolstoy's horse in "Kholstomer" or dis/ablist spatio-temporal distribution of entities, selves and others in the Troyan Monastery (Chapter 5). These conventions cause suffering. Perhaps, after accepting the invitation to perceive his or her familiar, lived environment as strange, even a walking person will start approaching staircases and uncut curbs differently. Perhaps she/he will start experiencing certain unease when encountering these elements of his or her habitual surroundings. It is such uneasiness that opens up possibilities for changes in thinking. And, as the stories about the woman who refused to be pulled up the stairs "like a sack of potatoes"[77] and about Petar Kichashki in Chapter 5 testify, it is such uneasiness that can also bring about resoluteness to change the world.

Notes

1 *This Morning*, bTV, May 19, 2011.
2 *The Hounds*, bTV, May 8, 2011.
3 *Hello Bulgaria*, Nova TV, June 8, 2011.
4 Michael Oliver, *Understanding Disability: From Theory to Practice* (London: Macmillan, 1996), 33. For an extended discussion, see Chapter 2 of the present investigation.

5 Tanya Titchkosky, "Disability in the news: a reconsideration of reading." *Disability & Society* 20, 6 (2005): 662.

6 Rod Michalko, *The Difference that Disability Makes* (Philadelphia: Temple University Press, 2002), 166.

7 Martin Heidegger, *Being and Time*, trans. John Macquarrie and Edward Robinson (Oxford: Blackwell, 1962 [1927]), 194–5.

8 Bat-Ami Bar On, "Marginality and epistemic privilege," in *Feminist Epistemologies*, eds. Linda Alcoff and Elizabeth Potter (New York: Routledge, 1993).

9 The following is the list of the media reports analyzed in this chapter. At the time when the analysis was done (October 2011), all of them were available on the internet:

- *The Day Begins*, BNT, May 5, 2011, http://bnt.bg/bg/news/view/52298/za_nedostypnata_gradska_sreda
- *The News*, bTV, May 5, 2011, http://www.btv.bg/news/bulgaria/obshtestvo/story/2087481388-S_kolichka_po_sofiyskite_ulitsi__misiya_nevazmojna
- *The News*, TV7, May 5, 2011, after the first 30.50 minutes, http://tv7.bg/newsVideoArchive/video321662.html
- *The Hounds*, bTV, May 8, 2011, http://www.btv.bg/action/predavania/hratkite/videos/video/631061484
- *This Morning*, bTV, May 19, 2011, http://www.btv.bg/shows/tazi-sutrin/reportazhi/story/1077580839
- *Hello Bulgaria*, Nova TV, June 8, 2011, http://novatv.bg/news/view/2011/06/08/17017 and http://novatv.bg/news/view/2011/06/08/17018
- *The News*, BBT, June 11, 2011, after the first 5.40 minutes, http://www.bbt.tv/video/section/2#video_6757
- *The News*, bTV, August 5, 2011, http://www.btv.bg/news/bulgaria/story/2075937116

10 Victor Shklovsky, "Art as technique," in *Russian Formalist Criticism: Four Essays*, eds. Lee T. Lemon and Marion J. Reis (Lincoln: University of Nebraska Press, 1965 [1917]).

11 Ibid., 12.

12 Ibid., 13–15.

13 Heidegger, *Being and Time*, 233–5.

14 Martin Heidegger, *The Fundamental Concepts of Metaphysics: World, Finitude, Solitude*, trans. William McNeill and Nicholas Walker (Bloomington and Indianapolis: Indiana University Press, 1995 [1929–30]).

15 Espen Hammer, *Philosophy and Temporality from Kant to Critical Theory* (Cambridge, UK: Cambridge University Press, 2011), 183.

16 Hubert L. Dreyfus, *Being-in-the-World. A Commentary on Heidegger's* Being and Time, *Division I* (Cambridge, MA: MIT Press, 1991), 177, original emphasis.

17 Sigmund Freud, "The uncanny," in *The Standard Edition of the Complete Psychological Works of Sigmund Freud, Volume XVII (1917–1919)*, trans. and ed. James Strachey, in collaboration with Anna Freud, assisted by Alix Strachey and Alan Tyson (London: Vintage, 2001 [1919]).

18 Heidegger, *Being and Time*, 234.

19 Masahiro Mori, "The uncanny valley [Bukimi no tani]." *Energy* 7, 4 (1970): 33–5.

20 Donna Haraway, *Simians, Cyborgs, and Women. The Reinvention of Nature* (London: Free Association Books, 1991).

21 Tom Shakespeare and Nicholas Watson, "The social model of disability: an outdated ideology," in *Research in Social Science and Disability, Vol. 2: Exploring Theories and Expanding Methodologies*, eds. Sharon N. Barnartt and Barbara M. Altman (Stamford, CT: JAI Press, 2001), 27.

22 Bill Hughes, "Being disabled: towards a critical social ontology for disability studies." *Disability & Society* 22, 7 (2007): 682.

23 Ibid., 681.

24 Ibid. Interestingly, more than a decade earlier Tom Shakespeare had defended a very similar position: "And it is not us, it is non-disabled people's embodiment which is the issue: disabled people remind non-disabled people of their own vulnerability" ("Cultural representation of disabled people: dustbins for disavowal?" *Disability & Society* 9, 3 (1994): 297). At that time Shakespeare had been interested in cultural representations of disability. Consequently, his point of departure had been different, perhaps more akin to the one taken by Hughes in 2007.

25 Victor Finkelstein, *Attitudes and Disabled People: Issues for Discussion* (New York: World Rehabilitation Fund, 1980); Michael Oliver, *Understanding Disability: From Theory to Practice* (London: Macmillan, 1996) and *The Politics of Disablement* (London: Macmillan, 1990).

26 For a North American overview, see Lennard J. Davis, *Bending over Backwards: Disability, Dismodernism, and Other Difficult Positions* (New York: New York University Press, 2002), 33–46.

27 For an overview, see Carol Thomas, *Sociologies of Disability and Illness: Contested Ideas in Disability Studies and Medical Sociology* (Basingstoke: Palgrave Macmillan, 2007), 120–53.

28 Hughes, "Being disabled," 681.

29 Oliver, *Understanding Disability*.

30 On this tactic of representing "flawed" bodily parts, see also Shakespeare, "Cultural representation," 288.

31 *Hello Bulgaria*, Nova TV, June 8, 2011.

32 *The News*, TV7, May 5, 2011.

33 *Hello Bulgaria*, Nova TV, June 8, 2011.

34 *The Day Begins*, BNT, May 5, 2011.

35 *The News*, BBT, June 11, 2011.

36 *The Hounds*, bTV, May 8, 2011.

37 For the meaning of such reversal of questioning, see Oliver, *Politics of Disablement*, 6–9.

38 Maurice Merleau-Ponty, *Phenomenology of Perception*, trans. Colin Smith (New York: Routledge, 2002 [1945]), 94.

39 See Oliver, *Understanding Disability*, 95–109.

40 Martin Heidegger, *Zollikon Seminars: Protocols, Conversations, Letters*, ed. Medard Boss, trans. Franz Mayr and Richard Askay (Evanston, IL: Northwestern University Press, 2001 [1959–69]), 232.

41 On the performative aspects of sightedness see Michalko, *Difference*, 26–7 and 168–72.

42 *The Day Begins*, BNT, May 5, 2011, emphases added.

43 *The News*, bTV, May 5, 2011.

44 *Hello Bulgaria*, Nova TV, June 8, 2011.

45 *This Morning*, bTV, May 19, 2011.

46 Heidegger, *Being and Time*, 120.

47 For a similar example, see Dreyfus, *Being-in-the-World*, 92.

48 *The News*, bTV, August 5, 2011.

49 *This Morning*, bTV, May 19, 2011.

50 *The Hounds*, bTV, May 8, 2011.

51 *Hello Bulgaria*, Nova TV, June 8, 2011.

52 Heidegger, *Being and Time*, 141–2.

53 Ibid., 105.

54 *This Morning*, bTV, May 19, 2011.

55 *Hello Bulgaria*, Nova TV, June 8, 2011.

56 *The News*, bTV, May 5, 2011.

57 *The Day Begins*, BNT, May 5, 2011.

58 *This Morning*, bTV, May 19, 2011.

59 *The Hounds*, bTV, May 8, 2011.

60 Shklovsky, "Art as technique," 21.

61 *The News*, bTV, August 5, 2011.

62 Similarly, in an essay on Bertolt Brecht, first published two decades after Shklovsky's "Art as technique," Walter Benjamin outlines the technique of making strange through "interruption" as key to Brecht's "epic theater" where the primary aim is to make the audience aware of its conditions of living: "The task of epic theatre, Brecht believes, is not so much to develop actions as to represent conditions. But 'represent' does not here signify 'reproduce' in the sense used by the theoreticians of Naturalism. Rather, the first point at issue is to *uncover* those conditions. (One could just as well say: to *make them strange* [*verfremden*].) This uncovering (making strange, or alienating) of conditions is brought about by processes being interrupted." Walter Benjamin, *Understanding Brecht*, trans. Anna Bostock (London: Verso, 1998 [1966]), 18.

63 *The Hounds*, bTV, May 8, 2011.

64 Rosemarie Garland Thomson, *Extraordinary Bodies: Figuring Physical Disability in American Culture and Literature* (New York: Columbia University Press, 1997), 60.

65 *Hello Bulgaria*, Nova TV, June 8, 2011, emphasis added.

66 *The News*, TV7, May 5, 2011.

67 *The News*, BBT, June 11, 2011.

68 Here, again, a parallel with Walter Benjamin's reflections on defamiliarization seems pertinent. In his groundbreaking essay "The work of art in the age of mechanical reproduction," originally published in 1936, Benjamin highlights the capacity of technologically mediated visual representation to defamiliarize our environment, thus making it possible for us to access hidden aspects of our worlds that otherwise rule over our lives—hence the transformative, even revolutionary potential that Benjamin sees in this technology:

"By close-ups of the things around us, by focusing on hidden details of familiar objects, by exploring commonplace milieus under the ingenious guidance of the camera, the film, on the one hand, extends our comprehension of the necessities which rule our lives; on the other hand, it manages to assure us of an immense and unexpected field of action. . . . With the close-up, space expands; with slow motion, movement is extended. The enlargement of a snapshot does not simply render more precise what in any case was visible, though unclear: it reveals entirely new structural formations of the subject." Walter Benjamin, "The work of art in the age of mechanical reproduction," in *Illuminations*, ed. Hannah Arendt, trans. Harry Zohn (New York: Schocken Books, 2007 [1936]), 236. The comparison between Benjamin's and Heidegger's views on technology goes well beyond the scope of the present study. I will only point out that in this chapter my argument is closer to Benjamin's valuation of the progressive potential of modern visual media than to Heidegger's deep skepticism about cinema, photography and television—indeed, Heidegger sees cinema as "a pernicious manifestation of technological en-framing" (Robert Sinnerbrink, "A Heideggerian cinema?: On Terrence Malick's *The Thin Red Line*." *Film-Philosophy* 10, 3 (2006): 27).

69 Ato Quayson, *Aesthetic Nervousness: Disability and the Crisis of Representation* (New York: Columbia University Press, 2007).

70 Ibid., 17.

71 Kevin Paterson and Bill Hughes, "Disability studies and phenomenology: the carnal politics of everyday life." *Disability & Society* 14, 5 (1999): 597–610.

72 Finkelstein, *Attitudes*, 25–6; see also Chapter 4 of the present investigation.

73 Fiona Kumari Campbell, *Contours of Ableism: The Production of Disability and Abledness* (Basingstoke: Palgrave Macmillan, 2009), 56.

74 Ibid., 70.

75 Rob Imrie, "Disability, embodiment and the meaning of the home." *Housing Studies* 19, 5 (2004): 753.

76 See Michalko, *Difference*, 43–4.

77 *The News*, bTV, August 5, 2011.

7

Sexuality

State socialism was reluctant to talk about sex. As Phillips points out in relation to the former Soviet Union, "questions of gender and especially sex were a closed book throughout much of Soviet history."[1] This reluctance characterized the Soviet Bloc as a whole, where silence was imposed on public discussion of these issues and even on the open admission of sexuality.[2] Such silencing was even more pronounced in Bulgaria than in East Germany or Hungary, for example, because of the relatively greater degree to which the country was closed off from Western cultural influences. After 1989, discourses on sex and sexuality in Bulgaria were quickly and effectively normalized and liberalized. Nevertheless, disabled people have remained excluded from such liberalization, as if continuing to live under the state socialist taboo.[3] Of course, cultural desexualization of disabled people is by no means a specifically state-socialist or specifically Bulgarian phenomenon. It is characteristic of Western modernity in general, where disabled people have consistently been regarded as "sexless beings"—"aesthetically neutered objects of benevolence and assistance."[4] Yet the Bulgarian case can furnish important insights into the mechanisms of rendering disabled people "sexless." In such an analysis, differences from Western countries may be easier to spot than those from the countries of the former Soviet Bloc, where similarities seem to prevail, although the available information is scarce.[5]

By daring to speak publicly about disabled people's sexuality, Bulgarians break an important cultural taboo that, although genealogically traceable to state socialist "puritanism," transcends its boundaries. This is the tacit prohibition on associating issues related to sex with issues related to disability. Western modernity has exempted certain groups from this interdiction, but their membership has almost exclusively been confined to experts in the "helping" domain: "There is quite an industry producing work around the issue of sexuality and disability, but it is an industry controlled by professionals from medical and psychological and sexological backgrounds."[6] Hughes also points out that, apart from popular prejudice, the "sexual invalidation of disabled people is mediated by medical knowledge."[7] The corollary is that discourses related to disabled people's sexuality have been heavily individualized, professionalized and/or pathologized. A "regime of truth"[8] has been constituted, regulating *what* can legitimately be said and *who* can legitimately say it. This regime regulates Bulgarian public discourse too, perhaps to a greater extent than in most other European countries, including some of the Eastern European ones, for reasons outlined in the discussion of the specific physiognomy of the Bulgarian disability-related context in Chapter 1. Consequently, the mere bringing of the topic of disability and sexuality in a non-expert public context is already a subversive act, a challenge of dominant mechanisms of truth production.[9] Such an act becomes even more subversive when the person speaking is himself or herself (self-identified as) disabled, for it then becomes an instance of "reclaiming the voice"—a cornerstone of individual and collective empowerment and emancipation.[10]

This chapter regards desexualization of disabled people in existential-ontological terms. From such a perspective, desexualization is among those dis/ablist practices that translate the bodily difference of "impairment" into undermining of disabled persons' very existence. Against the background of systematic desexualization sustained by expert-dominated regimes of truth, the occasional instances of non-expert discourses on disabled people's sexuality are not only subversive, but also revelatory. They reveal and challenge taken-for-granted notions about people's own and others' bodies, and particularly about the bodily differences usually identified as "impairments." Proceeding from these presumptions, in what follows I will explore how Bulgarians discuss sexuality in relation to disability in non-expert, public contexts. My sources of information will be an autobiographical essay and an internet discussion. In the analysis, I will be guided by the phenomenological notion of "lived body," according to which *pure* physicality is an abstraction—an objectifying detachment from the meaning-engendering context of the world, as also emphasized in Chapter 6. This phenomenological understanding of the human body will allow me to suspend or "bracket" the taken-for-granted negativity of the bodily difference of "impairment" without disembodying the human being (see also the concluding section of Chapter 2).

"I, my impairment and sex"

In the Bulgarian context of systematic desexualization of disabled people and the attendant professionalized "regimes of truth," spaces for alternative public deliberation on the topic in question are scarce. Such spaces provide discursive "clearings" where the relationship between sexuality and disability can be addressed in nonexpert—and, accordingly, nonpathologized and/or nonpaternalistic—ways. Few such "clearings" have existed in Bulgaria in the decades since the fall of state socialism in 1989. Among them were the periodicals edited and published by the Center for Independent Living—Sofia, the Bulgarian disabled people's organization that figures as the main civil society protagonist of the present investigation. The Center's periodicals included the monthly newsletter *Independent Living*, of which 52 issues were published in 1999–2004; the magazine *Integral*, of which nine issues were published in 2001–04; and the monthly magazine *Independent Living*, intended to succeed the previous two, of which six issues were published in the second half of 2004. This prolific publishing endeavor came to a halt in December 2004. As noted in Chapter 1, I collaborated with the organization throughout the first decade of the new millennium, although I was not directly involved in its publishing program. All of the periodicals of the Center were supported by foreign donors through programs for civil society development in Bulgaria—none enjoyed financial support from the Bulgarian state. Consequently, when the foreign programs ended, the Center's periodicals disappeared, for they could not sustain themselves through free-market mechanisms. As in other cases related to cultural and social policy issues, the market proved to be a problematic "regulator." For as far as the public good was concerned, the Center's publications had an important and pioneering function—to open up public spaces for the articulation of subjugated knowledges. In a similar fashion to state socialist taboos or outright repressions—and similar to the "regime of truth" of medicalization—the instrumental rationality of the market can also silence voices.

The Center's periodicals contained a special section titled "Taboo." It was explicitly designated for discussing openly and publicly disability-related issues that usually remain silenced, including issues related to disabled people's sexuality. I will take as my example an autobiographical essay that first appeared in the *Integral* magazine in 2002 and was subsequently reprinted in the *Independent Living* newsletter in 2003. The four-page essay, entitled "I, my impairment and sex" (in Bulgarian: *Az, moeto uvrezhdane i seksat*),[11] was written by Nina Zhisheva and appeared in the "Taboo" section of both periodicals. This piece deserves to be read not only as a text, but also as an event. It was a venture not simply into uncharted territory, but also into one which has for a long time been dominated by expert knowledge and power. The rich and multi-layered essay is thus an instance of the aforementioned "reclaiming the voice."

Zhisheva identifies from the outset the two interrelated issues that I have already singled out—desexualization of disabled people and silence on the topic of disabled people's sexuality:

> Interestingly, has it ever occurred to you that disabled people need sex too? No? According to many they are so "impaired" and the sex is so "normal" and natural that it is as if they are mutually exclusive. Moreover, for disabled people themselves sex is almost always Taboo Number One. I have a severe physical impairment myself and I know it, alas, from my own experience. I know many people like myself and I admit in anguish that I have rarely heard these people speak frankly among themselves on the topic of sex.[12]

These two issues of desexualization and silencing are aspects of the same existential-ontological problem. Zhisheva regards sexuality as an essential dimension of the full human being—"sex really incorporates the beauty of everything human."[13] She thus hints at the mechanism for denying the status of subjects,[14] or, more generally, the "ontological invalidation"[15] of disabled people that is put in operation by the denial of sexuality. Such dis/ablist violence is not targeted at a specific feature of the individual but at his or her very being. As argued in the study of the Troyan Monastery case in Chapter 5, such violence is experienced by the person who comes to inhabit a world where there is "no place" for her/him—an uncanny or unhomely dwelling. "Exclusion, even oppression is a kind of homelessness. It implies a world of bodily discomfort, of being left out in the cold," write Paterson and Hughes.[16] Zhisheva's point is that a profound existential-ontological crisis develops when an essential aspect of one's being is denied a place through desexualization: "The woman in me had to fall asleep in order for me to live. . . . Do you understand what I was doing? Allegedly in order to live, I was slowly killing myself."[17]

Where does this desexualization of disabled people come from? What causes it? Zhisheva suggests that it comes from culture and not from nature—disabled people are not naturally a-sexual. This is the main thrust of her argument and it is rearticulated at several points throughout the essay:

> with time I also found out something that perhaps will seem preposterous or intolerable [*nelepo i nedopustimo*] . . . or grotesque. I found out that I, a woman with impairment, think, desire, seek and have a need—a real and completely normal need—for sex. . . . I was a normal person and needed sex just as much as I needed food when I was hungry or medical assistance when in pain. I needed sex just as much as everyone else.[18]

For Zhisheva, desexualization of disabled people is a question of "upbringing," "attitudes," "societal perception."[19] It is made, not given. Zhisheva also identifies the particular socio-cultural construct that is responsible for desexualization—the perception of impairment as inherently negative, as "something ugly that, with its very essence [*sas samata si sashtnost*], kills the desire for beauty."[20] "I was ugly. I was crippled. I was prejudged as being no good. I was not entitled to sex."[21] This negative understanding is tied to a stifling charity attitude: "Just about that time—as if from the Salvation Army . . .—good relatives and friends visited and labored to convince me that one can live without sex."[22] But most importantly, this negative understanding is solidified through internalization: "I was slowly killing myself, day after day going down, deeper and deeper into the sticky swamp of self-pity."[23] If one is not able to disregard the part of one's self that is invested with negativity, this negativity tends to take over one's whole being. Silence becomes self-imposed, negativity transforms into self-hatred and oppression is internalized:

> I resented life, fate, God, the physicians who injected me with the live vaccine against polio. I resented my doom, my ugliness, myself, nature for creating male and female persons, my natural desires. . . . I came to hate my breasts that disobediently continued to react as an erogenous zone whenever unwittingly touched. I wanted to vanish from this world, not to be there, to have never existed. . . . My God, I came to be ashamed of myself—I was deformed, incomplete, useless! I was so convinced of this ugliness and uselessness of mine that even if someone told me he had feelings about me, I just did not believe him—I thought that he did it solely out of courtesy, because he realized how much it would hurt me if he disregarded me too.[24]

The self-hatred related to "internalized oppression"[25] comes with cynicism and is self-perpetuating—one tends to unwittingly treat others in such a way that they will react negatively: "I became evil and cruel and people did not like me."[26] What is the way out of this vicious self-negating trap? Zhisheva's text suggests that the solution is to recognize its imposed or constructed character and thus to restore the externality of this negativity—in other words, to denaturalize existential-ontological negation. In disability studies, this has been aided by pointing out the disabling features of the built environment that people with impairments inhabit (see Chapter 6). Some poststructuralist disability scholars have also highlighted the disabling features of knowledge/power constructs, including those concerning "impairment."[27] Another option, suggested by the feminist strand of disability studies, has been to locate negativity in the objectifying "male gaze."[28] This last possibility is actually hinted at by Zhisheva when she refers bitterly to "those who did not see the woman in me but noticed only my deformed bottom and the apparatuses"[29]— "[b]ecause men judge whether a woman is 'good' by the size of her breasts, the length of the legs and the behind."[30] But Zhisheva does not elaborate this critique of sexual objectification and its relation to disability. Instead, she chooses to focus on the technical aids—the orthopedic leg braces—she utilizes in order to get about:

> I found out that in order to have sex, I have to take off my iron apparatuses . . . and they are ugly. They have never been part of me, yet they are my physical independence—I can move from here to there only with them. I came to hate them and I have hated them to date. . . . I hated these iron things, I regarded them as fetters, they enveloped [*obvivaha*] not only my body, but also my soul. Yes, I felt pain in my apparatuses [*moite aparati me bolyaha*].[31]

This attitude toward the leg braces is ambivalent. On the one hand, they provide independence, on the other hand, they are "fetters." Zhisheva asserts that they are not part of her, but they still "envelope" her body and her soul to the point where she can feel pain in them. The reason for this ambivalence is that, while technical aids enable a person to exercise agency on one level, on another level they also "help to disable by working to reproduce the conditions for the making of difference and disability in the first instance."[32] Similar to the everyday environment from the case study in Chapter 6, assistive technology embodies a corporeal norm. Consequently, it can cause the bodily difference of "impairment" to seem *problematic* or, in other words, to *dys*-appear by *appearing as* dys-functional.[33] Indeed, it is not simply that the "iron apparatuses" are themselves "ugly," the problem is that they make the person who uses them "ugly": "In the beginning I tried to hide them by all means, but I was never successful—they always meanly exposed themselves and betrayed my incompleteness, my difference. They made me ugly."[34] Yet being *detachable*, in both material *and* cultural sense, mobility aids can also disburden the person and her body from self-hatred; they can translate self-directed hatred into object-directed discontent. More generally, as something made, as something constructed, technology testifies that the "ugliness" of the impaired body is itself not given.

The turning point comes with an encounter. A young man approaches Zhisheva in a disco club and asks her whether she dances. Still trapped in the self-perpetuating pattern of internalized oppression, she immediately assumes that he is mocking at her and retorts: "I do not dance. Don't you see that I am an invalid [*invalid*]."[35] Yet it turns out that he is not interested in her body, but in her soul: "I did not ask about your body. I asked about your soul. I cannot dance either, and I am not an invalid. No, believe me, beautiful music can make my soul really dance."[36] At that, the man looks at Zhisheva in a special way—his eyes are "childishly sincere" and he does not detach them from her eyes while speaking to her. It is this nonobjectifying look, coupled with the unexpected reply, that sets Zhisheva free from self-negation. She is able, for the first time, to detach herself from the negativity carried by her orthopedic devices: "Then, in this infinitely short moment, I understood—I loved through my soul and not through my legs, ugly as they were in the iron apparatuses."[37]

Notwithstanding the personal transformation, it seems that this new, emancipated self is still radically disembodied. Furthermore, the detachment of the soul from the body seems to reproduce the very pattern of desexualization that Zhisheva has criticized at the outset. Consequently, existential-ontological invalidation returns through the proverbial back door—the dis/ablist negation of bodily difference is re-inscribed at the very moment of its alleged overcoming. This problem predates every attempt at disability emancipation that relies on emphasizing *personhood*—or what has been criticized in the disability studies literature as the "'person first' ideology." As Michalko has argued, "[c]hoosing personhood over disability emphasises both the strength of personhood and its separation from the body."[38] The corollary is *inclusive exclusion* that effaces the difference able to make a difference:

Inclusion on the basis of privileging personhood over disability is thus never inclusionary. The difference-of-disability is always excluded in this version of inclusion. Social change is never part of such an inclusion.[39]

There are two considerations that at least complicate such a reading of Zhisheva's text. The first is that Zhisheva does not actually distance herself from her *body* but rather from her *technical aids*: "there are no orthopedic apparatuses for the soul. The free soul just does not need them."[40] The second consideration is related to Zhisheva's understanding of "soul." It seems that her use of the notion mirrors the phenomenological concept of "lived body" because Zhisheva actually proposes an *embodied* understanding of the soul: "Yes, I had a soul—and *she was able to dance*! Yes, I had a soul and she was able to love, to make love—and to be made love to [*Da, az imah dusha i tya umeeshe da obicha, da lyubi—i da bade lyubena*]."[41] It is this insight that leads to the conclusive reclaiming of positive self-identity. Importantly, this newly found identity is a sexually integrated identity, one which does not deny one's body and sexuality, but accepts and enacts them:

> Why did I allow myself to perceive myself as ugly, useless, deformed? This was absolutely not me! This was some other Nina, different from myself. I am Nina—with a fragrance of endless hot meadows, the ardent Nina, who also can burn hearts with her look, the exceptional Nina, the one and only, the unique. Nina, who can caress gently, who can whisper the sweetest words and make the loved one pulsate with happiness and desires. With the same happiness and desires that fill me.[42]

Zhisheva enhances this affirmative statement with a proud assertion of her motherhood: "Both of my children were conceived as a result of hot sexual experiences."[43] Thus she challenges another widespread stigma—that disabled persons, and particularly women, cannot be (good) parents: "Whereas motherhood is often seen as compulsory for women, disabled women are often denied or discouraged from the reproductive role that some feminists find oppressive."[44] The relationship between disability, sexuality, femininity and motherhood will be explored in the next section. I will finish this one with Zhisheva's last sentence that rearticulates the fundamental existential-ontological importance attributed to sexuality: "I don't know whether this is sex or joy, or love. . . . The only thing I know is that it is something wonderful, something that makes us human, us—women and men."[45]

"We talk about sex"

Let me now turn towards a collective reflection on the topic of sexuality and disability. The discussion took place in an internet forum hosted by the Bulgarian web portal dir.bg. It was held under the rubric "We talk about sex" (in Bulgarian: *Govorim za seks*). Neither the website, nor the forum, not even the rubric were specifically focused on disability-related issues—the setting was nonprofessional, nonspecialized and as mainstream as one can get. The mere fact that disability was discussed in the context of sexuality, rather than sexuality in the context of disability, made a difference. The discussion happened in 2004 and was renewed for a short while in 2007 with some of the original participants taking part in the later exchange as well. All the discussants participated anonymously, using nicknames instead of their real names. The personal information disclosed occasionally suggests that many of them had only a marginal interest in the topic of disability while some were relatives or friends of disabled people and only few were disability professionals (service providers). Most importantly, several participants identified themselves as disabled, thus enacting—like Zhisheva—the aforementioned "reclaiming the voice." Both male and female participants took part and no gender seems to have dominated the discussion, although gender-specific understandings did (as will be explained below). The number of participants can be estimated at 35, presuming that nobody used more than one nickname, which seems unlikely. The number of comments exchanged in 2004 was 71, with further 25 added in 2007, or 96 in total. All this testifies that the topic attracted significant interest.[46]

There are no indications that the discussion was triggered by a specific event. It was initiated by one of the participants who formulated its subject as "On bodily deficiencies" and its guiding question as "How many of you would accept your partner having physical impairments without this embarrassing you?" At some point during the discussion Zhisheva's essay was posted in full by another participant (judging by the personal information disclosed by this participant, it seem unlikely that it was Zhisheva herself). This posting stimulated further debate and testifies that the *Integral* magazine reached the mainstream. The collective and open nature of the dir.bg forum, coupled with participants' anonymity, elicited tacit yet widespread understandings of impairment, disability and sexuality. Even statements that were deliberately provocative or purposefully exaggerated drew on culturally available knowledges. While it is questionable that this open, collective and anonymous discussion produced more truth on the topic, it does seem that it did—and it still can—stimulate reflexive awareness of the mechanisms that produce and sustain such truths. As was the case with Zhisheva's essay, the material is too rich to be comprehensively covered within the thematic and material confines of this chapter. Therefore, I will restrict myself to outlining several important themes that relate directly to the foregoing analysis—silencing and desexualization, the meaning of impairment, medicalization, and gender. The translation of all the comments from Bulgarian is mine; they are referenced with the Latinized participants' nicknames in brackets.

Silencing and desexualization

The reflexivity hinted at in the preceding paragraph manifests itself at an early stage of the discussion. Echoing Zhisheva's essay, the silencing of discourses that bring together sexuality and disability is explicitly recognized and thematized: "what you are talking about is one of the many taboos. . . . And as a taboo it causes a spontaneous dread [*uzhas*] and/or denial [*otrichane*] in most people." (*Lilit*) The dread and/or denial brought about by the topic are seen as existentially motivated. Invoking a logic that reminds one of Tom Shakespeare's reflections on disability and the disavowal of frailty,[47] *Lilit* points out that impairment produces uneasiness because it is a reminder of human finitude: "physical impairments confront us with our own vulnerability and fragility." Reluctance to engage with the topic is openly expressed by another participant who regards the issue of disability as "too serious and important," concluding: "I do not see it as appropriate for this club [that is, the online discussion club 'We talk about sex']. People with impairments have too many problems for us to try to disentangle them here" (*GROZNIK 1*). This statement unwittingly reproduces the already highlighted "regime of truth" that regulates discourses on disability. It implies that "serious matters" should be addressed by "serious people" (read "experts") in "serious settings" (a number of such *special* places have existed in Bulgaria for a long time). As such, the statement is an instance of both desexualization and silencing—in response, the initiator of the discussion retorts: "the unwillingness to discuss such a topic here is also a form of discrimination against people with physical problems. They too have a right to sex and they have a right to speak about it" (*High Carbon Steel*). Accordingly, breaking the silence surrounding disabled people's sexuality is aptly regarded as a prerequisite for social change, where the very inclusion of disabled people in society is at stake:

> It is not enough to make the public transport and the public buildings accessible for them in order to integrate them [disabled people]. Social engagement is needed too. And a change of attitude, which has to do with the mind and begins with not disregarding the topic as a taboo. (*Kotkata Marta*)

This briefly sketched exchange revolves around the two issues that also served as points of departure for Zhisheva's essay: desexualization and silencing. In addition, it hints at the ways in which these dis/ablist operations are reproduced on an everyday level. People maintain regimes of truth by disciplining themselves and others with regard to what can be spoken, by whom and in what settings. The exchange also illuminates the possibility and importance of resistance to these everyday disciplinary pressures. Such resistance is important because it addresses sociopolitical and existential-ontological problems such as discrimination, exclusion and the disavowal of human finitude. Last but not least, the exchange testifies to the high degree of reflexivity of the discussants, facilitated, no doubt, by the possibility of publicly deliberating the issues of concern. Central among these issues is the meaning of impairment.

The meaning of impairment

From the outset of the discussion, impairment is regarded in negative terms, thus reproducing the hegemonic understanding of this type of bodily difference as a "limit without possibility"[48]—an understanding bound with the ontology of strong bodily realism, as argued in Chapter 2. The subject "On bodily deficiencies" (in Bulgarian: *Za telesnite nedostatatsi*) frames the corporeal differences to be discussed in terms of disadvantage or lack. The guiding question "How many of you would accept your partner having physical impairments without this embarrassing you [*bez tova da vi smuti*]?" implies that impairments themselves cause distress. The negativity conveyed by such wording becomes conspicuous if one considers alternative ways of posing the question, for example: "What are the physical characteristics of your partner that do not comply with the norm and that attract you?" One could also change the addressee of the utterance, again with significant consequences: "What are the physical oddities of yours that attract your partner?" Questioning, in other words, operates in a twofold manner. It is indispensable for opening up discursive "clearings" where phenomena can appear and become accessible. Yet questioning also *confines* the discoursing parties to the worlds thus disclosed. A symptom of such confinement is the production of tautologies such as this one: "Bodily deficiencies are misfortune for the people who have them" (*GROZNIK 1*). Even those discussants who attempt to challenge the presupposed negativity of impairment tend to fall back upon it. The reason is that this negativity is implied in the very terms that allow them to take part in the discussion in the first place: "It is not so much that the people themselves are those who do not accept the bodily deficiencies of their partner, but the surrounding ones, the others" (*razbiram*). Note that it would be very difficult for me to "accept" my bodily *difference* if it is regarded as *deficiency* in the first place.

On the other hand, the understanding of impairment as intrinsically negative does not—and *cannot*—hold absolute sway over participants. Even within the naturalized negativity of impairment a degree of uncertainty is present. For example, impairment is regarded as self-evidently problematic; it is *given* (not made) as problematic; it is conceived as problematic outside any interpretive economy, outside culture, language, understanding, meaning: "It is as though we are something disgusting that does not deserve to exist. It [what we are] does not deserve [to exist], but nevertheless it is a fact" (*High Carbon Steel*). And yet, *High Carbon Steel* also points out that "to have a physical problem practically means to be marked for life." Now, to denote impairment as a "mark" suggests that impairment *is* actually implicated in a particular interpretive economy. From such a perspective, impairment is a *sign*. Yet again, it is a special kind of a sign—one that cannot be effaced and has a fixed meaning. Nevertheless, such rendering suggests that the problem of impairment is an *interpretive problem*, a problem of an interpretation that has gone rigid, an interpretation lacking plasticity or flexibility: "my experience shows that they [disabled people] remain to a great extent confined in their own environment . . . mostly because other people avoid them, even if they do not want it—these are instincts" (*hose*).

Is then impairment something naturally negative or something culturally negative? Can it be one without being the other? Can it be both, without undermining the very distinction between "natural" and "cultural"? Such questions implicitly challenge the intrinsic negativity of the bodily difference of "impairment" within the very terms that take it for granted. In addition, there are discussants who challenge this negativity explicitly: "what I cannot understand is why you decided that impairment is a misfortune" (*she the wolf*). Some come even closer to the "affirmative model" of disability[49] by finding beauty in impairment: "One of the men who has impressed me most is blind—the curious thing is that his eyes are incredibly beautiful, beautiful blind eyes" (*SilentEnigma*). Chapter 2 linked the possibility for such articulations, the logic that guides them and the questions that motivate them to the ontology of weak bodily realism.

The negativity of impairment is also at stake in distinguishing between "minor" and "major" impairments, or between "physical" and "mental" impairments, where the former are regarded as acceptable or even as "charming extra[s]" (*alexbg67*), while the latter—as unacceptable, particularly in the context of intimate and/or sexual relations. A number of participants make such claims, for example: "Blindness and limping—OK. But imagine that you are in bed with a person who has chunks instead of arms; or with a woman who, instead of a breast, has a hole" (*seriozna 36*); "The only and most dangerous [impairments] are mental and emotional deficiency; everything else makes the loved one even more unique" (*Sex Maniac*). While as a rule such statements reproduce and reinforce dis/ablism, they nevertheless highlight another internal instability of meaning—the *scope* of the concept of "impairment" cannot be fixed and its boundary is subject to constant negotiations.[50] This is also reflected in the frequent uncertainties and disputes about what counts as "acceptable" or "unacceptable" impairments: "But otherwise I also know a family where the man has had both legs amputated at the knee. He was like that when they met. And they have lived harmoniously for many years" (*seriozna 36*); "My mother has a serious physical impairment of the right half of her body but I am always pleased to see how my father watches her with that carried-away look" (*SilentEnigma*).

To summarize, the online discussion incorporated numerous implicit and explicit challenges to the understanding of the bodily difference of "impairment" as intrinsically negative—an understanding that nevertheless marks the discussion's point of departure. Implicit challenges betray the inherent instability of attempts to fix the meaning of bodily difference. Explicit challenges testify to the subversive potential of collective reflection on disability and sexuality. In both cases, the mechanisms of subversion are similar to the ones mobilized by Zhisheva in her essay—they make corporeal negativity appear less private, less natural, and/or less fixed. Nevertheless, the understanding of the bodily difference of impairment as intrinsically negative retains its hegemony throughout the discussion. One of the main reasons for this is the pervasive medicalization of disability-related discourses and practices.

Medicalization

Drawing on their research with disabled people in the United Kingdom, Shakespeare, Gillespie-Sells and Davies point out that "[i]n the realm of sex and love, the generalised assumption that disability is a medical tragedy becomes dominant and inescapable."[51] The medicalization of disability is also hegemonic in Bulgaria, as argued in the analysis of Bulgarian disability assessment in Chapter 3, and is among the most consistent features of the discussions on disabled people's sexuality, even when they explicitly endeavor to challenge dis/ablism. Disabled people, their outlook, lifestyles, life chances and life choices are constantly counterposed to those of *healthy* people. Below are some examples of how medicalization manifests itself in everyday discourse, taken from the dir.bg discussion:

A healthy woman, who nevertheless is marked with huge purple spots on her skin, would agree much more readily to have a relation with a blind person than someone who is impeccably beautiful (otherwise who is going to admire her beauty). (*Kurator*)

it is not possible for a healthy person to fall in love with an impaired [*nedagav*] one, this only happens in the movies . . . (*GROZNIK 1*)

the truth is that even if someone has been born completely healthy, nobody, absolutely no person is insured that she or he won't be injured some day and go over to the category "invalid." (*Lilit*)

people with disabilities do not have problems . . . the healthy have problems with them . . . (*she the wolf*)

Every time [I visit the pool] I see how she swims more than all the healthy women in the pool. She has a great body, despite her problem. I admire her because of her incredible will . . . (*Idiotche*)

In these examples the distinction between those who are "healthy" and those who are not is used to organize different and even mutually challenging arguments about disability and intimacy. The first comment underlines the importance of appearance, engaging in what has been identified by Hughes as "aesthetic invalidation"[52] of disabled people. The argument is furthermore gendered—it is a woman who is expected to be worried about appearance, an issue that I will elaborate on below. Most importantly, the possibility for intimacy is *grounded* in deficiency. Thus not only individuals, but also their intimate relations are seen as governed by privation—it is not that Mariyka is attracted to Ivancho, it is that lack of beauty is attracted to lack of sight. The second comment rearticulates this conviction in negativity-driven intimacy. Disabled people are lumped together on the basis of pure and simple privation—they are alike because they all *lack* something.[53] The third comment is of a different sort—it highlights the universal precariousness of human condition, articulating a reminder of finitude that is supposed to enhance acceptance and understanding of difference. Similarly intended, the fourth comment points toward the attitudinal barriers that create problems for disabled people. Finally, the fifth comment attempts to challenge negative perceptions of disability by rendering it in heroic terms, in terms of "overcoming"—a strategy that nevertheless takes the intrinsic negativity of impairment for granted. Notwithstanding their differences, all these statements about disabled people's bodies, identities, relationships and lives invoke the notion of "health." Crawford has pointed out that "[i]n modern societies, the meaningful practice of health is inextricably linked to the science, practice and layered meanings of biomedicine."[54] The persistent recourse to "health" is then both a manifestation and an effect of medicalization, especially when disability-related issues are concerned.

This becomes clear in cases when medicalization is bound up with the belief in reproduction as the ultimate purpose of life. Although pro-natalism has been in decline since the beginning of the Bulgarian "transition" in 1989, 74.2 percent of female and 67.9 percent of male Bulgarians, responding to the European Values Study of 2008, still maintained that a woman needs to have children in order to fulfill herself as a person.[55] Some of the participants in the dir.bg discussion reproduce these values in uncompromising terms: "the main aim of men and women getting together is to have children" (*Kradets na sartsa*). Accordingly, it is suggested that disabled people are excluded from sexual discourses and practices due to our instinctive striving to "pair" with healthy partners—in order to secure healthy genes, guaranteeing healthy offspring. True, not every physical impairment is genetic—and even if it is, it does not necessarily preclude the person from creating completely healthy children. But here we are speaking about instincts and primary reactions which for most of the people are not conscious and thought through [a]nd which serve the purpose of our survival as a biological species over the course of evolution. (*Lilit*)

In this vision, "offspring" provides a fixed teleological point of reference for human existence. The meaning of human life is to reproduce itself on the biological level—that is, "to secure healthy genes, guaranteeing healthy offspring" or, more generally, to survive as a species. Notably, such an understanding wholeheartedly espouses the norm of health and it is indeed hard to imagine modern reproduction outside the purview of medical professionals, institutions and technologies.[56] Steeped thus in medicalized biologism, *Lilit's* statement clearly incorporates the objective mode of existential-ontological reduction explored in the chapters on disability assessment (Chapter 3) and discrimination (Chapter 5). Against this reductive background, the difference of impairment is bound to seem problematic. According to *Lilit*, impairment is instinctively equated with lack of health—a lack that is seen as transferable to the offspring. Consequently, suggests *Lilit*, people with impairments tend to be automatically excluded from the reproductive equation, and with it—from discourses and practices of sexuality.

   In sum, the medicalized notion of health imposes a hierarchical classificatory order on human diversity through reference to a norm—"healthy partners," "healthy genes," "healthy offspring" or "healthy children." It thereby impairs the ability to imagine intimate and/or sexual relations without constantly referring to the "naturally given" ideal of able-bodiedness. This ideal feeds on reducing human beings to objectively measurable biological entities whose contribution to the "survival of the species" can be clearly determined in medical terms. Yet besides being medicalized, the normative ideal of the "healthy body" is also gendered, which significantly adds to its rigidity and power.

Gender

Despite the inclusion of women in nondomestic labor, the state-socialist regime remained patriarchal in many important respects.[57] Postsocialist societies have reasserted these patriarchal values in a process of "re-traditionalization . . ., where women have been ushered back into hearth and home, while men play the dominant roles in the new market economies and new political structures."[58] In her analysis of disability in present-day Ukraine, Phillips has convincingly shown how disabled Ukrainians negotiate their identities *within* this male-centered regime of knowledge/power, especially where sexuality is concerned.[59] Similar considerations have been put forward by Iarskaia-Smirnova with regard to disability and sexuality in contemporary Russia.[60] It is therefore unsurprising that many of the participants in the dir.bg discussion reproduced patriarchal understandings about the roles of men and women in society.

In a world dominated by masculinist visions and values, framing impairment in terms of "lack" parallels how the feminine is also understood in terms of "lack." As explained in Chapter 1, this hierarchical binary framework stems from the metaphysics of presence and reflects the work of privation that defines ontologically an entity as a lacking version of another, "ontologically complete" entity. Thus "[b]oth the female and the disabled body are cast as deviant and inferior; both are excluded from full participation in public as well as economic life; both are defined in opposition to a norm that is assumed to possess natural physical superiority."[61] On the one hand, the perception of disabled people, male and female alike, as weak, incapable or *lacking* is often enhanced by feminizing the bodily difference of impairment: "What better way to exclude a legally blind boy than to feminize the biology of his eyes? What better way to exclude me from the 'guys' than to castrate me—'cunt eyes'."[62] On the other hand, the *lack* associated with being a woman in a man's world is often perceived as the ultimate impairment. Take, for example, the following playful exchange, lavishly decorated with smiling and winking faces in the original: "Well done, lass!!!" (*she the wolf*, responding to a comment by *Jolee*)—"What lass, she has an internal impairment (of the hymen)" (*O!Sag*)—"I love people with a sense of humor. You are right, my hymen is irreparably impaired" (*Jolee*).

Another aspect of the male-centered culture is the association of masculinity with active agency and femininity with aesthetic appearance. Accordingly, the questions asked with regard to disabled people's sexuality tend to follow two distinct, gender-specific formulas: (a) Can disabled men be sexually *active* despite their impairments? (b) Can disabled women be sexually *attractive* despite their impairments?[63] On the one hand, disabled men's sexuality is defended with respect to potency or the ability to perform sexually: "We are greater lovers than some of the healthy who are filled with complexes to the edges of their hair" (*neponosim*). If the presentation of a man is important, it is so only insofar as it manifests an ability to display sexual potency, physical strength and/or economic power: "Well, as the saying goes, 'The true man is recognized even when naked', so why care about [bodily] deficiencies" (*Sex Maniac*). On the other hand, the sexuality of disabled women is defended (or denied) with respect to aesthetic appearance, as suggested in the comment cited above about the hypothetical woman with "huge purple spots on her skin" (*Kurator*). Feminine appearance is seen as important in order to *attract* sexual attention and action. Reproducing and embodying this pattern, the Bulgarian postsocialist "transition" has given birth and popularity to an odd couple: a stocky man dressed in trainers and track suit with a crew-cut hairstyle and an obligatory golden chain around his thick neck, accompanied by a slender woman with a fancy haircut, high heels, glossy clothing and expensive makeup. Disabled Bulgarians are excluded from this embodied ideal, where the masculine power to act complements and is complemented by the feminine ability to become an object of action. Indeed, similar to the feminine body, the impaired body is also objectified; but while the feminine body is objectified as a *sexual object*,[64] the impaired body is objectified as an *a-sexual object*,[65] mostly within the medicalized regimes of truth. This kind of asexual objectification is at the heart of the already discussed desexualization of disabled people.

Things get more complicated when familialist and reproductive expectations are added to the patriarchal mix. Familialism—the view that the nuclear family (comprising a father, a mother and child/ren) is the defining element of good life—is still strong in Bulgaria. Summarizing data from the European Values Study of 2008, Bulgarian sociologists point out that "[d]espite the crisis of the family institution, the family continues to be an absolute value [*bezprekoslovna tsennost*] for the Bulgarians."[66] In such a context, women are expected to be good mothers as well as attractive sexual objects. For some discussants these two roles collide: "It is just that I desire the woman who stays with me to be perfect, but if she is perfect, she will not be a good mother of her children. . . . You know the saying, better an 'unworthy' [*nestruvashta*] woman in your hands and in your home with the children than a beautiful, intelligent and bright one outside" (*Hishtnik*). Other discussants see women's sexual appeal as a prerequisite for reproduction: "A woman, no matter how hollow her nut is [sic], has no problems with reproducing given that she has big tits, a tight body and nice butt." (*High Carbon Steel*). Notably, "[t]he same goes for a man, but in this case it is money which can secure him reproduction" (*High Carbon Steel*). The appearance versus agency dichotomy is clearly expressed here. Women are sexually valuable when aesthetically attractive and men when they are economically potent. In addition, sexuality is reduced to an instrument for procreation—a position that, again, excludes disabled people, for they as a rule tend to be "instinctively" (*Lilit*) left out of the reproductive equation.

These gendered expectations are not fixed. Sometimes, it is disabled men's sexuality that is salvaged through recourse to "beauty": "Is a man like Andrea Bocelli not beautiful? Does the fact that he is blind make him ugly or rather different but still beautiful?" (*razbiram*). There are also those discussants who, similarly to Zhisheva, question the sexual objectification of women (but note the structural similarity with *Kurator*'s comment about "purple spots" and blindness): "Do you make love to a woman only because of her body? Aren't you attracted by her eyes, her radiance, her internal world, her sensibility, her principles, etc. Isn't it possible to fall in love with all these things and thus to become blind to her impairment?" (*debi*). Notwithstanding these occasional challenges, the gendered expectations of the male-centered worldview rooted in the metaphysics of presence remain hegemonic throughout the discussion. Together with the taken-for-granted negativity of impairment and medicalization, these rigid gendered expectations contribute to desexualization and the attendant existential-ontological invalidation of disabled people.

Concluding remarks

In this chapter, I explored the conjunction of sexuality and disability. I focused on the social, political and cultural aspects of this intertwining, but I also looked at it in existential-ontological terms. Similar to the practices of disability assessment, personal assistance, disability-based discrimination and media coverage of disability, explored in Chapters 3–6, nonexpert public discourses on sexuality and disability also incorporate existential-ontological reductions and translate bodily differences identified as "impairments" into undermining of disabled people's existence. I showed how such translation reproduces common, everyday understandings of the body. Two sources of information were used—an autobiographical essay and an internet discussion. Their analysis highlighted several general points.

First, the topic of sexuality and disability is overwhelmingly *silenced*, mainly by subjecting it to an expert-centered regime of truth. This silencing is directly related to a pervasive *desexualization* of disabled people that is existentially-ontologically invalidating. Second, in the rare instances when they take place, nonexpert public discourses on disability and sexuality tend to be medicalized, thus reflecting the hegemony of medical knowledge, experts, institutions, technologies and practices in the domain of disability in Bulgaria. Third, the bodily difference of impairment is as a rule understood in *negative* terms—as deficiency or lack. This understanding, supported by medicalization, pro-natalism and familialism in discussions on sexuality, adds to the perception of disabled people as asexual beings, and accordingly, to the undermining of their existence. Fourth, impairment-related discourses are gendered along *patriarchal* lines. Thus gender-specific expectations informed by a male-centered worldview (genealogically traceable to the metaphysics of presence) regulate the constitution of disabled people's identity, particularly when sexuality is concerned. All these mechanisms contribute to the (re) production of dis/ablism in Bulgaria and, on the ontological level, to the undermining of disabled people's being.

At the same time, various instances of resistance to dis/ablism were also highlighted in the context and content of Zhisheva's essay and the dir. bg discussion. Echoing the preceding two chapters, I underlined the crucial importance of *opening up spaces* or "clearings" that accommodate alternative meanings. In this chapter, such clearings were provided by nonexpert public reflection on sexuality and disability. The acts of disclosing and maintaining such clearings themselves work to subvert dis/ablist practices. This subversion is greatly enhanced when those who are usually "spoken about"—that is, disabled people themselves—*reclaim their voices* by speaking publicly on their own sexuality. My analysis also suggested that the negative meanings attributed to particular bodily differences are inherently unstable, thus reaffirming a key corollary drawn from the study of discrimination in Chapter 5. Consequently, dis/ablism can be undermined by exploiting and amplifying such inherent instability of meaning, particularly within discourses on sexuality where corporeal understandings are pivotal. In addition, it is also important to openly and explicitly challenge the taken-for-granted negativity of impairment. Yet such direct challenges are also prone to suffer the strongest repulse. In sum, each and every one of the aforementioned practices of resistance needs to be deliberately cherished in attempts at overcoming dis/ablism.

In this chapter, I relied on two major concepts—the notion of "dis/ablism" borrowed from disability studies and the notion of "lived body" borrowed from phenomenology. While the former was explicitly used throughout the analysis, the latter was mostly implied in the ongoing refusal to take the intrinsic negativity of impairment for granted. I see this refusal as crucial for challenging dis/ablism. The argument was fully developed in Chapter 2 where I explained in more detail how the notion of "lived body" provides for such a refusal while retaining an embodied understanding of human being. If it cannot be denied that physicality delimits human capacities, neither can it be denied that these limits appear as limits and do matter only within a world, a "context within which relations of objects and activities are organized and make sense."[67] In Chapter 2, the idea that bodily limits are always already mediated by inhabiting a world was linked to the position of weak bodily realism. From its perspective, any "excess" with respect to meaning is itself constituted within the meaning-engendering context.[68] Even if impairment is conceived in terms of such "excess," it still cannot be reduced to a "limit without possibility."[69] On the most general level, what exceeds meaning has the unique power to feedback and refresh it: "Encounters with excess can develop into crisis points, historical events in which meaning is refreshed or transformed; such events open new realms of meaning that, in turn, make it possible for us to encounter excess afresh."[70] More specifically, bodily differences—including those usually identified as "impairments"—bear the potential to refashion not only our customary identities and practices, but also the worlds we inhabit. In a dis/ablist culture there is a pressing need to realize this potential through strategies for recognition and affirmation. Key among these strategies is breaking the public silence on sexuality and disability by challenging expert-dominated regimes of truth. In Chapter 8, this argument about the importance of non-expert participation in public deliberations on disability will be applied to issues concerning legality.

Notes

1 Sarah D. Phillips, *Disability and Mobile Citizenship in Postsocialist Ukraine* (Bloomington, IN: Indiana University Press, 2011), 176.

2 Ilona Tomova, "Those who are different: between stigma and recognition," in *European Values in Bulgarian Society Today*, ed. Georgi Fotev (Sofia: St. Kliment Ohridski University Press, 2009), 146.

3 This situation suggestively parallels the one concerning homosexuality: "The prohibition of discrimination on the basis of sexual orientation is incorporated in a number of normative acts, and particularly in the Law for Protection against Discrimination. At the same time, in the country there is actually no public debate on the problems of homosexuals as problems of power relations in a society that is dominated by hierarchical sexist attitudes." Ibid., 147.

4 Harlan Hahn, "Can disability be beautiful?" in *Perspectives on Disability. Text and Readings on Disability*, ed. Mark Nagler (Palo Alto, CA: Health Markets Research, 1990), 314.

5 On the former, see Tom Shakespeare, Kath Gillespie-Sells and Dominic Davies, *The Sexual Politics of Disability: Untold Desires* (New York: Cassell, 1996); on the latter, see Phillips, *Disability*, 182–3, and Elena Iarskaia-Smirnova, "The stigma over the sexuality of 'invalids,'" in *In Search of Sexuality*, eds. Elena Zdravomyslova and Anna Temkina (St Petersburg: 'Dmitrii Bulanin' Publishing House, 2002).

6 Shakespeare, Gillespie-Sells and Davies, *Sexual Politics*, 3.

7 Bill Hughes, "Medicine and the aesthetic invalidation of disabled people." *Disability & Society* 15, 4 (2000): 564.

8 Michel Foucault, *Power/Knowledge: Selected Interviews and Other Writings, 1972–1977* (New York: Pantheon Books, 1980), 131.

9 See Hahn, "Can disability be beautiful?" 312–3.

10 Laura A. Milner, "Voice giving (way)," *Disability Studies Quarterly* 13, 3 (2011): n.p. The resolute action of Petar Kichashki discussed in Chapter 5, although unrelated to sexuality, can also be referred to as a case of emancipatory "reclaiming the voice."

11 Bulgarians usually use the word *uvrezhdane* to refer to the bodily difference denoted by British social model theorists as "impairment" (e.g., Michael Oliver, *Understanding Disability: From Theory to Practice*. London: Macmillan, 1996). In this sense, *uvrezhdane* is also used interchangeably with the word *nedag*. Following the social model of disability, I translate *uvrezhdane*, as well as *nedag*, as "impairment." Yet in the instances of more ambiguous usage I translate *uvrezhdane* as "disability" in order to preserve the allusion to the social aspects of the phenomenon implied in the original utterance. My translation is then simultaneously an interpretation informed by the British social model of disability. The relationship between translation and interpretation will be explored in more detail in Chapter 8.

12 Nina Zhisheva, "I, my impairment and sex." *Integral* 2 (2002): 6. The translation from Bulgarian is mine.

13 Ibid.

14 Shakespeare, Gillespie-Sells and Davies, *Sexual Politics*, 3.

15 Dan Goodley and Katherine Runswick-Cole, "The violence of disablism." *Sociology of Health & Illness* 33, 4 (2011): 608.

16 Kevin Paterson and Bill Hughes, "Disability studies and phenomenology: the carnal politics of everyday life." *Disability & Society* 14, 5 (1999): 604.

17 Zhisheva, "I, my impairment and sex," 8.

18 Ibid., 7–8.

19 Ibid., 6.

20 Ibid.

21 Ibid., 8.

22 Ibid.

23 Ibid.

24 Ibid., 7–8.

25 Micheline Mason, "Internalized oppression," in *Disability Equality in Education*, eds. Richard Rieser and Micheline Mason (London: Inner London Education, 1990). See also Fiona Kumari Campbell, *Contours of Ableism: The Production of Disability and Abledness* (Basingstoke: Palgrave Macmillan, 2009), 16–29.

26 Zhisheva, "I, my impairment and sex," 8; see also p. 9.

27 Shelley Tremain, "On the subject of impairment," in *Disability/Postmodernity: Embodying Disability Theory*, eds. Mairian Corker and Tom Shakespeare (London: Continuum, 2002).

28 Rosemarie Garland Thomson, *Extraordinary Bodies: Figuring Physical Disability in American Culture and Literature* (New York: Columbia University Press, 1997), 26.

29 Zhisheva, "I, my impairment and sex," 8.

30 Ibid., 7.

31 Ibid.

32 Ingunn Moser, "Disability and the promises of technology: technology, subjectivity and embodiment within an order of the normal." *Information, Communication & Society* 9, 3 (2006): 388–9.

33 Paterson and Hughes, "Disability studies and phenomenology," 602–4; see also Chapter 2 of the present investigation.

34 Zhisheva, "I, my impairment and sex," 7.

35 Ibid., 9.

36 Ibid.

37 Ibid.

38 Rod Michalko, *The Difference that Disability Makes* (Philadelphia: Temple University Press, 2002), 10–11.

39 Ibid., 155; see also the discussion of "ontological privation" in Chapter 1.

40 Zhisheva, "I, my impairment and sex," 9.

41 Ibid., emphasis in the original.

42 Ibid.

43 Ibid.

44 Thomson, *Extraordinary Bodies*, 26.

45 Zhisheva, "I, my impairment and sex," 9.

46 The archive can be found online at http://clubs.dir.bg/showthreaded.php?Board=talkabout&Number=1942347955, accessed September 27, 2013.

47 Tom Shakespeare, "Cultural representation of disabled people: dustbins for disavowal?" *Disability & Society* 9, 3 (1994): 283–99.

48 Tanya Titchkosky, "Disability in the news: a reconsideration of reading." *Disability & Society* 20, 6 (2005): 657.

49 John Swain and Sally French, "Towards an affirmation model of disability." *Disability & Society* 15, 4 (2000): 569–82.

50 See Thomson, *Extraordinary Bodies*, 12–15.

51 Shakespeare, Gillespie-Sells and Davies, *Sexual Politics*, 10.

52 Bill Hughes, "Medicine and the aesthetic invalidation of disabled people." *Disability & Society* 15, 4 (2000): 555–68.

53 The implications of this logic were outlined in Chapters 1 and 2 and were revisited in the chapters on disability assessment (Chapter 3) and discrimination (Chapter 5).

54 Robert Crawford, "Health as a meaningful social practice." *Health: An Interdisciplinary Journal for the Social Study of Health, Illness and Medicine* 10, 4 (2006): 403.

55 Alexey Pamporov, "The crisis of marriage as an institution, familialism, and the new forms of family," in *European Values in Bulgarian Society Today*, ed. Georgi Fotev (Sofia: St. Kliment Ohridski University Press, 2009), 162. The European Values Study is available online at www.europeanvaluesstudy.eu.

56 See Soren Holm, "The medicalization of reproduction—a 30 year retrospective," in *Reprogen-Ethics and the Future of Gender*, ed. Frida Simonstein (London & New York: Springer, 2009).

57 Tomova, "Those who are different," 134–6.

58 Phillips, *Disability*, 178.

59 Ibid.

60 Iarskaia-Smirnova, "The stigma over the sexuality of 'invalids.'"

61 Thomson, *Extraordinary Bodies*, 19.

62 Michalko, *Difference*, 20–1.

63 Phillips makes the following observation, reflecting on a mobility seminar for wheelchair users in Ukraine: "whereas most of the men at the meeting used active wheelchairs, the majority of women participants used large, so-called 'room' or home wheelchairs, or lever-drive chairs operated by pumping two levers with the hands" (Phillips, *Disability*, 176). Thus the assignment of gendered lifestyles is mediated by assistive technology. What are these lifestyles? According to Phillips, "[g]oing out in public (being mobile) is seen as an important aspect of masculinity, but women seem more worried by their visible imperfections and are given more leeway to stay at home in their 'traditional' setting" (Ibid., 186).

64 Iris Marion Young, *On Female Body Experience: "Throwing Like a Girl" and Other Essays* (Oxford: Oxford University Press, 2005), 38–44. Young's reflections on the sexual objectification of women are clearly homologous to the analyses of the medicalized objectification of disabled people developed in the present work: "the woman lives her body as object as well as subject. The source of this is that patriarchal society defines woman as object, as a mere body, and that in sexist society women are in fact frequently regarded by others as objects and mere bodies. An essential part of the situation of being a woman is that of living the ever-present possibility that one will be gazed upon as a mere body, as shape and flesh that presents itself as the potential object of another subject's intentions and manipulations, rather than as a living manifestation of action and intention" (Ibid., 44).

65 Hahn, "Can disability be beautiful?" 315.

66 Pamporov, "The crisis of marriage," 167; see also Tomova, "Those who are different," 143.

67 Mark A. Wrathall, "Existential phenomenology," in *A Companion to Phenomenology and Existentialism*, ed. Hubert L. Dreyfus and Mark A. Wrathall (Oxford: Blackwell, 2006), 38.

68 See also Richard Polt, "Meaning, excess, and event," *Gatherings: The Heidegger Circle Annual* 1 (2011).

69 Titchkosky, "Disability in the news," 657.

70 Polt, "Meaning, excess, and event," 28.

8

The UN Convention
on the Rights of Persons
with Disabilities

So far, the analyses of the United Nations Convention on the Rights of Persons with Disabilities (CRPD) have been dominated by juridical commentary. The papers collected in the volume under the editorship of Arnardóttir and Quinn might serve as an authoritative example.[1] Legal expertise has led the way in thinking about the treaty, informed mainly by readings of international and national regulations and court decisions. Indispensable in its own right, this focus on legality has nevertheless left important issues related to the meaning of the CRPD unexplored. Proceeding from the presumption that the interpretation of legal instruments such as the CRPD has an irreducible extra-juridical dimension, in this chapter I will seek to complement the juridical approach to the CRPD with a phenomenologically informed study of the constitution of its meaning.

The initial stimulus came from critical disability scholarship. In her analysis of the US disability rights legislation, Marta Russell highlights the inefficiency of positive provisions in a system that promotes *laissez faire* and deregulation.[2] Furthermore, the interpretation of rights is said to be influenced by the material and/or symbolic inequalities that permeate society. Some groups wield more economic, social and cultural power than others because of their positions defined along axes such as class, ethnicity, gender, and disability. Those with more power are more likely to influence interpretation, to "bend" it in accordance with their own positions. This social and political aspect can remain inconspicuous, which on its behalf serves to maintain the *status quo* of power inequalities. One strategy to keep the politics of interpretation covered up is by uncritically regarding meaning as *fixed* or *pre-given*; another strategy is to represent the procedures involved in interpreting as *neutral* or *immaterial*. But even in cases when neutrality of procedure can be taken at face value, the *access* to it might still be problematic:

> Civil rights, for instance, are based on the premise that the individual citizen is an equal actor in the judicial process with the legal power to redress injustice through court challenges to discrimination, but what if the individual, due to her class position, lacks the money to hire an attorney, or has not the education or circumstance to secure those rights?[3]

This critical reasoning has made some disability scholars inclined toward materialist explanations to doubt the possibility of redressing disability-related injustices through recourse to purely legal means.[4] The historical-materialist analysis is usually deployed on the *macro-level* of the social, political and economic organization of society. It regards the situation of disabled people in terms of oppression and traces it to issues such as ideology, relations of production, structural unemployment, class exploitation, conflict of interests and so forth. To approach disability in these terms is politically poignant and analytically relevant, yet not without its limitations and risks. In its extreme versions, the materialist critique is predated by determinism and reductionism, whose corollaries are reified analytical categories, exclusionary identity politics that imposes rigid divisions between "us" and "them," and insufficient reflexivity. Such issues can effectively be addressed without abandoning the critical project by complementing it with analyses deployed on the *micro-level*. Proceeding from this methodological presumption, the case studies presented in the preceding chapters endeavored to combine critical reasoning with phenomenologically informed attention to detail.

In this chapter, I would like to propose an analysis of the CRPD that attends to the extra-juridical details of the way its meaning is achieved. On the one hand, the *ends* of my analysis will be similar to the ones pursued by Russell— to highlight the irreducibility of the extra-juridical dimension of meaning so that the gap between abstract liberal rights and concrete privations experienced by disabled people can effectively be bridged.[5] This, in my opinion, requires the active involvement in the interpretation of disability rights on behalf of organizationally and conceptually strong disabled people's collectives. By the latter I mean, first and foremost, nongovernmental, nonprofit organizations of disabled people working for social change in the disability area. I do not exclude informal civil society groups and networks, neither do I underestimate the role of publicly active individuals, yet I take formal organizations to be better positioned in terms of legitimacy and bargaining power. My argument is that such disabled people's collectives should be recognized and admitted as important stakeholders and contributors in the community of interpretation that gives the CRPD its meaning. This argument builds on a number of observations about the pivotal role of civil society with regard to disability issues that have already been put forward in the preceding chapters of the book.

On the other hand, the *means* of my analysis will be different from the ones applied by the historical materialists. Instead of tracing interpretation back to class divisions, conflict of interests and relations of production, I will attempt to phenomenologically trace it back "to the things themselves." The idea has its origins in Husserl's philosophy and is subsequently developed by Heidegger.[6] The crucial point is that "entities are constituted—allowed to show themselves as they are in themselves—when they have a place in a whole context of relations to other worldly entities and human activities."[7] The phenomenological call to return "to the things themselves" encourages one to explore this meaning-engendering context, which does not mean to find grounds for meaning in a domain extrinsic to it but to affirm the primacy of interpretation by uncovering its workings. As Gadamer, the leading proponent of hermeneutic phenomenology, puts it: "We are always taking something *as* something. That is the primordial givenness of our world orientation, and we cannot reduce it to anything simpler or more immediate."[8] From such a perspective, what is originally given is meaning, not meaningless reality.

The corollaries of this argument were extensively discussed in Chapter 2 with regard to corporeality; the attendant weakly realist ontology informed the case studies that followed. Thus the methodological guideline to return (hermeneutically) "to the things themselves" underlines all the analyses of disability-related practices presented so far. It suggests that the meaning-engendering mediation of inhabiting a world cannot be circumvented—consequently, research into disability should explore its workings, as well as its existential-ontological implications. In this chapter, I will apply this approach to the domain of juridical regulation concerning disability rights. First, I will briefly introduce the CRPD. Then, I will explore its significance as a "paradigm shift" in the disability area. It will be argued that such a shift is best grasped through the phenomenological notion of being-in-the-world. This will prepare the ground for discussing the ubiquity of the interpretation of human rights provisions and the limits of regulating it through purely juridical means. In the second part of the chapter, I will explore the extra-juridical dimension of the treaty's interpretation by highlighting its socially embedded materiality and by discussing issues related to its translation between languages. I will specifically look at two Bulgarian versions of the CRPD, using the English version as a reference but also consulting the French and the Russian versions. The conclusion will present some tentative methodological and programmatic inferences to be drawn from the analysis and will also reiterate the core argument of the chapter about the importance of disabled people's collectives for the interpretation of the CRPD.

The Convention

The CRPD is an international legally binding human rights instrument of the United Nations (UN). It was unanimously adopted, together with its Optional Protocol, by the UN General Assembly on December 13, 2006, and was opened for signature on March 30, 2007. Following its twentieth ratification, it came into force on May 3, 2008. Since then, the treaty has promptly gained international recognition with a rapidly increasing number of ratifications. All of this suggests that, first, the CRPD is still at its early stages of realization, and second, that it is quickly gaining acceptance (at least formally) as *the* legal standard in the disability area all over the world. These two facts alone should suffice to attract the attention of disability studies scholarship, but there is more to make the study of the CRPD timely.

According to the UN website (www.un.org/disabilities), the CRPD has broken a number of records. Its negotiations were the fastest in the history of the UN human rights treaties. They were conducted between 2002 and 2006, within eight sessions of an Ad Hoc Committee established by the General Assembly. In addition, the number of signatories on the first day of the CRPD's opening for signature was the highest in UN history—82 (with 44 signatories of the Optional Protocol). These figures suggest a significant consensus on the disability-related definitions, problems and solutions put forward by the CRPD. It seems that the ground for such a consensus had been consolidated by the long-lasting efforts of the UN to promote the human rights of disabled people[9]—the CRPD is an heir of the UN Standard Rules on the Equalization of Opportunities for Persons with Disabilities, adopted in 1993. Yet it should also be reminded that the consensus over the CRPD is built upon decades of sustained activism on behalf of disabled people's organizations,[10] which supports the argument about the pivotal role of civil society actors for the constitution of CRPD's meaning. The drafting of the document has been assessed as open and participatory, with disability rights organizations actively involved in all of its stages.[11]

Unlike the aforementioned UN Standard Rules, the CRPD is legally binding. It has been argued that the CRPD does not create new rights but clarifies the application of the existing human rights provisions in the context of disability.[12] Upon ratifying the document, the States Parties are obliged to amend their legislation and to implement disability-related policies in compliance with the provisions of the CRPD; ratifying the Optional Protocol brings about the possibility for individual or collective complaints on issues covered by the CRPD. It seems clear that in the coming years and possibly decades the CRPD will significantly shape disability thinking and policy worldwide. Moreover, such an influence is expected to bring about a *radical change* in the domain of disability.

The paradigm shift

The CRPD is praised as representing a "paradigm shift."[13] Such a shift is concerned with nothing less than a transformation of the very understanding of disabled people's *way of being*—in other words, it has profound existential-ontological consequences. The UN website states that the document

> takes to a new height the movement from viewing persons with disabil-
> ities as "objects" of charity, medical treatment and social protection
> towards viewing persons with disabilities as "subjects" with rights,
> who are capable of claiming those rights and making decisions for their
> lives based on their free and informed consent as well as being active
> members of society. (http://www.un.org/disabilities/default.asp?navid=
> 14&pid=150)

A fundamental philosophical dichotomy—the subject/object distinction—is recruited in order to interpret "the movement" that the CRPD has taken to a "new height." The three practices highlighted with regard to the objectifying framework are charity, medical treatment and social protection. They correspond to the apparatuses of personal tragedy, medicalization and paternalism that have already been extensively analyzed in the preceding chapters of the book. On the other hand, the new understanding of disabled people's way of being—as subjects of rights rather than as objects of charity, treatment and protection—is clearly informed by an emphasis on *individual autonomy*. Indeed, the first of the general principles enshrined by the CRPD in its Article 3 reads: "Respect for inherent dignity, individual autonomy including the freedom to make one's own choices, and independence of persons."

This overarching emphasis on individuals as right-holders and autonomous decision-makers should be put in the wider context of the CRPD's provisions though. At least some of the measures envisioned to promote subject-hood are unequivocally *positive*—the most widely discussed example being the provision of reasonable accommodation. Accordingly, it is often underlined that the CRPD covers both sets of rights—civil and political, on the one hand, and economic, social and cultural, on the other:

> In truth, all persons (whether disabled or not) depend on social supports at least at some point in their lives (especially when young or at the onset of old age) to make freedom and choice a reality. This underlying reality is simply more obvious in the case of persons with disabilities (though not for all of them). If one sought tangible proof of the interconnectedness of both sets of rights [i.e., civil and political, on the one hand, and economic, social and cultural, on the other] then *disability is the obvious example*. It is plainly not enough to enact anti-discrimination laws to break down arbitrary barriers. It is also necessary to assist people in getting past those barriers. *The deeper paradox—one that obtains for all persons—is that personal freedom ultimately relies on social solidarity.*[14]

A clear parallel can be drawn between this comprehensiveness of the CRPD and the logic of the personal assistance scheme explored in Chapter 4—both emphasize individual freedom and both pay heed to the infrastructures of support underlying this freedom. This means that the CRPD exceeds the classical liberal focus on autonomy and "negative liberty."[15] Moreover, the model of agency promoted by the CRPD is very similar to the one promoted by the personal assistance scheme from Chapter 4 in being much more *distributed* than a straightforward reading of the principle of individual autonomy would readily admit:

> The vision of rights embodied in the Convention is thus based upon the recognition that individuals with disabilities are not self-sufficient monist entities, but rather depend upon collective social action to make provision for their basic rights. The Convention therefore articulates a very different vision of rights from that embedded in the US Constitution, for example, where individual rights are primarily conceived as imposing negative constraints upon the state in order to maximise individual autonomy.[16]

This distributed or contextualized understanding of agency is easily discernible in Article 12 concerning "legal capacity," in Article 19 concerning "independent living," and at the places where "peer support" is promoted. In other words, the understanding of human being that is enshrined by the CRPD is much more complex than the traditional philosophical subject/object distinction would suggest. Taking such complexity on board is inevitable whenever one wants to address both "subjectivity" and "objectivity" seriously. The phenomenological contextualization of human existence, captured in the notion of being-in-the-world (see Chapter 1), would provide for a more fruitful point of departure in disclosing the full scope of CRPD's meaning and significance. The analytical value of this approach in exploring national and international regulations has already been emphasized with regard to personal assistance in Chapter 4. There, I also underlined that the perspective informed by the notion of being-in-the-world does not undermine agency—rather, it highlights the social and material conditions that make agency possible. It is telling that, besides the *individualist* emphasis on subjectivity, autonomy, informed consent, and sovereign decision-making, the paradigm shift promoted by the CRPD is also explained through a *context-oriented* recourse to the social model of disability. To this end, for example, the guidance for monitoring the CRPD, issued by the UN Office of the High Commissioner for Human Rights, cites from Michael Oliver's *The Politics of Disablement*.[17] The social model is used to highlight the contextual factors that constitute disability—the so-called barriers to participation—and also to substantiate the necessity to shift the focus of interventions from the individual toward his/her environing world. Yet unlike individual autonomy and its cognates, the social model is not explicitly mentioned in the CRPD. Instead, it is used as an *interpretive device* in commentaries and guidelines that seek to clarify the meaning of CRPD's principles and provisions (examples abound). Importantly, this interpretive device emerged out of the organized movement of disabled people for social change, which, again, supports the argument about the key role of civil society in the constitution of CRPD's meaning:

> The politics of the disability rights movement has its roots in a family of social explanations of disability which have been developed by disability studies scholars and activists. This new social-contextual understanding of disability, most commonly referred to as "the social model," has created a new vision of disability and has influenced policy making at local and international levels. . . . Disability studies scholars have been instrumental in developing this new understanding of disability which has provided a foundation for legal development worldwide, including the adoption of the UN Convention on the Rights of Persons with Disabilities (CRPD).[18]

I will now explore briefly the juridical dimension of CRPD's interpretation. Then, I will proceed with the exploration of the latter's extra-juridical dimension and, more specifically, with highlighting the role of disabled people's collectives for interpreting the document.

The juridical dimension of interpretation

International law posits its own guidelines for interpretation. The Vienna Convention on the Law of Treaties (VCLT), adopted in 1969 and in force since 1980, provides the general framework for the operation of international legal instruments such as the CRPD. Its Articles 31–33 set the meta-rules for the interpretation of such treaties. According to Article 31, interpretation should be honest ("in good faith") and should be guided by the "ordinary meaning" of the terms, circumscribed by their own context and the object and purpose of the treaty. It is also recognized that this context is not bounded but extends beyond the text of the treaty and includes, *inter alia*, reservations and interpretive declarations formulated by the parties to the treaty. Moreover, when the meaning remains "ambiguous or obscure," interpretation may resort to "preparatory work of the treaty and the circumstances of its conclusion" (Article 32). Finally, in cases when the text is recognized as authentic in two or more languages, the Vienna Convention regards these versions as "equally authoritative" (Article 33). If, upon comparison, differences of meaning between or among the authentic texts are disclosed, then "the meaning which best reconciles the texts, having regard to the object and purpose of the treaty, shall be adopted" (Article 33, paragraph 4). The significance of this provision will become clear when discussing the different language versions of the CRPD.

Articles 31–33 of the VCLT disclose that the legislator explicitly recognizes and strives to regulate issues related to interpretation, including those that arise with regard to translation of international treaties. The extent to which such juridical meta-rules can effectively arrest the dynamics of meaning and cope with "ambiguity and obscurity" is a matter that needs to be resolved on a case-by-case basis. Notwithstanding concrete cases though, interpretation always involves a social and political aspect that cannot be effaced through purely juridical means. Historically, the separation of legality from power had a positive function in emancipating humanity from arbitrary command. Classical liberal thinkers of the seventeenth and eighteenth centuries such as Locke and Montesquieu insisted on the generality, abstractness and universality of the law in order to counter the arbitrariness and localness of monarchic power.[19] Yet the irreducible hermeneutic dimension of legality that stems from the law's embeddedness in language and communication has always complicated these principles.[20] The social and political dynamics of interpretation exceeds the scope of instruments such as the Vienna Convention that attempt to regulate it. It should also be reminded that the VCLT itself comes with a long list of interpretive declarations and reservations on behalf of its States Parties that reframe the meaning of its provisions in numerous ways.[21] Thus meta-rules *themselves* remain open to the interpretive contingencies they seek to eliminate.

Such stipulations are not meant to undermine the rule of law. Rather, the contrary is the case. Echoing the foregoing discussion of individual autonomy, the point is to contextualize legality and thus to gain a more active and responsible relationship to it. As already argued in the introduction to this chapter, meaning—even the meaning of legal provisions or, perhaps, *especially* this meaning (for it is unavoidably linguistic)—requires ongoing care on behalf of those concerned; it is never simply and factually given. Two examples related to the CRPD will illustrate this point. The interpretive declarations in relation to "legal capacity" (Article 12) that some states have already submitted or might be expected to submit were aptly regarded by some legal experts as "challenges" that would most probably hinder the implementation of the CRPD.[22] The same report states that EU members have interpreted key concepts such as "discrimination" and "reasonable accommodation" in an "inconsistent" manner.[23] The solutions to these interpretive problems are sought in the letter of the CRPD itself:

> If the wording of EU or national legislation is open to more than one *interpretation*, the EU and Member States should adhere, as far as possible, to the interpretation that renders the provision most consistent with the UN CRPD. Therefore, all EU and national governmental institutions, including the judiciary (EU and national Courts), should apply EU and national law in a manner that is most consistent with the UN CRPD.[24]

Yet the letter of the CRPD *in itself* is not enough to secure its meaning—Gerard Quinn makes a similar point, linking it to the insights of legal realism.[25] It is reports such as the one by the European Foundation Centre just cited that actually take care of the interpretation of the CRPD, as well as the active involvement of the disabled people's organizations in all the stages of the CRPD's development and implementation. In a number of areas crucial for disability equality—for example, with regard to reasonable accommodation, independent living, or legal capacity—the CRPD can only *invite* certain responses and *open up* possibilities for the deployment of certain meanings and practices, but it cannot *determine* these responses, meanings and practices. Neither is it possible to fix them through legal instruments such as the VCLT. This last point calls for an account of the extra-juridical dimension of interpretation.

The extra-juridical dimension of interpretation

Besides a juridical dimension, the interpretation of legal instruments such as the CRPD has an *irreducible* extra-juridical dimension. This means that no system of legal provisions and/or practices, no matter how comprehensive, can fix and secure, once and for all, the meaning of the key terms of the CRPD. The extra-juridical dimension of interpretation becomes evident when one considers the socially embedded materiality of interpretation; it also comes clearly into view when one attends to translation between languages. In this section, I start with providing a brief example for the former. Afterwards, I discuss some interpretive issues that arise when one compares different language versions of the CRPD. These considerations are not meant to be exhaustive but are intended as illustrations whose aim is to indicate possible directions for future research.

The socially embedded materiality of interpretation

The socially embedded materiality of interpretation is traceable at the micro-level by highlighting the networks of heterogeneous (human and nonhuman, material and ideal) entities involved in interpreting. Such assemblages have already been studied in Chapter 3 with regard to disability assessment, as well as in Chapter 5 with regard to nonhuman entities in the Troyan Monastery event. In the domain of interpretation, the actuality of assemblages suggests that, while human-related, interpretation is never totally human-centered or human-controlled. As far as the CRPD is concerned, a fecund area for tracing the socially embedded materiality of interpretation is the functioning of the Committee on the Rights of Persons with Disabilities. This is an UN-level body but similar enquiries could focus on national bodies set up within the framework of the CRPD.

Presently, the Committee consists of eighteen experts who monitor the implementation of the CRPD by considering national reports submitted at regular intervals by the States Parties.[26] According to Article 36, paragraph 1 of the CRPD, "[e]ach report shall be considered by the Committee, which shall make such suggestions and general recommendations on the report as it may consider appropriate and shall forward these to the State Party concerned." This means that the main task of the Committee is to *interpret* the national reports in light of the provisions made by the CRPD (themselves subject to interpretation). What does this formidable work of interpreting involve? A draft resolution of the UN General Assembly, dated November 9, 2011, provides some hints.[27] It states that "document and translation costs for the reports of States parties constitute the largest part of the budget for the Committee."[28] An additional issue identified by the resolution is that "the Committee currently meets for only two sessions of one week per year."[29] Addressing these issues, the General Assembly invites "States parties to adhere to the page limit established by the Committee for reports of States parties, and notes that this would reduce the operating costs of the Committee."[30] Also, the General Assembly extends the working time of the Committee to three weeks per year, providing for "an additional week of meeting time per year to be used consecutive to an existing regular session, bearing in mind the requirements of the Committee for reasonable accommodation."[31]

These considerations indicate that (and how) the interpretative work of the Committee is socially and materially mediated. In order to be considered by the Committee (i.e., in order to be interpreted), the national CRPD reports have to be translated, which incurs translation costs in need of approval by the General Assembly. Further, the members of the Committee need to meet—clearly, the amount and quality of their "meeting time" has impact on the quality of their findings and recommendations. In addition, in order to be manageable, the reports of the States Parties need to adhere to a prescribed page limit; the volume of the reports is also bound to the operating costs of the Committee's work. Last but not least, the Committee requires "reasonable accommodation," a fact that introduces a whole new aspect of socially embedded materiality into the considerations of its interpretive work. The report on the status of the CRPD, presented by the UN Secretary-General before the General Assembly on July 7, 2011, states:

> Among its major decisions, the Committee requested that measures be taken to ensure that all persons with disabilities have full access to meetings of human rights bodies. The Committee also requested that all aspects of accessibility should be taken into account, including training, the provision of documents in Braille and easy-to-read and comprehensible formats, the provision of sign-language interpretation and other appropriate forms of support, as well as relevant information and communications technologies and systems.[32]

This statement is made immediately after reporting on the "days of general discussion" held by the Committee in 2009 and 2010. Thus the Committee's work highlights issues of material accessibility not only due to its thematic focus, but also due to the physical presence of disabled people, be it

Committee members or other people attending the open events held by it. Chapter 6 explored a similar effect—related there to media representations of inaccessibility—of illuminating as problematic what is usually taken for granted in the materiality of the environing world. Here, this indirect outcome of the Committee's work reaffirms the importance of disabled people's participation in the interpretation of CRPD. Besides architectural adaptation, the demands for accessibility put forward in the statement of the UN Secretary-General include the need to transform the written word into alternative systems of signification and to provide appropriate information and communication support. The corollary is that disability tends *of itself* to illuminate social-material assemblages that mediate human agency. This point has crucial implications for human rights legislation because it emphasizes the importance of bridging the gap between "negative" and "positive" liberties.[33] In the case of the CRPD, it has also been reflected in its contextualized understanding of human being, as discussed above.

Interpretation and translation

The ubiquity and embeddedness of interpretation can also be demonstrated with regard to translation between languages. Proceeding from the presumption that *every translation is an instance of interpretation,*[34] I would like to highlight some of the interpretive issues arising between and among different language versions of the CRPD. Article 50—the last article of the treaty—enlists as "authentic" versions of the CRPD those written in Arabic, Chinese, English, French, Russian and Spanish. In accordance with the Vienna Convention (discussed above), the UN provides the following disclaimer with regard to the translations of the CRPD available on the UN website:

> The non-official versions of the Convention are provided by other sources and are for informational purposes only; they do not constitute endorsement of, or an approval by, the United Nations of any of the text or products, services, or opinions of the organization or individual. The United Nations bears no responsibility for the accuracy, legality or content of their statements and opinions. (http://www.un.org/disabilities/default.asp?navid=14&pid=150)

Two questions ensue, as far as the constitution of meaning and the work of interpretation are concerned. First, what are the relationships among the authentic versions of the CRPD? Second, what are the relationships among the authentic versions and those in other languages? Comprehensive answers to these questions exceed the confines of this chapter. I will limit myself to providing a few examples, utilizing the languages I have command of. Among the nonauthentic versions of the CRPD I will specifically focus on the Bulgarian ones, drawing on my native-speaker competence and my professional knowledge of the Bulgarian disability policy context. The discussion of CRPD's translation in relation to the treaty's interpretation will add another case in support of the argument that disabled people and their civil society organizations are key stakeholders in the constitution of CRPD's meaning.

Two Bulgarian versions

At the time of writing this text, two different versions of the Bulgarian translation of the CRPD were publicly available. One was accompanying the Decision of the Bulgarian Council of Ministers, number 967 from December 30, 2011, that recommended to the Bulgarian National Assembly to ratify the CRPD (the Optional Protocol was not included).[35] Following the submission of this Decision, the CRPD was unanimously ratified, without reservations, by the National Assembly on January 26, 2012, and the law for its ratification was promulgated in the *State Gazette*, number 12 from February 10, 2012. I will refer to the Bulgarian translation of the CRPD that accompanied this process of ratification as "translation B." The other Bulgarian translation—what I will accordingly refer to as "translation A"—was part of an earlier ratification process. It was annexed to the Decision of the Council of the European Union for the conclusion of the CRPD, dated November 26, 2009 (2010/48/EC), that was promulgated in the *Official Journal of the European Union* on January 27, 2010.[36]

Translation B is an edited version of translation A. The edits that transformed translation A into translation B were taken on board after a consultative process organized by the Bulgarian government that involved a number of civil society organizations, including organizations of disabled people. Thus the edits illuminate the social and political dynamics of interpretation and the role of civil society actors in its constitution. I will return to this point in my discussion of Article 19 of the CRPD.

Defining disability: Preambular paragraph (e) and Article 1

According to authoritative interpretations, the CRPD does not provide a definition of disability but rather only "guidance" that is intended to clarify

CRPD's application.[37] This guidance is contained in the preambular paragraph (e) and in Article 1 of the CRPD. Nevertheless, it seems legitimate to regard these two statements as definitions, albeit tentative ones, for at least two reasons. First, they serve as a pivotal point of reference for the whole conceptual edifice of the CRPD. Second, even if in theory they are not regarded as definitions, in practice they will most probably be used as such by policy-makers and civil society activists alike.

The preambular paragraph (e) of the English version of the CRPD states

> that disability is an evolving concept and that disability results from the interaction between persons with impairments and attitudinal and environmental barriers that hinders their full and effective participation in society on an equal basis with others.

The first thing to be noticed here is that, following the social model of disability,[38] the English version distinguishes between "disability" and "impairment." This distinction is regarded as of utmost importance, because it goes to the heart of the paradigm shift of the CRPD:

> The *challenge*, when applying the paradigm shift at domestic level, is the subtle, and not always acknowledged, difference between the terms "impairment" and "disability." The notion of "disability" used in the UN CRPD focuses on barriers, which may hinder full and effective participation in society on an equal basis with others, and not on individual impairments. This is particularly important for the application of certain rights, such as legal capacity (Article 12 UN CRPD).[39]

The two Bulgarian translations take up this challenge of differentiating between "impairment" and "disability" with varying degrees of success. Translation B erases the distinction by rendering both "disability" and "impairment" with the same word—*uvrezhdane* (the meaning of this word in Bulgarian is explained in an endnote in Chapter 7). Translation A copes with the challenge by rendering "disability" as *uvrezhdane* and "impairments" as *narusheni fizicheski funktsii* ("impaired physical functions"). Indeed, reducing "impairments" to "physical functions" may create another problem if it is taken as exclusive of mental and intellectual differences, explicitly enlisted among the "impairments" in Article 1 of the CRPD. Nevertheless, on this point translation A seems less problematic than translation B.

Further, in the English version of the preambular paragraph (e), the third person singular of the verb "hinder" (indicated by the suffix -s: "hinder*s*") suggests that it is the *interaction* between the person with impairments and the attitudinal and environmental barriers that prevents disabled people from equal participation in society—rather than the barriers themselves. This subtle difference becomes conspicuous when the English version is compared with, for example, the French one: *le handicap résulte de l'interaction entre des personnes présentant des incapacités et les barrières comportementales et environnementales qui font obstacle à leur pleine et effective participation à la société.* The third person plural of the verb *faire*—that is, *font*—indicates that the French version identifies the barriers themselves (*les barrières*) as hindering participation—rather than the *interaction* between persons with impairments and the barriers, as is the case in the English version. Both Bulgarian translations B and A concur with the French version on this point.[40]

The aforementioned issues do not arise when considering Article 1 of the CRPD—the other place in the CRPD where the meaning of "disability" is explicitly addressed, this time through a tentative definition of "persons with disabilities." According to the English version of Article 1:

> Persons with disabilities include those who have long-term physical, mental, intellectual or sensory impairments which in interaction with various barriers may hinder their full and effective participation in society on an equal basis with others.

The text suggests that what "may hinder" disabled people's participation in society are *impairments*-in-their-interaction-with-environmental-barriers. Article 1 makes it impossible to disentangle the interactional assemblage that is identified as preventing disabled people from participating—hence my hyphenation. Notwithstanding the relatively stronger emphasis on the role of impairments here in comparison with the preambular paragraph (e), the English version remains consistent in its interpretation of the hindrances to participation. At this point, the French and the two Bulgarian versions concur with the English one. It should also be added that in Article 1, both Bulgarian translations A and B distinguish between "disability" and "impairment" by rendering these terms, accordingly, as *uvrezhdane* ("disability"), and *nedostatachnost* ("deficiency").

These comments are not intended as critiques of particular language versions of the CRPD, although such criticisms are possible and, in some cases, desirable. For example, as early as in 2008, issues were reported in relation to the Hungarian and the German versions of the text.[41] In the case of the latter, Virtanen more specifically pointed out that "[t]he German Disability Council is trying to lobby changes in the translation because there are mistakes in the German translation. For example, the word *inclusion* in the context of education has been translated as *Integration* instead of *Inklusion.*"[42]

A similar intervention on behalf of a civil society organization of disabled people in the CRPD's translation will be discussed below, with regard to the Bulgarian translation of Article 19. Yet rather than criticize different language versions of the CRPD, my aim here is to emphasize the ambiguities that persist even in highly codified juridical contexts and that become conspicuous when comparing different language versions of the same text. It would be misleading to regard such ambiguities as *mere* errors or inconsistencies that can be rectified once and for all. Rather, they should be regarded as invitations for social and political engagement with ostensibly self-enclosed and expert-dominated domains of meaning. The CRPD itself embraces this spirit of civic involvement in its Articles 4(3) that states:

> In the development and implementation of legislation and policies to implement the present Convention, and in other decision-making processes concerning issues relating to persons with disabilities, States Parties shall closely consult with and actively involve persons with disabilities, including children with disabilities, through their representative organisations.

Independent living: Article 19

Article 19 of the CRPD concerns issues related to independent living, community services, personal assistance and, by implication, deinstitutionalization. The significance of these concepts for disability equality cannot be overstated. As also pointed out in Chapter 4, they constitute the main preoccupation of international organizations of disabled people such as the European Network on Independent Living (www.enil.eu) and the Independent Living Institute (www.independentliving.org). On the national level, Centers for Independent Living—organizations run and controlled by disabled people—focus exclusively on the issues circumscribed by these concepts.[43]

The English title of Article 19 is "Living independently and being included in the community." Bulgarian translation A renders "living independently" as *samostoyatelen zhivot*, but the word *samostoyatelen* is much closer to the English "selfstanding" or "autonomous" than to "independent"—hence *samostoyatelen zhivot* would be translated back to English as "selfstanding living" or "autonomous living." This makes translation A problematic from the perspective of the independent living philosophy, as outlined in Chapter 4. Before recalling this argument, it is worth pointing out that a similar problem can be discerned in the French and the Russian versions as well, where "living independently" is rendered as *autonomie de vie* ("autonomy of living") and *samostoyatel'nyi obraz zhizni* ("selfstanding/autonomous way of living") respectively. It should be noted that there are other provisions of the CRPD where both the French and the Russian versions render "independence" differently. For example, in the preambular paragraph (n) the English "autonomy and independence" corresponds in the French version to *autonomie et . . . indépendance* and in the Russian to *samostoyatel'nost' i nezavisimost'*—that is, the French and Russian words or their cognates used in Article 19 to refer to "independent" are used here to refer to "autonomy." (In the preambular paragraph (n) both Bulgarian translations A and B render the English "autonomy and independence" as *samostoyatelnost i nezavisimost*.)

What is the problem with rendering "independent" as "selfstanding/ autonomous"—or with obliterating the difference between the two concepts? Chapter 4 made clear that from the perspective of the independent living philosophy, the concept of independent living does not imply coping without assistance, as might be suggested by terms such as "selfstanding" and "autonomous." Instead, independent living requires the assistance to be organized in such a ways so that the person who utilizes it is enabled to exercise choice and control over his or her everyday activities. Proceeding from similar presumptions, the Center for Independent Living—Sofia, the Bulgarian organization of disabled people that figures prominently in the foregoing case studies, insisted on changing the Bulgarian translation A of the CRPD before its ratification by the Bulgarian National Assembly. As a result of this advocacy, in the ensuing translation B "living independently" was rendered as *nezavisim zhivot* ("independent living"). The same advocacy efforts resulted in some other important changes in Article 19, for example the substitution of *sluzhbi za sotsialno podpomagane* ("offices for social assistance," Bulgarian translation A) with *uslugi za podkrepa v obshtnostta* ("services for support in the community," Bulgarian translation B) in its paragraph (b), corresponding to the English "community support services." The motivation for these changes stems from concerns similar to those mentioned above.

Let me summarize the more general points on translation made so far: (a) by comparing different language versions of the CRPD, one is able to see how (b) translation is intrinsically related to interpretation, while (c) interpretation is rooted in different and sometimes conflicting understandings of disabled people's problems and their solutions. These differences can be traced to different understandings of human being, as shown in Chapter 4 with regard to personal assistance. They continue to have an impact even when—as I take it to be the case with the CRPD—the juridical norm is formulated with precision, insight and sensitivity; they bend it towards diverging and sometimes mutually exclusive outcomes. The role of the Center for Independent Living—Sofia in changing the Bulgarian translation of the CRPD illustrates how the involvement of civil society actors can have a decisive impact on the interpretation of human rights provisions. After all—and as already pointed out—the CRPD is itself to a great extent a result of such an involvement of civil society in policy- and law-making.

Concluding remarks

In conclusion, I would like to draw two inferences from the foregoing analysis—a methodological and a programmatic one, as well as to rearticulate the argument about the role of disabled people's collectives in the CRPD's interpretation.

In terms of methodology, the analysis of the CRPD provided additional support for the claim that critical disability scholarship would greatly benefit from micro-level investigations of meaning constitution. In phenomenology, such investigations are intrinsically related to a contextualized understanding of human being, conceived as being-in-the-world. Besides emphasizing "distributed" aspects of human agency, the phenomenological perspective informed by the notion of being-in-the-world suggests that interpretation is "the basic structure of our experience of life,"[44] rather than just one human activity among others. As demonstrated in the preceding chapters, these metatheoretical and methodological points constitute a fertile ground for innovative developments within disability studies.

The second point is related to circumscribing themes for future research on the CRPD and other similar legal instruments concerning disability. One area for future study that promises important insights is the extra-juridical constitution of the meaning of legal instruments. Within it, close attention needs to be paid to the socially embedded materiality of interpretation of legal instruments such as the CRPD, both on international and national levels. This chapter provides some preliminary clues but much more could be done. The other theme for future research is translation. Comparing different language versions of a treaty such as the CRPD would stimulate new analytical insights. It should be noted that issues related to national translations of the CRPD have already been highlighted by some commentators,[45] but to my knowledge no systematic research in this direction has been undertaken.

The central argument of this chapter concerns the importance of the active participation of civil society actors in the interpretation of juridical provisions such as those contained in the CRPD. The treatment of disability—and, as argued in Chapter 2, of impairment too—should not be abandoned to medical experts. Similarly, the interpretation of disability rights should not be fully conceded to legal experts—a position with which, I believe, many of the legal experts involved in the drafting and subsequent exegesis of the CRPD would agree. The CRPD Committee itself openly recognizes the need for involving civil society actors in the interpretation of the CRPD—for example, by inviting submissions for comments on particular CRPD provisions, a practice that is to be commended and sustained. A recent call addressed Article 9 of the CRPD that deals with states' obligations with regard to accessibility. In response, strong and influential disabled people's organizations such as the European Disability Forum (www.edf-feph.org) have submitted their proposals for interpreting Article 9, highlighting subtle but politically crucial distinctions such as the one between "reasonable accommodation" and "general accessibility."[46]

The struggle over CRPD's meaning(s) is yet to be deployed on the terrains of national and international law-making, policy planning, implementation and monitoring. Different groups will appropriate the treaty's provisions in different ways, bending them to fit their own sociopolitical positions.[47] Gadamer points out that "[i]t is in the service of just decisions that one reinterprets the law and finds the most adequate solution of the juristic problem."[48] My contention is that, besides competent jurists, administrators and politicians, just decisions require active, politically engaged communities. This does not invalidate the rule of law but highlights a crucial condition for its realization. Applied to the domain of disability, this means that political decisions can be and remain *just* only in the vicinity of collectively organized disabled people. The forms of these collectives may vary, but they are most effective when constituted as nongovernmental, nonprofit organizations *of* (rather than *for*) disabled people. This does not exclude informal groups or individuals, yet the capacity of the formally constituted organizations to influence interpretation is greater, as is their legitimacy within the conventional frameworks of policy-making and policy implementation. In other words, only organizationally and conceptually strong disabled people's collectives can further the transformative and emancipatory potential inherent in the CRPD.

Notes

1 Oddný Mjöll Arnardóttir and Gerard Quinn (eds), *The UN Convention on the Rights of Persons with Disabilities: European and Scandinavian Perspectives* (Leiden and Boston: Martinus Nijhoff Publishers, 2009).

2 Marta Russell, "What disability civil rights cannot do: employment and political economy." *Disability & Society* 17, 2 (2002): 117–35.

3 Ibid., 122.

4 Colin Barnes and Mike Oliver, "Disability rights: rhetoric and reality in the UK." *Disability & Society* 10, 1 (1995): 111–6; Mike Oliver and Colin Barnes, "Disability politics and the disability movement in Britain: where did it all go wrong?" *Coalition*, August (2006): n.p.

5 Russell, "What disability civil rights cannot do."

6 Martin Heidegger, *Being and Time*, trans. John Macquarrie and Edward Robinson (Oxford: Blackwell, 1962 [1927]), 49–50.

7 Mark A. Wrathall, "Existential phenomenology," in *A Companion to Phenomenology and Existentialism*, eds. Hubert L. Dreyfus and Mark A. Wrathall (Oxford: Blackwell, 2006), 33.

8 Hans-Georg Gadamer, "The hermeneutics of suspicion." *Man and World* 17, 3–4 (1984): 317.

9 I prefer the term "disabled people" to "people/persons with disabilities" for reasons similar to the ones articulated by Oliver in *The Politics of Disablement* (London: Macmillan, 1990), xiii. The CRPD uses "persons with disabilities." This confounds the issue but whenever possible, I will stick to "disabled people."

10 Rannveig Traustadóttir, "Disability studies, the social model and legal developments," in *The UN Convention on the Rights of Persons with Disabilities: European and Scandinavian Perspectives*, eds. Oddný Mjöll Arnardóttir and Gerard Quinn (Leiden and Boston: Martinus Nijhoff Publishers, 2009).

11 Lana Moriarity and Kevin Dew, "The United Nations Convention on the Rights of Persons with Disabilities and participation in Aotearoa New Zealand." *Disability & Society* 26, 6 (2011): 683–97.

12 Arnardóttir and Quinn, *UN Convention*, xvii; European Foundation Centre, *Study on Challenges and Good Practices in the Implementation of the UN Convention on the Rights of Persons with Disabilities VC/2008/1214* (Brussels: European Foundation Centre, 2010), 22–3.

13 Arnardóttir and Quinn, *UN Convention*, xvii; Paul Harpur, "Embracing the new disability rights paradigm: the importance of the Convention on the Rights of Persons with Disabilities." *Disability & Society* 27, 1 (2012): 1–14; Moriarity and Dew, "The United Nations Convention," 686–7.

14 Arnardóttir and Quinn, *UN Convention*, xviii, emphases added.

15 On the distinction between "positive" and "negative" liberty see Isaiah Berlin, "Two concepts of liberty," in *Four Essays on Liberty*, ed. Isaiah Berlin (Oxford: Oxford University Press, 1969 [1958]).

16 Colm O'Cinneide, "Extracting protection for the rights of persons with disabilities from human rights frameworks: established limits and new possibilities," in *The UN Convention on the Rights of Persons with Disabilities: European and Scandinavian Perspectives*, eds. Oddný Mjöll Arnardóttir and Gerard Quinn (Leiden and Boston: Martinus Nijhoff Publishers, 2009), 164.

17 UN Office of the High Commissioner for Human Rights, *Monitoring the Convention on the Rights of Persons with Disabilities: Guidance for Human Rights Monitors* (New York and Geneva: United Nations, 2010), 9.

18 Traustadóttir, "Disability studies," 3.

19 Jürgen Habermas, *The Structural Transformation of the Public Sphere: An Inquiry into a Category of Bourgeois Society*, trans. Thomas Burger with the assistance of Frederick Lawrence (Cambridge, MA: The MIT Press, 1993 [1962]), 53–4.

20 See Gadamer, "The hermeneutics of suspicion," 315.

21 The list is available online at http://treaties.un.org/doc/Publication/MTDSG/Volume%20II/Chapter%20XXIII/XXIII-1.en.pdf, accessed September 27, 2013.
22 European Foundation Centre, *Study*, 10.
23 Ibid., 11. For a list of interpretive declarations and reservations made by the States Parties upon ratification, formal confirmation or accession to the CRPD see http://treaties.un.org/doc/Publication/MTDSG/Volume%20I/Chapter%20IV/IV-15.en.pdf, accessed September 27, 2013.
24 Ibid., 15–16.
25 Gerard Quinn, "Resisting the 'temptation of elegance': can the Convention on the Rights of Persons with Disabilities socialise states to right behaviour?" in *The UN Convention on the Rights of Persons with Disabilities: European and Scandinavian Perspectives*, eds. Oddný Mjöll Arnardóttir and Gerard Quinn (Leiden and Boston: Martinus Nijhoff Publishers, 2009), 217.
26 The Committee's work is presented online at http://www.ohchr.org/EN/HRBodies/CRPD/Pages/CRPDIndex.aspx, accessed September 27, 2013.
27 UN General Assembly, *Report of the Secretary-General on the Status of the Convention on the Rights of Persons with Disabilities and the Optional Protocol thereto, A/66/121, of 7 July 2011* (New York and Geneva: United Nations, 2011).
28 Ibid., 1.
29 Ibid.
30 Ibid., 2.
31 Ibid.
32 UN General Assembly, *Resolution A/C.3/66/L.29/Rev.1 of 9 November 2011* (New York and Geneva: United Nations, 2011), 4–5.
33 See Ida E. Koch, "From invisibility to indivisibility: the international Convention on the Rights of Persons with Disabilities," in *The UN Convention on the Rights of Persons with Disabilities: European and Scandinavian Perspectives*, eds. Oddný Mjöll Arnardóttir and Gerard Quinn (Leiden and Boston: Martinus Nijhoff Publishers, 2009), 70–2.
34 Martin Müller, "What's in a word? Problematizing translation between languages." *Area* 39, 2 (2007): 206–13.
35 The Decision is available online at pris.government.bg, accessed September 27, 2013.
36 The Decision is available online at eur-lex.europa.eu, accessed September 27, 2013.
37 UN Office of the High Commissioner for Human Rights, *Monitoring the Convention*, 15.
38 Ibid., 8–9.
39 European Foundation Centre, *Study*, 42.
40 Another one of the authentic versions that I checked—the Russian one—concurs with the English version.
41 Riku Virtanen, *The Survey on the Ratification Processes of the Convention on the Rights of Persons with Disabilities in Seven States* (Helsinki: VIKE—The Center for Human Rights of Persons with Disabilities, 2008).
42 Ibid., 35. The German disabled people's organization *Netzwerk Artikel 3* (www.netzwerk-artikel-3.de) has developed and promoted an alternative, "shadow" version of the official German translation of the CRPD and its Optional Protocol.

43 Colin Barnes, "Direct payments and their future: an ethical concern?" *Ethics & Social Welfare* 1, 3 (2007): 348–54.

44 Gadamer, "The hermeneutics of suspicion," 317.

45 For example, Virtanen, *Survey*.

46 The Committee's call is available at http://www2.ohchr.org/SPdocs/CRPD/ CallSubmissionsArticle9.doc; EDF's submission is available at http://www. edf-feph.org/Page_Generale.asp?DocID=13855&thebloc=29617, accessed September September 27, 2013.

47 See Quinn "Resisting the 'temptation of elegance,'" 216–17.

48 Gadamer, "The hermeneutics of suspicion," 315.

9

Conclusions

Since its inception in the 1980s, the discipline of disability studies has been highly effective in illuminating the social and political aspects of the problems faced by disabled people. Yet the questions of ontology have remained largely unaddressed, leaving the methodological holism that grounds the discipline amenable to internal conceptual contradictions and external charges of inconsistency and neglect. The present inquiry attempted to fill this gap. Chapter 1 defended the case for recognizing ontologically—and not only sociopolitically—the contextual embeddedness of disability. Chapter 2 complemented this thesis by developing a weakly realist view of the body informed by phenomenology. Taken together, the first two chapters elaborated the theoretical framework that guided the case studies developed throughout the rest of the book.

The praxis-oriented suggestions resulting from this critical investigation can be summarized on a case-by-case basis. To begin with, the discussion in Chapter 3 argued for de-medicalization of disability assessment and a decoupling of its methodology from productivist considerations. Such a change can be achieved by shifting the focus of the assessment from the individual deficiencies of the person being assessed toward the deficiencies of his or her environing world. Notably, the shift will not succeed until the productivist ethos reducing humans to resources is also critically addressed, which is likely to require a much wider sociopolitical transformation than simply changing the disability assessment.

Chapter 4 argued in support of personal assistance (direct payments) schemes for disabled persons that create conditions for their independent living. The very meaning of "independence" was subjected to critical scrutiny that underlined the collective and distributive aspects of the phenomenon. Accordingly, it was suggested that it is vital for personal assistance schemes to provide for peer support. It was also argued that the long-term viability of such schemes depends on disabled people's ability and willingness to organize collectively for public, political action. Thus besides personal assistance,

Chapter 4 also made the case for a strong disabled people's movement—an argument that was further backed up by the analyses developed in subsequent chapters.

The case study of disability-based discrimination presented in Chapter 5 highlighted the need and promise of individual resolution and empowerment, where antidiscrimination legislation undeniably plays a significant role. Yet the analysis did not embrace individualist explanations of dis/ablist discrimination and did not focus on juridical redress. Instead, it looked phenomenologically at the embeddedness of dis/ablism into that which is mundane, everyday, homely—in other words, all too familiar to be ordinarily noticed. It is not only in the courtroom (or on the street or the square, as suggested in the preceding paragraph) but also at home that emancipation is to be achieved. To this end, the experience of unhomeliness bears a significant transformative potential— a point whose articulation was prepared in Chapter 5 and fully achieved in Chapter 6, with the discussion of defamiliarization and the "uncanny."

Chapter 6 underlined the importance of media representations of disabling contexts and, more specifically, of architectural inaccessibility. Such media practices should be praised and actively promoted because they highlight the contextual aspects of ostensibly individual problems by making strange the familiar details of our everyday, lived world. The attendant experience of uncanniness changes the audience's perception not only of disabled people's problems but also of its own relationship with the world it inhabits. This can undermine the hegemony of individualism[1] by making people attentive to what is beyond themselves and yet makes their own being possible. It should also be emphasized that most of the media reports analyzed in Chapter 6 happened in response to a collectively organized public action of disabled people who protested against inaccessible built environment. This suggests a strong relationship between public engagement and the possibility of enlightened criticism.

This point was further elaborated in Chapter 7, which argued for the need to provide opportunities for public deliberation on challenging disability-related topics such as sexuality and disability. Discourses on the latter are overwhelmingly silenced or else dominated by medicalized expertise. Accordingly, opening up and sustaining spaces for nonmedicalized discussions on sexuality in its relation to disability is a major condition for transforming patterns of thought and action that undermine disabled people's existence— especially when disabled people themselves participate and/or take the lead in such instances of public deliberation. Moreover, inviting the general public to articulate their views on sexuality and disability may bring to the surface other tacit assumptions directly linked to dis/ablism, thus making them amenable to change. For example, challenging dis/ablism in the domain of sexuality is intrinsically related to questioning medicalization and patriarchy.

The relationship between expert and nonexpert domains of knowledge/power was the main concern of the final case study in the book, presented in Chapter 8. In practical terms, it argued for involvement of disabled people and their organizations in the processes of interpreting juridical documents such as the United Nations Convention on the Rights of Persons with Disabilities (CRPD). Chapter 8 grounded this suggestion in a phenomenologically informed understanding of the ubiquity of interpretation and the constitutive role of its extra-juridical dimension. Proceeding from these theoretical presumptions, it claimed that the institutional infrastructures facilitating extra-juridical involvement in interpreting juridical provisions need to be deliberately developed and sustained. In this sense, the practice of the Committee on the Rights of Persons with Disabilities to announce open invitations for submissions of interpretive comments on different CRPD provisions is to be welcomed. Such mechanisms should be created on the national level as well, which seems particularly timely given the early stage of CRPD's implementation. The process is most likely to be propelled by grassroots initiatives of disabled people and supported by international civil society networks such as the European Network on Independent Living (www.enil.eu).

In sum, the praxis-oriented conclusions of the preceding chapters were formulated with regard to several different domains of disability-related practices: disability assessment, personal assistance, disability-based discrimination, media representations of disability, public deliberations on sexuality and disability, and juridical approaches to disability. In each of these domains, practical measures for overcoming dis/ablism were proposed: de-medicalization of the disability assessment, provision of properly organized personal assistance for independent living, resistance against dis/ablist patterns embedded in the familiar everyday world, focusing of media attention on disabling contexts, public engagement with silenced and/or expert-dominated issues such as sexuality and disability and involvement of disabled people and their organizations in the interpretation of juridical provisions concerning disability rights. The analyses of the different cases also demonstrated that a major condition for the possibility of articulating and implementing these measures is the collective organizing of disabled people for social change.

In each of these studies of disability-related practices, I emphasized the existential-ontological significance of the phenomena under investigation. Let me remind the reader of the main argument of the book, as formulated in Chapter 1: (a) bodily differences usually identified as "impairments" are (b) mediated through inhabiting a world constituted by disability-related practices that incorporate existential-ontological reductions, and thus get translated into (c) restrictions of activity and, on an ontological level, into undermining of disabled people's very existence. The practical measures summarized above concern mediation (element b). Their ontological significance lies in incorporating alternative, nonreductive existential-ontological patterns so that bodily differences (element a) are no longer translated into undermining of disabled people's existence (element c) but are positively affirmed. Indeed, it is possible to imagine that these progressive (from the perspective of the present study) practices can themselves invite ontological reductions. For example, de-medicalization can open up possibilities for commodification, thus enhancing the instrumental rationality of the productivist/consumerist order—an issue that is likely to become more pressing with the increasing "mainstreaming" of impairments in education, sports, media and so forth. Personal assistance for independent living bears the potential to bring about what Roulstone and Morgan term "enforced individualism,"[2] given its emphasis on consumer choice as highlighted in Chapter 4. On their behalf, collective forms of support and organizing can end up enforcing collectivism[3] and incorporating paternalistic and/or productivist patterns, as testified by the history of state socialism and its response to disability in Eastern Europe. These examples suggest that, albeit urgent, the positive measures enlisted above cannot guarantee progressive policies—in the long run, they need to be accompanied by reflexive analyses of their own existential-ontological implications. Although the present study did not engage with such analyses, it developed a theoretical basis for their elaboration.

The study also touched on a number of important issues related to disability, without engaging with them directly. While remaining outside the scope of the present work, these issues can be regarded as useful points of departure for future investigations of disability informed by critical phenomenology. To begin with, questions concerning mental and psychological impairments remained largely unaddressed within the book, although hints on approaching these phenomena from an existential-ontological perspective can be found throughout the work, and particularly in the chapter on personal assistance (Chapter 4). The relationship between these impairments and the body is less obvious than in other instances of disability—still, it is hard to deny the bodily aspect, no matter whether conceived as constructed or given.[4] Thus it seems that the position of weak bodily realism developed in Chapter 2 is equally applicable to mental and psychological differences as it is to physical and sensory ones. Furthermore, explorations of these phenomena may illuminate dis/ablist mediation with even greater clarity than explorations of more straightforwardly bodily impairments. With their emphasis on individualism and knowledge production/consumption, post-industrial societies put immense pressures on people to be cognitively efficient and self-sufficient. Those who do not conform to this ideal of autonomous cognitive agency are likely to experience symbolic and physical violence. It is therefore both analytically promising and politically important to expand the existential-ontological analysis of disability developed in this work toward issues related to cognitive and emotional difference.

A closely related set of questions concerns old age. Considering the current demographic trends and the advances in biomedicine, these issues are likely to become crucial in the decades to come. Their answers have been sought predominantly in economic and welfare terms, leaving the ontological aspects of old age unattended to. In this sense, it would be advisable to inquire about the relationship between the meaning of old age and the meaning of human being in general. Old age intersects with disability in many respects—hence it is important to study the ways in which bodily differences associated with aging are mediated within dis/abling contexts. For example, elderly people have an uneasy relationship with economic productivity, which tends to undermine their existence in a society driven by instrumental imperatives. This point is also closely related to the medicalization of old age. Such preliminary observations suggest that the analyses developed within the framework of the present inquiry contain ideas that can easily be applied to old age. No doubt, an endeavor of this kind will have to address the question of time, and particularly of the relationship between lived time and calendar time. To this end, existential phenomenology seems an indispensable resource for analytical insights. More generally, questions of intersectionality are of crucial importance to disability studies and emancipatory praxis. Besides the intersection between disability and old age, it is also important to consider the intersection of disability and ethnicity, class and sexuality. Suggestions on how to approach these issues phenomenologically and how to consider their existential-ontological implications can be found in Chapter 7, although it focuses mainly on the intersection between disability and gender.

Another area that received only marginal attention in the book but stands in need of further elaboration concerns pain and illness. Sociological analyses of these phenomena are deployed on a contested terrain where different disciplines such as disability studies, sociology of the body and medical sociology fight for authority, engaging in sometimes fierce boundary-work. Questions of power aside, the very consistency of the methodological holism underlying the greatest majority of works within disability studies requires addressing the issues of pain and illness. The position of weak bodily realism developed in Chapter 2 may provide a useful conceptual point of reference for such analyses. The crucial question concerns the very relationship between pain, illness and impairment. For example, pain can accompany illness and impairment, but it is not necessarily tied to them; one can have an impairment without experiencing pain and *vice versa*; pain can be experienced as a positive thing (e.g., as a sign of progress in sport or of healing in therapy); and so on. As far as illness is concerned, the debate about the relationships between disability, impairment and illness (and chronic illness in particular) has a long and turbulent history of disagreements and mutual accusations of intellectual fallacy routinely exchanged among scholars within disability studies and medical sociology. It is my contention that phenomenology provides excellent opportunities for advancing the knowledge in this highly contested area. Nevertheless, such explorations will by no means be unproblematic. Among the numerous disciplinary and methodological difficulties, they will inevitably have to face the major question about the relationship between the micro- and macro-levels of inquiry.

This issue was addressed several times throughout the book, and particularly in the chapters on sexuality (Chapter 7) and the UN Convention (Chapter 8). It circumscribes an important conceptual tension *within* disability studies. The quarrel is between those who focus on the minute details of everyday interaction and those who insist on exploring wider sociopolitical structures. Paterson and Hughes describe the predicament thus:

> just as interactionist perspectives can be criticised for their micro-analysis of disability at the expense of any macro analysis, the converse can be said of disability studies' approach to understanding disability. . . . Here, the everyday reality of lived experience is neglected in favour of a purely structural analysis of disability.[5]

In the present inquiry I sought to incorporate the macro-level perspective into my phenomenological micro-level analyses. I believe that it is possible and even desirable to focus on the everyday and the (seemingly) minor and still support emancipatory political projects for large-scale structural transformations. One can even go a step further and argue that it is impossible to understand power without looking at its mundane operations; on the other hand, if one focuses exclusively on the micro-level, one risks disregarding issues of power altogether. A properly critical inquiry then is self-consciously circular—the macro-perspective triggers specific micro-analyses that in turn reshape the macro-perspective.

This book started with a critical analysis of the general patterns of modern existential-ontological reductions. The development of the position of weak bodily realism shed new light on these existential-ontological issues by putting them in the perspective of bodily difference. The analysis then proceeded by studying the ways in which the everyday, involved and engaged being-in-the-world incorporates existential-ontological reductions that have fundamental significance for the lives of disabled people. The framework thus elaborated and applied provides a good basis for future research on disability that is critical, emancipatory *and* attentive to the details that constitute the disabling contexts of present-day modernity.

Notes

1 Radical individualism of the type promoted by contemporary neoliberalism erodes society and, by extension, democracy (William Outhwaite, "How much capitalism can democracy stand (and vice versa)?" *Radical Politics Today*, May, 2009, 17–19). Ontologically, it coincides with the reduction of the human being to a self-contained, self-present and self-sufficient subjectivity. Yet such a reduction is also *self-denying*—it undermines the very conditions that make the constitution of subjectivity possible. This point was most clearly formulated in the discussion of personal assistance in Chapter 4.

2 Alan Roulstone and Hannah Morgan, "Neo-liberal individualism or self-directed support: are we all speaking the same language on modernising adult social care?" *Social Policy & Society* 8, 3 (2009): 333–45.

3 Ibid.

4 Not long ago, Carol Thomas made the following programmatic observation: "The growth in interest in 'difference' and 'the impaired body' has only just begun to turn disability studies writers' attention to the workings of "the mind." Carol Thomas, *Sociologies of Disability and Illness: Contested Ideas in Disability Studies and Medical Sociology* (Basingstoke: Palgrave Macmillan, 2007), 131.

5 Kevin Paterson and Bill Hughes, "Disability studies and phenomenology: the carnal politics of everyday life." *Disability & Society* 14, 5 (1999): 601.

Bibliography

Abberley, Paul. "The concept of oppression and the development of a social theory of disability." *Disability, Handicap & Society* 2, 1 (1987): 5–19.

Agamben, Giorgio. *Homo Sacer: Sovereign Power and Bare Life*, trans. Daniel Heller-Roazen (Stanford, CA: Stanford University Press, 1998 [1995]).

Anderberg, Peter. "ANED country report on the implementation of policies supporting independent living for disabled people. Report on Sweden." Academic Network of European Disability experts (ANED), 2009, accessed September 27, 2013, http://www.disability-europe.net/theme/independent-living.

Anderson, Damon. "Productivism, vocational and professional education, and the ecological question." *Vocations and Learning* 1, 2 (2008): 105–29.

Angelova, Liliya. "The road to Mogilino: the ideology of normality and Bulgaria's abandoned children" (Sofia: Center for Independent Living, 2008). In Bulgarian, accessed September 27, 2013, http://www.cil.bg/userfiles/nabliudatelnitsa/Putqt_kum_Mogilino.pdf.

Arnardóttir, Oddný Mjöll and Gerard Quinn (eds), *The UN Convention on the Rights of Persons with Disabilities: European and Scandinavian Perspectives* (Leiden and Boston: Martinus Nijhoff Publishers, 2009).

Askay, Richard R. "Heidegger, the body, and the French philosophers." *Continental Philosophy Review* 32, 1 (1999): 29–35.

Austin, John L. *How to Do Things with Words? The William James Lectures Delivered at Harvard University in 1955*, ed. J. O. Urmson (Oxford: Oxford University Press, 1962).

Barnes, Barry. *The Elements of Social Theory* (London: UCL Press, 1995).

Barnes, Colin. "Independent Living, politics and implications." (Leeds: Centre for Disability Studies, 2004), accessed September 27, 2013. http://www.leeds.ac.uk/disability-studies/archiveuk/Barnes/Jane's%20paper.pdf.

—"Direct payments and their future: an ethical concern?" *Ethics & Social Welfare* 1, 3 (2007): 348–54.

Barnes, Colin and Mike Oliver. "Disability rights: rhetoric and reality in the UK." *Disability & Society* 10, 1 (1995): 111–16.

Barnes, Colin, Mike Oliver, and Len Barton. "Disability, the academy and the inclusive society," in *Disability Studies Today*, eds. Colin Barnes, Mike Oliver, and Len Barton (Cambridge: Polity Press, 2002), 250–9.

Bar On, Bat-Ami. "Marginality and epistemic privilege," in *Feminist Epistemologies*, eds. Linda Alcoff and Elizabeth Potter (New York: Routledge, 1993), 83–100.

Barton, Len. "The struggle for citizenship: the case of disabled people." *Disability & Society* 8, 3 (1993): 235–48.

—"Struggle, support and the politics of possibility." *Scandinavian Journal of Disability Research* 1, 1 (1999): 13–22.

—"Emancipatory research and disabled people: some observations and questions." *Educational Review* 57, 3 (2005): 317–27.

Benjamin, Walter. *Understanding Brecht*, trans. Anna Bostock (London: Verso, 1998 [1966]).

—"The work of art in the age of mechanical reproduction," in *Illuminations*, ed. Hannah Arendt, trans. Harry Zohn (New York: Schocken Books, 2007 [1936]), 217–51.

Beresford, Peter and Jane Campbell. "Disabled people, service users, user involvement and representation." *Disability & Society* 9, 3 (1993): 315–25.

Berlin, Isaiah. "Two concepts of liberty," in *Four Essays on Liberty*, ed. Isaiah Berlin (Oxford: Oxford University Press, 1969 [1958]), 118–72.

Blattner, William. "Existence and self-understanding in *Being and Time*." *Philosophy and Phenomenological Research* 56, 1 (1996): 97–110.

—"Heidegger's Kantian idealism revisited." *Inquiry* 47, 4 (2004): 321–37.

—"Temporality," in *A Companion to Heidegger*, eds. Hubert L. Dreyfus and Mark A. Wrathall (Oxford: Blackwell, 2005), 311–24.

—*Heidegger's* Being and Time*: A Reader's Guide* (London: Continuum, 2006).

Boss, Medard. *Existential Foundations of Medicine and Psychology*, trans. Stephen Conway and Anne Cleaves (New York and London: Jason Aronson, 1979 [1971]).

Braddock, David L. and Susan L. Parish. "An institutional history of disability," in *Handbook of Disability Studies*, eds. Gary L. Albrecht, Katherine D. Seelman, and Michael Bury (London: SAGE, 2001), 11–68.

Brenner, Andreas. "The lived-body and the dignity of human beings," in *A Companion to Phenomenology and Existentialism*, eds. Hubert L. Dreyfus and Mark A. Wrathall (Oxford: Blackwell, 2006), 478–88.

Brisenden, Simon. "Young, gifted and disabled: entering the employment market." *Disability, Handicap & Society* 4, 3 (1989): 217–20.

Bulgarian Helsinki Committee. *Human Rights in Bulgaria in 2010* (Sofia: Bulgarian Helsinki Committee, 2011), accessed September 27, 2013, http://www.bghelsinki.org/media/uploads/annual_reports/2010-en.pdf.

Cameron, Colin. "Not our problem: impairment as difference, disability as role." *The Journal of Inclusive Practice in Further and Higher Education* 3, 2 (2011): 10–24.

Campbell, Fiona Kumari. "Legislating disability: negative ontologies and the government of legal identities," in *Foucault and the Government of Disability*, ed. Shelley Tremain (Ann Arbor: The University of Michigan Press, 2005), 108–30.

—*Contours of Ableism: The Production of Disability and Abledness* (Basingstoke: Palgrave Macmillan, 2009).

Carman, Taylor. "Heidegger's concept of presence." *Inquiry: An Interdisciplinary Journal of Philosophy* 38, 4 (1995): 431–53.

—*Merleau-Ponty* (New York: Routledge, 2008).

Center for Independent Living. *From Handicapped People to Persons with Disabilities (Disability Rights in Bulgaria: A Survey, 2001)* (Sofia: Center for Independent Living, 2002), accessed September 27, 2013, http://www.cil.bg/userfiles/english_docs/survey_2001_en.pdf.

—*Disability—A Deficit or a Survival Means (Disability Rights in Bulgaria: A Survey, 2002)* (Sofia: Center for Independent Living, 2003), accessed September 27, 2013, http://www.cil.bg/userfiles/english_docs/survey_2002_ en.pdf.

—*Equal Opportunities through Access to Social Services (Disability Rights in Bulgaria: A Survey, 2003)* (Sofia: Center for Independent Living, 2004), accessed September 27, 2013, http://www.cil.bg/userfiles/english_docs/ survey_2003_en.pdf.

—*Assessment of the "Assistant for Independent Living" Service* (Sofia: Center for Independent Living, 2009). In Bulgarian, accessed September 27, 2013, http://cil.bg/userfiles/nabliudatelnitsa/Report_ANJ_final.doc.

—*Assessment of the Assistant Services for People with Disabilities in Bulgaria* (Sofia: Center for Independent Living, 2009). In Bulgarian, accessed September 27, 2013, http://cil.bg/userfiles/nabliudatelnitsa/ocenka_asistentski_ uslugi_BG.rar.

Cerbone, David R. "Heidegger and Dasein's 'bodily nature': what is the hidden problematic?" *International Journal of Philosophical Studies* 8, 2 (2000): 209–30.

Clarke, Adele E., Janet K. Shim, Laura Mamo, Jennifer R. Fosket, and Jennifer R. Fishman. "Biomedicalization: technoscientific transformations of health, illness, and U. S. biomedicine." *American Sociological Review* 68, 2 (2003): 161–94.

Conrad, Peter. "The shifting engines of medicalisation." *Journal of Health and Social Behavior* 46, 1 (2005): 3–14.

Corker, Mairian and Tom Shakespeare (eds), *Disability/Postmodernity: Embodying Disability Theory* (London: Continuum, 2002).

Crawford, Robert. "Health as a meaningful social practice." *Health: An Interdisciplinary Journal for the Social Study of Health, Illness and Medicine* 10, 4 (2006): 401–20.

Critchley, Simon. "Introduction: What is continental philosophy?" in *A Companion to Continental Philosophy*, eds. Simon Critchley and William R. Schroeder (Oxford: Blackwell, 1998), 1–17.

Crossley, Nick. *The Social Body: Habit, Identity and Desire* (London: SAGE, 2001).

Crow, Liz. "Renewing the social model of disability." *Coalition News*, July (1992): n.p, accessed September 27, 2013, http://www.leeds.ac.uk/disability-studies/ archiveuk/Crow/Social%20model.pdf.

Curtis, Glenn E. (ed.), *Bulgaria: A Country Study* (Washington: Library of Congress, 1992), accessed September 27, 2013, http://lcweb2.loc.gov/frd/cs/ bgtoc.html.

Dakova, Vera. *For Functionaries and People, Part 1* (Sofia: Center for Independent Living, 2004). In Bulgarian, accessed September 27, 2013, http://www.cil.bg/ userfiles/library/otdelni/za_chinovnitsite_i_horata_1_2004.pdf.

Dale, Gareth. "Introduction: The transition in Central and Eastern Europe," in *First the Transition, Then the Crash: Eastern Europe in 2000s*, ed. Gareth Dale (London: Pluto Press, 2011), 1–20.

Davis, Lennard J. *Bending over Backwards: Disability, Dismodernism, and Other Difficult Positions* (New York: New York University Press, 2002).

DeJong, Gerben. "Independent Living: from social movement to analytic paradigm." *Archives of Physical Medicine and Rehabilitation* 60, 10 (1979): 435–46.

DeJong, Gerben, Andrew I. Batavia, and Louise B. McKnew. "The independent living model of personal assistance in national long-term-care policy." *Generations: Journal of the American Society on Aging* 16, 1 (1992): 89–95.

Deleuze, Gilles and Félix Guattari. *A Thousand Plateaus: Capitalism and Schizophrenia*, trans. Brian Massumi (London: Continuum, 2004 [1980]).

Department for Work and Pensions. "Differences and similarities between Disability Living Allowance (DLA) and PIP," in *Personal Independence Payment: Fact Sheet Pack (Version 4.0: October 2013)* (London: Department for Work and Pensions), accessed December 19, 2013, https://www.gov.uk/government/uploads/system/uploads/attachment_data/file/266752/pip-toolkit-all-factsheets.pdf.

—*PIP Assessment Guide* (London: Department for Work and Pensions, 2013), accessed December 19, 2013, https://www.gov.uk/government/uploads/system/uploads/attachment_data/file/210722/pip-assessment-guide.pdf.

Derrida, Jacques. "Heidegger's ear: Philopolemology (*Geschlecht* IV)," in *Reading Heidegger: Commemorations*, ed. John Sallis, trans. John P. Leavey, Jr. (Bloomington and Indianapolis: Indiana University Press, 1993), 163–218.

—*The Politics of Friendship*, trans. George Collins (London: Verso, 2005 [1994]).

Descartes, René. *Key Philosophical Writings*, ed. Enrique Chávez-Arvizo, trans. Elizabeth S. Haldane and G. R. T. Ross (Hertfordshire: Wordsworth Editions, 1997).

de Shazer, Steve. *Putting Difference to Work* (New York: Norton, 1991).

—*Words Were Originally Magic* (New York: Norton, 1994).

Dowse, Leanne. "'Some people are never going to be able to do that'. Challenges for people with intellectual disability in the 21st century." *Disability & Society* 24, 5 (2009): 571–84.

Dreyfus, Hubert L. *Being-in-the-World. A Commentary on Heidegger's* Being and Time, *Division I* (Cambridge, MA: MIT Press, 1991).

—"How Heidegger defends the possibility of a correspondence theory of truth with respect to the entities of natural science," in *Heidegger Reexamined. Vol. 2: Truth, Realism, and the History of Being*, eds. Hubert L. Dreyfus and Mark A. Wrathall (New York: Routledge, 2002), 219–30.

Duckett, Paul S. "What are you doing here? 'Non-disabled' people and the disability movement: a response to Fran Branfield." *Disability & Society* 13, 4 (1998): 625–28.

European Foundation Centre. *Study on Challenges and Good Practices in the Implementation of the UN Convention on the Rights of Persons with Disabilities VC/2008/1214* (Brussels: European Foundation Centre, 2010).

Finkelstein, Victor. *Attitudes and Disabled People: Issues for Discussion* (New York: World Rehabilitation Fund, 1980).

Fisher, Pamela. "Experiential knowledge challenges 'normality' and individualized citizenship: towards 'another way of being'." *Disability & Society* 22, 3 (2007): 283–98.

Flyvbjerg, Bent. "Five misunderstandings about case-study research." *Qualitative Inquiry* 12, 2 (2006): 219–45.

Foucault, Michel. *Power/Knowledge: Selected Interviews and Other Writings, 1972–1977* (New York: Pantheon Books, 1980).

—"Afterword: the subject and power," in *Michel Foucault: Beyond Structuralism and Hermeneutics*, eds. Hubert L. Dreyfus and Paul Rabinow (Brighton: The Harvester Press, 1982), 208–26.

—"Nietzsche, genealogy, history," in *The Foucault Reader*, ed. Paul Rabinow (London: Penguin, 1984 [1971]), 76–100.

—*Discipline and Punish: The Birth of the Prison*, trans. Alan Sheridan (London: Penguin, 1991 [1975]).

—"The birth of social medicine," in *Power. Essential Works of Foucault, 1954–1984*, ed. James D. Faubion, trans. Robert Hurley and others (New York: The New York Press, 2000 [1974]), 134–56.

Fraser, Nancy. *Justice Interruptus: Critical Reflections on the "Postsocialist" Condition* (New York: Routledge, 1997).

Freire, Paulo. *Pedagogy of the Oppressed*, trans. Myra B. Ramos (London: Continuum, 2006 [1968]).

Freud, Sigmund. "The uncanny," in *The Standard Edition of the Complete Psychological Works of Sigmund Freud, Volume XVII (1917–1919)*, trans. and ed. James Strachey, in collaboration with Anna Freud, assisted by Alix Strachey and Alan Tyson (London: Vintage, 2001 [1919]), 217–56.

Fried, Gregory and Richard Polt. "Translators' introduction," in *Introduction to Metaphysics*, ed. Martin Heidegger, trans. Gregory Fried and Richard Polt (New Haven and London: Yale University Press, 2000), vii–xix.

Fujimura, Joan H. "Crafting science: standardized packages, boundary objects and 'translations'," in *Science as Practice and Culture*, ed. Andrew Pickering (Chicago: University of Chicago Press, 1992), 168–211.

Gadamer, Hans-Georg. "The hermeneutics of suspicion." *Man and World* 17, 3–4 (1984): 313–23.

Garfinkel, Harold. *Studies in Ethnomethodology* (Englewood Cliffs, NJ: Prentice-Hall, 1967).

—*Ethnomethodology's Program. Working Out the Durkheim's Aphorism*, ed. Anne W. Rawls (Oxford: Rowman & Littlefield Publishers, 2002).

Gerring, John. *Case Study Research: Principles and Practices* (Cambridge: Cambridge University Press, 2007).

Gibbs, David. "Public policy and organisations of disabled people." Text of a seminar presentation (Leeds: Centre for Disability Studies), accessed September 27, 2013, http://www.leeds.ac.uk/disability-studies/archiveuk/Gibbs/Leeds-0504.text.pdf.

Giddens, Anthony. *Beyond Left and Right: The Future of Radical Politics* (Cambridge: Polity Press, 1994).

Gieryn, Thomas F. "Boundary-work and the demarcation of science from non-science: strains and interests in professional ideologies of scientists." *American Sociological Review* 48, 6 (1983): 781–95.

Glendinning, Simon. "What is phenomenology?" *Think* (Summer 2004): 33–41.

—*The Idea of Continental Philosophy: A Philosophical Chronicle* (Edinburgh: Edinburgh University Press, 2006).

Goodley, Dan. "Becoming rhizomatic parents: Deleuze, Guattari and disabled babies." *Disability & Society* 22, 2 (2007): 145–60.

Goodley, Dan and Katherine Runswick-Cole. "The violence of disablism." *Sociology of Health & Illness* 33, 4 (2011): 602–17.

Grigorenko, Elena L. "Russian 'defectology': anticipating *Perestroika* in the field." *Journal of Learning Disabilities* 31, 2 (1998): 193–207.

Gross, Elizabeth. "What is feminist theory?" in *Feminist Challenges: Social and Political Theory*, eds. Carole Pateman and Elizabeth Gross (Sydney: Allen & Unwin, 1986), 190–204.

Guignon, Charles. "Being as appearing: retrieving the Greek experience of Phusis," in *A Companion to Heidegger's* Introduction to Metaphysics, eds. Richard Polt and Gregory Fried (New Haven and London: Yale University Press, 2001), 34–56.

Gurevitch, Zali D. "The other side of dialogue: on making the other strange and the experience of otherness." *American Journal of Sociology* 93, 5 (1988): 1179–99.

Habermas, Jürgen. *The Structural Transformation of the Public Sphere: An Inquiry into a Category of Bourgeois Society*, trans. Thomas Burger with the assistance of Frederick Lawrence (Cambridge, MA: The MIT Press, 1993 [1962]).

Hacking, Ian. *The Social Construction of What?* (Cambridge, MA: Harvard University Press, 1999).

Hahn, Harlan. "Can disability be beautiful?" in *Perspectives on Disability. Text and Readings on Disability*, ed. Mark Nagler (Palo Alto, CA: Health Markets Research, 1990), 310–19.

Hall, Budd L. "In from the cold? Reflections on participatory research from 1970–2005." *Convergence* 38, 1 (2005): 5–24.

Hammer, Espen. *Philosophy and Temporality from Kant to Critical Theory* (Cambridge, UK: Cambridge University Press, 2011).

Hancock, Philip, Bill Hughes, Elizabeth Jagger, Kevin Paterson, Rachel Russel, Emmanuelle Tulle-Winton, and Melissa Tyler. *The Body, Culture and Society* (Buckingham: Open University Press, 2000).

Han-Pile, Béatrice. "Early Heidegger's appropriation of Kant," in *A Companion to Heidegger*, eds. Hubert L. Dreyfus and Mark A. Wrathall (Oxford: Blackwell, 2005), 80–101.

Haraway, Donna. *Simians, Cyborgs, and Women. The Reinvention of Nature* (London: Free Association Books, 1991).

Harding, Sandra. *The Science Question in Feminism* (Ithaca, NY: Cornell University Press, 1986).

Harpur, Paul. "Embracing the new disability rights paradigm: the importance of the Convention on the Rights of Persons with Disabilities." *Disability & Society* 27, 1 (2012): 1–14.

Hasler, Frances. "Developments in the disabled people's movement," in *Disabling Barriers—Enabling Environments*, eds. John Swain, Vic Finkelstein, Sally French, and Mike Oliver (London: SAGE, 1993).

Heidegger, Martin. *Being and Time*, trans. John Macquarrie and Edward Robinson (Oxford: Blackwell, 1962 [1927]).

—*Poetry, Language, Thought*, trans. Albert Hofstadter (New York: Harper & Row, 1971).

—*The Question Concerning Technology, and Other Essays*, trans. William Lovitt (New York: Harper & Row, 1977).

—*The Fundamental Concepts of Metaphysics: World, Finitude, Solitude*, trans. William McNeill and Nicholas Walker (Bloomington and Indianapolis: Indiana University Press, 1995 [1929–30]).

—*Plato's* Sophist, trans. Richard Rojcewicz and André Schuwer (Bloomington and Indianapolis: Indiana University Press, 1997 [1924–25]).

—*Zollikon Seminars: Protocols, Conversations, Letters*, ed. Medard Boss, trans. Franz Mayr and Richard Askay (Evanston, IL: Northwestern University Press, 2001 [1959–69]).

—*Off the Beaten Track*, ed. and trans. Julian Young and Kenneth Haynes (Cambridge: Cambridge University Press, 2002).

Holm, Soren. "The medicalization of reproduction—a 30 year retrospective," in *Reprogen-Ethics and the Future of Gender*, ed. Frida Simonstein (London & New York: Springer, 2009), 29–36.

Howard, Marc Morjé. *The Weakness of Civil Society in Post-Communist Europe* (Cambridge: Cambridge University Press, 2003).

Hughes, Bill. "Medicalized bodies," in *The Body, Culture and Society*, eds. Philip Hancock, Bill Hughes, Elizabeth Jagger, Kevin Paterson, Rachel Russel, Emmanuelle Tulle-Winton, and Melissa Tyler (Buckingham: Open University Press, 2000), 12–28.

—"Medicine and the aesthetic invalidation of disabled people." *Disability & Society* 15, 4 (2000): 555–68.

—"Being disabled: towards a critical social ontology for disability studies." *Disability & Society* 22, 7 (2007): 673–84.

—"Wounded/monstrous/abject: a critique of the disabled body in the sociological imaginary." *Disability & Society* 24, 4 (2009): 399–410.

Hughes, Bill and Kevin Paterson. "The social model of disability and the disappearing body: towards a sociology of impairment." *Disability & Society* 12, 3 (1997): 325–40.

Hunt, Paul. "A Critical Condition," in *The Disability Reader: Social Science Perspectives*, ed. Tom Shakespeare (London: Cassell, 1998 [1966]), 7–19.

Husserl, Edmund. *The Basic Problems of Phenomenology: From the Lectures, Winter Semester, 1910–1911*, trans. Ingo Farin and James G. Hart (Dordrecht: Springer, 2006 [1910–11]).

Iarskaia-Smirnova, Elena. "The stigma over the sexuality of 'invalids'," in *In Search of Sexuality*, eds. Elena Zdravomyslova and Anna Temkina. In Russian. (St Petersburg: "Dmitrii Bulanin" Publishing House, 2002), 223–44.

—"'A girl who liked to dance': life experiences of Russian women with motor impairments," in *Gazing at Welfare, Gender and Agency in Post-socialist Countries*, eds. Maija Jäppinen, Meri Kulmala, and Aino Saarinen (Newcastle upon Tyne: Cambridge Scholars Publishing, 2011), 104–24.

Imrie, Rob. "Demystifying disability: a review of the *International Classification of Functioning, Disability and Health*." *Sociology of Health & Illness* 26, 3 (2004): 287–305.

—"Disability, embodiment and the meaning of the home." *Housing Studies* 19, 5 (2004): 745–63.

Inahara, Minae. "This body which is not one: the body, femininity and disability." *Body & Society* 15, 1 (2009): 47–62.

International Disability Network. *International Disability Rights Monitor (IDRM): Regional Report of Europe, 2007* (Chicago: International Disability Network, 2007), accessed September 27, 2013, http://www.idrmnet.org/pdfs/IDRM_Europe_2007.pdf.

Irigaray, Luce. *This Sex Which is Not One*, trans. Catherine Porter with Carolyn Burke (Ithaca, NY: Cornell University Press, 1985 [1977]).

Kanev, Alexander. *Heidegger and the Philosophical Tradition*. In Bulgarian (Sofia: East-West, 2011).

Kant, Immanuel. "An answer to the question: 'What is Enlightenment?'" in *Kant: Political Writings*, 2nd edn, ed. Hans S. Reiss, trans. H. B. Nisbet (Cambridge: Cambridge University Press, 1991 [1784]), 54–60.

—"On the common saying: 'This may be true in theory, but it does not apply in practice'," in *Kant: Political Writings*, 2nd edn, ed. Hans S. Reiss, trans. H. B. Nisbet (Cambridge: Cambridge University Press, 1991 [1793]), 61–92.

—*The Critique of Pure Reason*, 2nd edn, trans. Norman Kemp Smith (London: Palgrave Macmillan, 2003 [1787]).

Karpin, Isabel and Roxanne Mykitiuk. "Going out on a limb: prosthetics, normalcy and disputing the therapy/enhancement distinction." *Medical Law Review* 16, 3 (2008): 413–36.

Khong, Lynnette. "Actants and enframing: Heidegger and Latour on technology." *Studies in History and Philosophy of Science* 34, 4 (2003): 693–704.

Koch, Ida E. "From invisibility to indivisibility: the international Convention on the Rights of Persons with Disabilities," in *The UN Convention on the Rights of Persons with Disabilities: European and Scandinavian Perspectives*, eds. Oddný Mjöll Arnardóttir and Gerard Quinn (Leiden and Boston: Martinus Nijhoff Publishers, 2009), 67–77.

Latour, Bruno. *We Have Never Been Modern*, trans. Catherine Porter (Cambridge, MA: Harvard University Press, 1993 [1991]).

—*Reassembling the Social: An Introduction to Actor-Network-Theory* (Oxford: Oxford University Press, 2005).

Law, John. "Notes on the theory of the actor network: ordering, strategy, and heterogeneity." *Systems Practice* 5, 4 (1992): 379–93.

Law, John and Michel Callon. "Engineering and sociology in a military aircraft project: a network analysis of technological change." *Social Problems* 35, 3 (1988): 284–97.

Leder, Drew. *The Absent Body* (Chicago: The University of Chicago Press, 1990).

—"A tale of two bodies: the Cartesian corpse and the lived body," in *Body and Flesh: A Philosophical Reader*, ed. Donn Welton (Oxford: Blackwell, 1998), 117–29.

Levinas, Emmanuel. *Totality and Infinity: An Essay on Exteriority*, trans. Alphonso Lingis (The Hague: Martinus Nijhoff Publishers, 1979 [1961]).

Mason, Micheline. "Internalized oppression," in *Disability Equality in Education*, eds. Richard Rieser and Micheline Mason (London: Inner London Education, 1990), accessed September 27, 2013, http://disability-studies.leeds.ac.uk/files/library/Mason-Michelene-mason.pdf.

Meekosha, Helen and Leanne Dowse. "Enabling citizenship: gender, disability and citizenship in Australia." *Feminist Review* 57, 1 (1997): 49–72.

Merleau-Ponty, Maurice. *Phenomenology of Perception*, trans. Colin Smith (New York: Routledge, 2002 [1945]).

Michalko, Rod. *The Difference that Disability Makes* (Philadelphia: Temple University Press, 2002).

Miller, Gale and Steve de Shazer. "Have you heard the latest rumor about…? Solution-focused therapy as a rumor." *Family Process* 37, 3 (1998): 363–77.

Milner, Laura A. "Voice giving (way)." *Disability Studies Quarterly* 13, 3 (2011): n.p.

Mladenov, Teodor. *Of People and People. Analysis of the "Assistant for Independent Living" Campaign of the Center for Independent Living— Sofia*. In Bulgarian (Sofia: Center for Independent Living, 2004), accessed September 27, 2013, http://www.cil.bg/userfiles/library/otdelni/za_horata_i_ horata_2004.pdf.

—"Institutional woes of participation: Bulgarian disabled people's organisations and policy-making." *Disability & Society* 24, 1 (2009): 33–45.

Mori, Masahiro. "The uncanny valley [Bukimi no tani]." *Energy* 7, 4 (1970): 33–5. In Japanese. An English translation by Karl F. MacDorman and Takashi Minato is available online, accessed September 27, 2013, http://www.androidscience. com/theuncannyvalley/proceedings2005/uncannyvalley.html.

Moriarity, Lana and Kevin Dew. "The United Nations Convention on the Rights of Persons with Disabilities and participation in Aotearoa New Zealand." *Disability & Society* 26, 6 (2011): 683–97.

Morris, Jenny. "Independent living and community care: a disempowering framework." *Disability & Society* 19, 5 (2004): 427–42.

Moser, Ingunn. "Disability and the promises of technology: technology, subjectivity and embodiment within an order of the normal." *Information, Communication & Society* 9, 3 (2006): 373–95.

Müller, Martin. "What's in a word? Problematizing translation between languages." *Area* 39, 2 (2007): 206–13.

O'Cinneide, Colm. "Extracting protection for the rights of persons with disabilities from human rights frameworks: established limits and new possibilities," in *The UN Convention on the Rights of Persons with Disabilities: European and Scandinavian Perspectives*, eds. Oddný Mjöll Arnardóttir and Gerard Quinn (Leiden and Boston: Martinus Nijhoff Publishers, 2009), 163–98.

Oliver, Michael. *The Politics of Disablement* (London: Macmillan, 1990).

—*Understanding Disability: From Theory to Practice* (London: Macmillan, 1996).

Oliver, Mike and Colin Barnes. "Disability politics and the disability movement in Britain: where did it all go wrong?" *Coalition*, August (2006): n.p.

Oliver, Mike and Gerry Zarb. "The politics of disability: a new approach." *Disability, Handicap & Society* 4, 3 (1989): 221–39.

Outhwaite, William. "How much capitalism can democracy stand (and vice versa)?" *Radical Politics Today*, May (2009): 1–26.

—"Postcommunist capitalism and democracy: cutting the postcommunist cake." *Democratic Socialism* 1, 1 (2011): 1–23.

Pamporov, Alexey. "The crisis of marriage as an institution, familialism, and the new forms of family," in *European Values in Bulgarian Society Today*.

In Bulgarian. ed. Georgi Fotev (Sofia: St. Kliment Ohridski University Press, 2009), 154–71.

Panayotova, Kapka and Kolyu Todorov. *Integration and the Law for the Integration of People with Disabilities.* In Bulgarian. (Sofia: Center for Independent Living, 2007), accessed September 27, 2013, http://www.cil.bg/userfiles/library/otdelni/integratsiqta_i_zakonut.pdf.

Panov, Lyuben and Georgi Genchev. *Assessment of the Mechanism for Allocating Subsidies from the Budget of the Republic of Bulgaria to NGOs.* In Bulgarian (Sofia: Bulgarian Center for Not-for-Profit Law, 2011), accessed September 27, 2013, http://www.bcnl.org/uploadfiles/documents/report_budget_subsidies_in_bg_with_all.doc.

Paterson, Kevin and Bill Hughes. "Disability studies and phenomenology: the carnal politics of everyday life." *Disability & Society* 14, 5 (1999): 597–610.

Pearson, Charlotte. "Money talks? Competing discourses in the implementation of direct payments." *Critical Social Policy* 20, 4 (2000): 459–77.

Peters, Susan. "Is there a disability culture? A syncretisation of three possible world views." *Disability & Society* 15, 4 (2000): 583–601.

Pfeiffer, David. "The devils are in the details: the ICIDH2 and the disability movement." *Disability & Society* 15, 7 (2000): 1079–82.

Phillips, Sarah D. *Disability and Mobile Citizenship in Postsocialist Ukraine* (Bloomington, IN: Indiana University Press, 2011).

Pickles, John. *Phenomenology, Science and Geography: Spatiality and the Human Sciences* (Cambridge: Cambridge University Press, 1985).

Pippin, Robert B. *Modernism as a Philosophical Problem*, 2nd edn (Oxford: Blackwell, 1999).

Platform "Social Policies." *White Paper: Basic Principles of Effective Support for Vulnerable Social Groups in Bulgaria trough Social Services.* In Bulgarian. (Sofia: Platform "Social Policies," 2009), accessed September 27, 2013, http://bcnl.biz/uploadfiles/documents/news_docs/doc_91.doc.

Polt, Richard. "Meaning, excess, and event." *Gatherings: The Heidegger Circle Annual* 1 (2011): 26–53.

Powell, Walter W. and Kaisa Snellman. "The knowledge economy." *Annual Review of Sociology* 30, 1 (2004): 199–220.

Quayson, Ato. *Aesthetic Nervousness: Disability and the Crisis of Representation* (New York: Columbia University Press, 2007).

Quinn, Gerard. "Resisting the 'temptation of elegance': can the Convention on the Rights of Persons with Disabilities socialise states to right behaviour?" in *The UN Convention on the Rights of Persons with Disabilities: European and Scandinavian Perspectives*, eds. Oddný Mjöll Arnardóttir and Gerard Quinn (Leiden and Boston: Martinus Nijhoff Publishers, 2009), 215–56.

Ratzka, Adolf. "Model national personal assistance policy." A project of the European Center for Excellence in Personal Assistance (ECEPA), 2004, accessed September 27, 2013, http://www.independentliving.org/docs6/ratzka200410a.pdf.

—"The Swedish Personal Assistance Act of 1994." (Stockholm: The Independent Living Institute, 2004), accessed September 27, 2013, http://www.independentliving.org/docs6/ratzka20040623.html.

Reindal, Solveig M. "Independence, dependence, interdependence: some reflections on the subject and personal autonomy." *Disability & Society* 14, 3 (1999): 353–67.

Riis, Soren. "The symmetry between Bruno Latour and Martin Heidegger: the technique of turning a police officer into a speed bump." *Social Studies of Science* 38, 2 (2008): 285–301.

Ritzer, George. *Modern Sociological Theory*, 5th edn (Boston: McGraw-Hill, 2000).

Rorty, Richard. "Wittgenstein, Heidegger, and the reification of language," in *The Cambridge Companion to Heidegger*, ed. Charles Guignon (Cambridge: Cambridge University Press, 1993), 337–57.

Roulstone, Alan and Hannah Morgan. "Neo-liberal individualism or self-directed support: are we all speaking the same language on modernising adult social care?" *Social Policy & Society* 8, 3 (2009): 333–45.

Rush, Fred. "Conceptual foundations of early Critical Theory," in *The Cambridge Companion to Critical Theory*, ed. Fred Rush (Cambridge: Cambridge University Press, 2004), 6–39.

—"Introduction," in *The Cambridge Companion to Critical Theory*, ed. Fred Rush (Cambridge: Cambridge University Press, 2004), 1–5.

Russell, Marta. "What disability civil rights cannot do: employment and political economy." *Disability & Society* 17, 2 (2002): 117–35.

Ryle, Gilbert. *The Concept of Mind* (Harmondsworth: Penguin Books, 1963 [1949]).

Said, Edward W. *Orientalism* (New York: Vintage Books, 1978).

Sandel, Michael J. *Liberalism and the Limits of Justice* (Cambridge: Cambridge University Press, 1998 [1982]).

Sandford, Stella. "Levinas, feminism and the feminine," in *The Cambridge Companion to Levinas*, eds. Simon Critchley and Robert Bernasconi (Cambridge: Cambridge University Press, 2002), 139–60.

Sayer, Andrew. *Realism and Social Science* (London: SAGE, 2000).

Schatzki, Theodore. "Introduction: Practice theory," in *The Practice Turn in Contemporary Theory*, eds. Theodore Schatzki, Karin Knorr Cetina, and Eike von Savigny (New York: Routledge, 2001), 1–14.

Schecter, Darrow. "Liberalisms and the limits of knowledge and freedom: on the epistemological and social bases of negative liberty." *History of European Ideas* 33, 2 (2007): 195–211.

—*The Critique of Instrumental Reason from Weber to Habermas* (London: Continuum, 2010).

Schillmeier, Michael. *Rethinking Disability: Bodies, Senses, and Things* (New York: Routledge, 2010).

Scully, Jackie Leach. "Disability and the thinking body," in *Arguing About Disability: Philosophical Perspectives*, eds. Kristjana Kristiansen, Simo Vehmas, and Tom Shakespeare (New York: Routledge, 2009), 57–73.

Shakespeare, Tom. "Cultural representation of disabled people: dustbins for disavowal?" *Disability & Society* 9, 3 (1994): 283–99.

—*Disability Rights and Wrongs* (New York: Routledge, 2006).

Shakespeare, Tom and Nicholas Watson. "The social model of disability: an outdated ideology," in *Research in Social Science and Disability, Vol. 2:*

Exploring Theories and Expanding Methodologies, eds. Sharon N. Barnartt and Barbara M. Altman (Stamford, CT: JAI Press, 2001), 9–28.

Shakespeare, Tom, Kath Gillespie-Sells, and Dominic Davies. *The Sexual Politics of Disability: Untold Desires* (New York: Cassell, 1996).

Shildrick, Margrit. "The disabled body, genealogy and undecidability." *Cultural Studies* 19, 6 (2005): 755–70.

Shklovsky, Victor. "Art as technique," in *Russian Formalist Criticism: Four Essays*, eds. Lee T. Lemon and Marion J. Reis (Lincoln: University of Nebraska Press, 1965 [1917]), 3–24.

Sinnerbrink, Robert. "A Heideggerian cinema?: On Terrence Malick's *The Thin Red Line*." *Film-Philosophy* 10, 3 (2006): 26–37.

Sismondo, Sergio. *An Introduction to Science and Technology Studies* (Oxford: Blackwell, 2004).

Smart, Andrew, Richard Tutton, Paul Martin, George T. H. Ellison, and Richard Ashcroft. "The standardization of race and ethnicity in biomedical science editorials and UK biobanks." *Social Studies of Science* 38, 3 (2008): 407–23.

Solomon, Robert C. "Introduction," in *The Blackwell Guide to Continental Philosophy*, eds. Robert C. Solomon and David Sherman (Oxford: Blackwell, 2003), 1–7.

Spandler, Helen. "Friend or foe? Towards a critical assessment of direct payments." *Critical Social Policy* 24, 2 (2004): 187–209.

Stainton, Tim and Steve Boyce. "'I have got my life back': users' experience of direct payments." *Disability & Society* 19, 5 (2004): 443–54.

Stammers, Neil. "Social movements and the social construction of human rights." *Human Rights Quarterly* 21, 4 (1999): 980–1008.

Star, Susan Leigh and James R. Griesemer. "Institutional ecology, 'translations' and boundary objects: amateurs and professionals in Berkeley's Museum of Vertebrate Zoology, 1907–39." *Social Studies of Science* 19, 3 (1989): 387–420.

Sturdy, Steve and Roger Cooter. "Science, scientific management and the transformation of medicine in Britain c. 1870–1950." *History of Science* 36, 114 (1998): 1–47.

Swain, John and Sally French. "Towards an affirmation model of disability." *Disability & Society* 15, 4 (2000): 569–82.

Thomä, Dieter. "The name on the edge of language: a complication in Heidegger's theory of language and its consequences," in *A Companion to Heidegger's* Introduction to Metaphysics, eds. Richard Polt and Gregory Fried (New Haven and London: Yale University Press, 2001), 103–22.

Thomas, Carol. "Disability theory: key ideas, issues and thinkers," in *Disability Studies Today*, eds. Colin Barnes, Mike Oliver, and Len Barton (Cambridge: Polity Press, 2002), 38–57.

—*Sociologies of Disability and Illness: Contested Ideas in Disability Studies and Medical Sociology* (Basingstoke: Palgrave Macmillan, 2007).

Thomson, Rosemarie Garland. *Extraordinary Bodies: Figuring Physical Disability in American Culture and Literature* (New York: Columbia University Press, 1997).

Tierney, Thomas F. *The Value of Convenience: A Genealogy of Technical Culture* (Albany: State University of New York Press, 1993).

Titchkosky, Tanya. "Disability in the news: a reconsideration of reading." *Disability & Society* 20, 6 (2005): 655–68.

Tomova, Ilona. "Those who are different: between stigma and recognition," in *European Values in Bulgarian Society Today*. In Bulgarian. ed. Georgi Fotev (Sofia: St. Kliment Ohridski University Press, 2009), 119–53.

Tradigo, Alfredo. *Icons and Saints of the Eastern Orthodox Church: A Guide to Imagery*, trans. Stephen Sartarelli (Los Angeles: Getty Publications, 2006).

Traustadóttir, Rannveig. "Disability studies, the social model and legal developments," in *The UN Convention on the Rights of Persons with Disabilities: European and Scandinavian Perspectives*, eds. Oddný Mjöll Arnardóttir and Gerard Quinn (Leiden and Boston: Martinus Nijhoff Publishers, 2009), 3–16.

Tremain, Shelley. "On the subject of impairment," in *Disability/Postmodernity: Embodying Disability Theory*, eds. Mairian Corker and Tom Shakespeare (London: Continuum, 2002), 32–47.

—(ed.), *Foucault and the Government of Disability* (Ann Arbor: The University of Michigan Press, 2005).

UN General Assembly. *Report of the Secretary-General on the Status of the Convention on the Rights of Persons with Disabilities and the Optional Protocol thereto, A/66/121, of 7 July 2011*. New York and Geneva: United Nations, 2011, accessed September 27, 2013, http://www.un.org/disabilities/documents/gadocs/a_66_121.pdf.

—*Resolution A/C.3/66/L.29/Rev.1 of 9 November 2011*. New York and Geneva: United Nations, 2011, accessed September 27, 2013, http://www.un.org/disabilities/documents/resolutions/draft_ga66_crpd.pdf.

Union of the Physically Impaired Against Segregation. *Fundamental Principles of Disability*. London: Union of the Physically Impaired Against Segregation, 1976, accessed September 27, 2013, http://www.leeds.ac.uk/disability-studies/archiveuk/UPIAS/fundamental%20principles.pdf.

UN Office of the High Commissioner for Human Rights. *Monitoring the Convention on the Rights of Persons with Disabilities. Guidance for Human Rights Monitors*. New York and Geneva: United Nations, 2010, accessed September 27, 2013, http://www.ohchr.org/Documents/Publications/Disabilities_training_17EN.pdf.

Vattimo, Gianni and Santiago Zabala. *Hermeneutic Communism. From Heidegger to Marx* (New York: Columbia University Press, 2011).

Virtanen, Riku. *The Survey on the Ratification Processes of the Convention on the Rights of Persons with Disabilities in Seven States* (Helsinki: VIKE—The Center for Human Rights of Persons with Disabilities, 2008), accessed September 27, 2013, http://www.kynnys.fi/images/stories/Lakinetti/crpd-survey.pdf.

Williams, Clare, Steven P. Wainwright, Kathryn Ehrich, and Mike Michael. "Human embryos as boundary objects? Some reflections on the biomedical worlds of embryonic stem cells and pre-implantation genetic diagnosis." *New Genetics and Society* 27, 1 (2008): 7–18.

Williams, Gareth H. "The movement for Independent Living: an evaluation and critique." *Social Science & Medicine* 17, 15 (1983): 1003–10.

Winance, Myriam. "Trying out the wheelchair: the mutual shaping of people and devices through adjustment." *Science, Technology & Human Values* 31, 1 (2006): 52–72.

Wittgenstein, Ludwig. *Philosophical Investigations*, trans. G. E. M. Amscombe (Oxford: Basil Blackwell, 1986 [1953]).

World Health Organization. *International Classification of Functioning, Disability and Health* (Geneva: World Health Organization, 2001).

Wrathall, Mark A. "Existential phenomenology," in *A Companion to Phenomenology and Existentialism*, eds. Hubert L. Dreyfus and Mark A. Wrathall (Oxford: Blackwell, 2006), 31–47.

Wrathall, Mark A. and Hubert L. Dreyfus. "A brief introduction to phenomenology and existentialism," in *A Companion to Phenomenology and Existentialism*, eds. Hubert L. Dreyfus and Mark A. Wrathall (Oxford: Blackwell, 2006), 1–6.

Young, Iris Marion. *On Female Body Experience: "Throwing Like a Girl" and Other Essays* (Oxford: Oxford University Press, 2005).

Zhisheva, Nina. "I, my impairment and sex." In Bulgarian. *Integral* 2 (2002): 6–9.

Žižek, Slavoj. *The Ticklish Subject: The Absent Centre of Political Ontology* (London: Verso, 1999).

Index